Gaston Boissier, Arabella Ward

Roman Africa

Archaeological Walks in Algeria and Tunis

Gaston Boissier, Arabella Ward

Roman Africa
Archaeological Walks in Algeria and Tunis

ISBN/EAN: 9783337293918

Printed in Europe, USA, Canada, Australia, Japan

Cover: Foto ©ninafisch / pixelio.de

More available books at **www.hansebooks.com**

ROMAN AFRICA

ARCHÆOLOGICAL WALKS IN ALGERIA AND TUNIS

BY

GASTON BOISSIER

Author of "Cicero and His Friends," "Rome and Pompeii,"
"The Country of Horace and Virgil," etc.

AUTHORIZED ENGLISH VERSION BY

ARABELLA WARD

WITH FOUR MAPS

G. P. PUTNAM'S SONS
NEW YORK AND LONDON
The Knickerbocker Press
1899

COPYRIGHT, 1898
BY
G. P. PUTNAM'S SONS
Entered at Stationers' Hall, London

The Knickerbocker Press, New York

TRANSLATOR'S PREFACE.

IT is with great pleasure that I offer to the reading public the authorised English translation of Gaston Boissier's *L'Afrique Romaine*.

Monsieur Boissier needs no introduction to an English or American public. Those who have read his previous books are already familiar with the simplicity and clearness of the style, the picturesque descriptions of places and the vivid presentation of events which characterise Boissier's work, and have realised also that this work is based on a foundation of thorough scholarly knowledge.

The present volume deals with that part of Africa which came under the direct domination of Rome. The author transports the reader to Carthage, whence, at will, he may wander across the great stretch of surrounding country, visit the smaller cities and towns, and study, in the light of their past history, their inhabitants, their customs, their language and literature, their mode of living, their government, and the ruins of their ancient monuments, many of which are still standing.

I have followed for the spelling of the proper names the forms given by Heinrich Kiepert, Ph. D., in his *Manual of Ancient Geography*. In cases not mentioned by Kiepert, I have taken the authority of William Smith's *Ancient Geography* and *Classical Atlas*, appending to the ancient the modern name in all but a few instances in which I have been unable to find it. I have also occasionally been unable to discover the English equivalent of the ancient name as given by Boissier, and in these instances, I have left the word as it is in the French text. For further references, I have consulted: Polybius; Strabo; Herodotus; Pliny; Livy; Appian; Homer's *Iliad* and *Odyssey;* Sallust's *Jugurtha;* Virgil's *Æneid* and *Georgics;* Chateaubriand's *Itinéraire;* Mommsen's *History of Rome;* E. H. Bunberry's *Rome;* R. Bosworth Smith's *Carthage and the Carthaginians;* G. L. Ditson's *North Coast of Africa;* Church's *Story of Carthage;* Davis's *Carthage and her Remains;* Henty's *Carthage and the Carthaginians;* Morris's *Life of Hannibal;* J. Marcel's *Tunis;* General Daumas's *Mœurs;* Thompson's *History of Roman Literature;* Cruttwell's *History of Roman Literature;* Napoleon's *Correspondence;* Anthon's *Ancient Geography*, and Lippincott's *Gazetteer*.

I have devoted to the work painstaking and conscientious study, and if in certain instances I have erred, if the English rendering mars or misinterprets the original, I can only ask the indulgence of the author as well as that of his readers.

ARABELLA WARD.

SOUTH ORANGE, N. J.,
December 1, 1898.

AUTHOR'S PREFACE

WHEN I visited Africa, in 1891, I met on my route a number of senators and deputies, who were travelling through the country in order to become acquainted with its resources and needs. The Algerian question had just been brought up again in the Chamber of Deputies; it had been discussed for a long time without result, and, as is the custom when an understanding cannot be reached, they succeeded in deciding to make an investigation. The politicians came therefore to seek, on the very spot, light on the discussions which they foresaw.

Naturally they set to work to study the actual condition of Algeria and Tunis; they computed the hectares of cultivated land, they looked into the yield of the crops and the vines, and the state of the shipping; they talked with the colonists and the natives; they strove to take account of that which has been accomplished in half a century, and that which remains to be done. Nothing is better; but is this all? In order to know the future of our African possessions, and to understand the true condition of their prosperity, is it sufficient to enquire into the present? I think not. It seems to me that the past also has the right to be heard. We are not the first who came from the countries of the

North to settle in Africa; we have had, on this soil, illustrious predecessors, who conquered it, as we did, and governed it with glory for more than five centuries. They encountered almost the same obstacles there that we did; they had to overcome the same resistance of nature, which was no kinder then than now; the same opposition of warlike races, which occupied the soil, and which were willing to share it with no one. How did they accomplish it? By what miracles of courage, of patience, and of skill did they make of this arid and oftentimes uninhabitable soil one of the richest provinces of their Empire and of the world? What means did they employ in order to implant their civilisation in the midst of these barbarians, and render it so flourishing there that Africa succeeded in producing Latin writers in abundance, and that in a short time it seemed more Roman than Italy and Rome? All that, it is important for us to know; we cannot neglect the lessons and the examples that the past is able to furnish us. In order that the desired investigation may be complete, it is necessary to call upon the Romans also to take part in it: I believe that, if we knew how to question them, they would have much to tell us.

Yet at first I hesitated to do this; it seemed to me that, in order to appreciate the work of the Romans in Africa, it was not sufficient to have merely glanced at the monuments that they left there, and to have spent a few weeks in travelling through the country. Happily, the very careful and exhaustive research, which lack of time has not

Author's Preface

allowed me to finish, has been taken up by others. Ernest Renan was right in saying that " the scientific exploration of Algeria would be one of the titles to glory of France in the nineteenth century." It began almost the day after the conquest, and has been carried on without interruption to the present time. Thanks to the devotion of all those who have helped in this great work, we have, on every question on which it is important for us to be informed, an incredible number of documents,—the only objection to them being that they are scattered about almost everywhere and difficult to collect. I have no merit other than that of having taken them from their hiding-places and culled from them that which they contain. Therefore, it is right for me in the beginning of this study to thank those travellers, often unknown,—officers of our army, employees of our Government, workmen, landowners, whom the sight of and love for the monuments have made archæologists,—for what they have taught me. I owe to them almost all that I know, and my first duty is to say to the reader that, if he takes any interest in looking over these pages, it is to them that he should show his gratitude.

CONTENTS

CHAPTER I

PAGES

THE NATIVES 1–39

I.—Origin of the Numidians according to King Hiempsal, 2. Whence he derived these accounts, 3. What, in the account of Hiempsal, comes from the Greeks and Numidians, 4. Difference in the physiognomy of the natives, 5. Unity of their language, 6. The Libyan alphabet, 8. The Berbers, 9.

II.—How the Berber kingdoms were organised, 10. Masinissa, 12. He defeats Syphax and takes possession of Cirta, 14. Constantine, 15. Death of Sophonisba, 17.

III.—Jugurtha, 20. Character of Sallust's history, 20. Information it contains concerning the natives and their country, 24.

IV.—Juba I. conquered at Thapsus by Cæsar, 26. Juba II. King of Mauretania, 27. Queen Cleopatra, 29. Cæsarea, 30. The Museum of Juba II., 34. End of the dynasty of Masinissa, 35.

CHAPTER II

CARTHAGE 40–91

I.—The Phœnicians, 40. Their character, 41. Their commerce, 42. The colonies they founded, 45. Carthage, 46.

II.—The Byrsa, 48. The site of Carthage, 49. What remains of the Punic city, 52. Carthaginian tombs, 54. The *steles* of Tanit, 55.

III.—The Fourth Book of the *Æneid*, 59. Why Virgil portrays Dido in love, 61. Description of her passion, 64. Why she resists it, 68. Character of Æneas, 70.

IV.—Scipio the Younger at Carthage, 73. Surprise at the Megara, 74. Carthage cut off on the land side, 75. Then on the sea, 75. The harbours of Carthage, 75. The Carthaginians equip their last fleet, 80. The siege of Carthage, 81.

CHAPTER III

THE GOVERNMENT AND THE ARMY . 92–141

I.—Timid policy of the Republic in Africa, 92. How this may be explained, 93. System of the protectorate, 96. Limited occupation, 97. How the Romans renounced it under the Empire, 98. Extent of their possessions, 100.

II.—The Proconsular Province, 102. Numidia, 103. How the Romans settled the question of civil and of military government, 103. The two Mauretanias, 104.

III.—The Roman army in Africa, 108. Number of the soldiers, 109. Site of the stations, 109. *Castella* and *burgi*, 110. Telegraphic communications, 111. The great highway, 112. Call for foreign troops, 113. The "goums," 115.

IV.—The third *Augustan* legion, 117. It is stationed at Lambèse, 118. Inspection of Emperor Hadrian, 119. The legionaries obtain the right to marry, 120. The camp at Lambèse, 121. The prætorium, 123. The camp was the home neither of the soldiers nor of the officers, 124.

V.—The town of Lambèse, 125. Its history, 125. The Temple of Æsculapius, 127. The soldiers and the officers in their private life, 127. Attitude of the soldiers towards their commanders, 129. Savings-banks, 132. Military associations, 133.

Contents

PAGES

VI.—Services rendered by the third legion, 135. Encounters in which it took part, 135. Tacfarinas, 135. Daily alarms, 136. Why Africa was not thoroughly subdued, 137.

CHAPTER IV

THE SURROUNDING COUNTRY . . . 142–191

I.—The large number of ruins in Africa proves the prosperity of the country in the time of the Romans, 142. Surprise at this, 144. Difficulties the Romans had to encounter, 145. Habits of the natives, 146. Natural obstacles, 149. How they were overcome, 150. Hydraulic works, 151. Wells and cisterns, 153. Dams, 154.

II.—The small estates, 156. The inhabitants of the Mapalia, 156. A rich peasant of Mactaris, 158. The principal products of Africa, 160. The markets, 161. Africa supplies Rome with corn, 163.

III.—The large estates of Africa, 165. The baths of Pompeianus, 168. His villa, 172. His stables, 173. The grove of the philosopher, 177.

IV.—The imperial domains, 178. The administration of the saltus, 179. The *Saltus Brunitanus*, 180. The *conductores*, 180. The *coloni*, 181. Origin of the colonat, 184. Officers in charge of the domains of the emperor, 188.

CHAPTER V

THE CITIES—TIMEGAD 192–237

I.—Thamugade, 196. The Triumphal Arch, 197. The highway between Lambèse and Theveste, 199. The Forum, 201. The Statues, 202. The Basilica, 203. The Altar of the Augusta Fortuna, 204. The Curia, 205. The *Rostrum*, 206.

Contents

    II.—Use of the Forum, 207. Games, 207. Elections, 208. The *summa honoraria*, 209. Extravagance of the candidates, 210. Danger of this extravagance, 212. The worship of Rome and of Augustus, 214.

    III.—The Market of Timegad, 218. The Capitol, 219. The Theatre, 221. The Byzantine Fortress, 226.

    IV.—Timegad seen from the Byzantine Fort, 227. Differences between the Roman cities and those we build in Africa, 228. Results of the prodigality of the Romans, 234. The effect it produces on visitors, 237.

CHAPTER VI

AFRICAN LITERATURE 238–287

    I.—The schools in Africa, 238. The education of the young, 237. How Rome encouraged it, 240. Rhetoric, 241.

    II.—Latin writers born in Africa, 243. Apuleius, 244. His early years, 244. Journey to Greece, 246. Sojourn at Rome, 246. Return to Carthage, 249. Marriage of Apuleius, 250. The *Apology*, 250. Lectures of Apuleius, 251. The *Florida*, 251.

    III.—The *Metamorphoses*, 256. Subject of the romance, 256. What is its hero? 257. Apuleius and Petronius, 258.

    IV.—What Apuleius owes to his fatherland, 261. Whence he derives the tales he tells, 262. Origin of the language he speaks, 264. Struggle of the schools against the patois, 265. The Latin of Apuleius, 266. African Literature, 269.

    V.—Latin poetry in Africa, 272. Meterical inscriptions, 273. The *Anthology*, 275.

    VI.—Dracontius, 277. His early poems, 278. Causes of his disgrace, 279. The *Satisfactio ad Regum Thrasamundum*, 279. The *Carmen de Deo*, 280.

Contents

CHAPTER VII

THE CONQUEST OF THE NATIVES . . 288–336

I.—Means of obtaining statistics of Roman Africa, 292. Latin inscriptions of Africa, 293. The Romans in the conquered countries, 294. Can the number of those who settled in Africa be estimated? 296.

II.—Policy of the Romans regarding conquered nations, 298. There was no national hatred between them and the Romans that could not be overcome, 299. Nor any real religious antipathy, 301.

III.—What the natives of Africa became, 307. How they succeeded in assuming Roman names, 310. The names they most willingly assumed, 313.

IV.—How Latin spread in Africa, 314. Christianity succeeded in spreading the use of it, 316. Popular Latin, 318. It resembles that of the other countries of the Occident, 320.

V.—Other languages spoken in Africa, 322. Punic, 322. Berber, 324. Independent tribes, 326. Under whose reign did they exist? 327. Did they remain complete strangers to Roman civilisation? 328.

VI.—Conclusion, 330–336.

INDEX 337

MAPS AND PLANS

	FACING PAGE
TERRITORY OF CARTHAGE	46
RUINS OF CARTHAGE	52
TIMEGAD	194
FORUM OF TIMEGAD	202

ROMAN AFRICA

CHAPTER I

THE NATIVES

I

THE Romans were not ignorant of the fact that the first condition of governing a country well consists in understanding it, and that one knows a country only when one is acquainted with its history. There are some present facts upon which the past alone can throw light: that which has been, explains what is.

It is probable that when they settled in Africa, the Romans were at first engrossed only by their ancient enemies, the Carthaginians, in almost the same way that the French, in the early periods of conquest, saw everywhere only Arabs. But, in reality, the Carthaginians formed only a very small portion of the population of Africa. Generally, they had settled in the large cities, about the seaports; at the most, they cultivated here and there a few fertile plains by a skilful agriculture. As soon as they penetrated into the interior of the country, climbed the plateaus, entered the desert, they met there other peoples, who had nothing in common with the Punic race. Rome could not remain in ignorance of them; before long she had to fight against them, and their resistance to her necessarily drew her attention to them. Who were they? Whence had they come? Did they belong to the same family or to different races? These questions naturally arose in the minds of those who, after having vanquished them, not without difficulty, began to look about for the best means of governing them.

Sallust was one of the first to take the trouble to answer these questions. He was an educated, intelligent man, very anxious to learn, and although he had not as yet written any of his historical works, he was very curious to know the past. Cæsar had entrusted to him the government of Numidia, and in this position he found the means of satisfying his curiosity. In order to be well informed as to the origin of the peoples he was governing, he conceived the idea of consulting them themselves. One of their kings, Hiempsal II., had written a history of them, in which he told whence they had come. Sallust translated the passage and has preserved it for us:

"In the beginning," said King Hiempsal in just about these words, "Africa was inhabited by the Gætuli and the Libyans, barbarians, who lived on the flesh of animals, and, like beasts, browsed on the grass of the fields.

The Natives

But later, Hercules [1]* having died in Spain, the various nations that composed his army, and which had lost their leader, could not understand one another and separated. Among them, the Persians, Medes, and Armenians crossed the strait, reached the coast of Africa, and settled along the shores of the sea. The Persians established themselves nearer the Ocean, mingled little by little in marriage with the Gætuli, and as, from a spirit of adventure, they crossed frequently from one country to another, they assumed the name of *Nomads*. The Medes and the Armenians settled near the Libyans, who, changing their name in their rude language, instead of *Medes* called them the *Moors*.[2] The Persians were those whose power became flourishing the most quickly; under this name of *Nomads* or *Numidians*, which they had given themselves, they left the land that they first inhabited, and which was overflowing with people, took possession of the country about Carthage, and called it Numidia." †

Such, in a few words, is the account given by King Hiempsal of the origin of his race. But from whom did he hear the strange story? Was it from his countrymen, as Sallust seems to think? I confess that I am loath to believe this. The Numidians of former ages did not possess long memories any more than did the Kabyles and the Tuaregs, their descendants. I doubt whether they troubled themselves greatly to know from what land their

---

* The numerals refer to the translator's notes at the end of the chapter.
† Sallust, *Jug.*, 18.

fathers had come. But there was at that time a bold, insinuating people, everywhere widely scattered, in Africa as elsewhere, who questioned nothing, who professed to be ignorant of nothing, who possessed a number of wonderful stories about themselves, and who gave of these generously to others: these were the Greeks. It was so natural for them to invent stories, that they filled not only their own history with them, but that of all peoples. From a few words which they heard spoken, their rich imagination created a whole legend; and, having once created it, they told it with so much grace that one could never forget it. It is evident that here, this intervention of Hercules and his army and these improbable changes in the form of words have a turn much more Greek than Numidian. The most one can admit is that these stories arose from some half-forgotten local tradition, and that there was, for instance, in the ancient religion of the country, which we scarcely know, some god, who, like the Melkart of the Phœnicians, might have been likened to Hercules. That which would go to prove this is the fact that Hercules became the protecting divinity of the dynasty of Masinissa, that these kings had his image stamped on their coins, and that they gloried in being called Heraclidæ.

How much then should we retain of the account of Hiempsal, so complaisantly translated by Sallust? One fact alone: namely, that there was perceived already, in the early ages, the difference in the aspect of the natives of Africa, since there had been felt the need of attributing to them various origins. Nothing is more noticeable at the present time when one travels through Algeria than this difference. I recall how I was impressed by it one day, while present at a great mart which was held at Souk-Arrhas (or Tagilt). It occupies the ruins of *Tagaste*. From all sides, the natives poured into the public square of the little town, where we have erected an iron market-shed. They came on foot, on horseback, on donkeys, and on camels. It was a pleasure to see them looking about for one another in that crowd, recognising one another, clasping hands, and embracing with cries of joy. There were men there of every height, form, and colour. From the shining black of the negroes of the Soudan, to the dull white of the Arab of the great tents,[3] they passed through all the shades that the human skin can assume. But that which was especially surprising to me, as I watched that crowd, was to find there, under the *chechia*, so many kindly faces that I thought I recognised. I noticed at every step small, thickset men, with blue eyes, blond or red hair, broad faces, and smiling mouths, who exactly resembled the inhabitants of our villages.

"Take a Kabyle *Djemâa*[4] in session," says Monsieur de la Blanchère, "remove the *bornous*, clothe them all in blue blouses and cloth coats, and you will have a municipal council of French peasants."*

* *Voyage d'étude dans une partie de la Maurétanie césarienne*, p. 34.

It must be confessed that this blond type, which is so common in Algeria,* forms a complete contrast to all the varieties of brown and negro shade among which one meets it. Therefore, the first idea that comes to one's mind, when one wishes to account for these differences, is to imagine that people who resemble one another so slightly must spring from different races, and that one sees before one not a single people only, but several. This was evidently the opinion of the ancients, and that which King Hiempsal meant in the passage quoted from Sallust.

And yet this theory encounters a serious objection. For a long time we had believed that the natives spoke only Arabic, and it was this language alone that we used in order to communicate with them; but as we became better acquainted with them, as we mingled with those who preserve their original characteristics and are freer from foreign elements, we noticed that in their private relations they used another. This is not, as one might suppose, a *patois* formed by the corruption of various dialects, but a distinct language, with a vocabulary and a grammar of its own. After having been in ignorance of it for a long time, or having but poorly understood it, we have finally given it its due, and our instructors teach it in connexion with Arabic in the schools of Kabylia.[5] But our surprise was greatly increased by this fact: this tongue, which

---

* It is no less so in Morocco, where, according to Tissot, it should form more than a third of the whole population.

we found living on the Jurjura* (*Djujura*), is spoken also in the villages of the Aurès (ancient *Audus*, or *Aurasius*). One can understand this, after all, for everything proves that the Kabyle and the Chaouia are brothers. But would one have suspected that it was spoken also among the Tuaregs and among the tribes of Morocco? The fact is, that with a few changes of vocabulary and pronunciation, it is spoken throughout the length and breadth of the Great Sahara (or Beled-el-Djerid), on the banks of the Niger, and almost as far as Senegal, by tribes that often bear but slight resemblance to one another, and of which at first it seems impossible to say that they belong to one and the same race.

From these contradictory facts, what must we conclude? It may be possible that the groundwork of this people is composed of elements of varied stock; that, originally, in epochs anterior to history, Africa was inhabited by tribes that came from the North and the South; that, as has been claimed, those of the blond type belong to the Aryan races and came from the Occident by the Strait of Gades (modern Straits of Gibraltar),* while the brown type came from Egypt by the Tripolitana Provincia, or from the Soudan by the Great Sahara; it is always possible that at a given time these tribes may have blended together and that for many years they lived the same life. If it is true, as a poet of the fifth

---

* This is about what King Hiempsal says when he tells that the Moors and the Numidians came from Spain into Africa, after the disbanding of the army of Hercules.

century says, that that which above all else makes a nation is a common language (*gentem lingua facit*), it must be admitted that all these people who understand one another when they speak, must have formed one nation.

This tongue not only is spoken, but is written also; it possesses even an advantage which the most important languages lack, namely, that while the Aryan nations are content to borrow their letters from the Phœnician alphabet, the natives of Africa originated, one knows not how, a system of writing, which belongs to them, and which is found nowhere else.* This is what is called the Libyan alphabet, which in our day has been the object of deep study.

At what epoch was it first used? One does not know; one has only the proof that it already existed in the times of the Carthaginians, two or three centuries before Christ, and nothing prevents our believing that it dates much farther back. It must have been greatly used at the time of the Numidian dynasty, when Masinissa strove to civilise his subjects, for remains of it have been found in the neighbouring countries of Cirta (Constantine, or Constantina). It may be said that it has been preserved until our day, since it has been shown that it is almost identical with the *tefinagh*, which the Tuaregs still use. It does not seem ever to have

---

* A specimen of Berber writing and a sketch of the attempts which have been made to decipher it may be found in the volume of Monsieur Philippe Berger, on *L'histoire de l'écriture dans l'antiquité*, p. 324, *et seq*.

been used in long-winded works: when King Hiempsal wished to write the history of the nation over which he was ruling, he wrote it in Punic. It was scarcely used except in short epitaphs and religious inscriptions. These inscriptions, which during the past few years have been searched for with the greatest care, are found not only in Algeria and Tunis: there are some also in the wilds of the Great Sahara, cut out by the point of a sword, written in tar or ochre, on the walls of caves, on the flat surfaces of rocks, near wells or springs, wherever the weary Nomad pauses, detained by the allurement of shade and water. What is more extraordinary, some have been discovered in the East, in Cyrenaica, in Egypt, and as far as the peninsula of Sinai; in the West, among the Sersous of Morocco,[1] and even in the Canaries.

Thus on that immense area of almost five thousand kilometres in length, a race has lived and still lives, divided to-day into a multitude of ever-jealous tribes, often enemies one with another and ready to tear one another to pieces, but which formerly was one nation, and which from its ancient unity has preserved a common language, the same that it spoke in the time of Jugurtha; these are the Berbers, to give them the name by which the Arabs designate them, those whom the Romans called Moors and Numidians, that is to say, the native groundwork on which outside nations came and settled, and which they towered above and covered over without destroying.

II

Independence has ever held the highest place in the Berber's affection. That which attaches the Tuaregs to the desert is the fact that they need acknowledge no masters there. It has been shown that the Kabyle *Djemâa* is of all governments the simplest, the most elementary, the one in which the people themselves act most directly, without need of courts, police, almost without magistrates.*

Such a kingdom can rise and continue only in a narrow space, in a small city; as soon as the latter expands, it is necessary for it to concentrate the authority in some hands, in order to strengthen it, and for each citizen to sacrifice a part of his personal independence in order to insure the safety of all. This is a sacrifice to which the Kabyle does not willingly consent; therefore he looks scarcely beyond his own village. At the most, several villages are occasionally united in order to form a tribe, yet the bond among them is always rather loose, and, beyond the tribe, there is nothing further. The Berbers knew no more in early times than now how to organise permanently those great dominions that allow a people to conquer others and to resist the invasions of the enemy.

Once only, for a few years, they appeared to give up their local quarrels, and joined together under the leadership of some valiant soldiers.† This

---

* See, in the *Mélanges d'histoire et de voyage*, the excellent study by Renan on " La Société berbère."

† Once again, however, in the seventh century of our era, the

is the most brilliant epoch of their history, but it did not last long. Toward the close of the Second Punic War, Rome and Carthage were engaging in their final battles. The Carthaginians, who levied armies of mercenaries, naturally had to think of recruiting them in the same country in which they had established their factories. Numidia furnished them with excellent cavalry which, together with the Balearic slingers [8] and the foot-soldiers from Spain and Gaul, kept the fortunes of Rome in doubt. One understands that during these long wars, some African chiefs may have had occasion to distinguish themselves above others; the renown that they won there followed them when they returned to their homes, and thus it was that there arose among these people, naturally friends of equality, a sort of military aristocracy. Among these petty kings (*reguli*, as they were called [9]), or these Sheiks, as we should say to-day, were some braver and cleverer ones who conquered the others by arms, or attached them to themselves through kindnesses: it was in this way that they succeeded in forming rather extensive kingdoms.

During the last years of the wars of Hannibal, there were two of these kingdoms in the country that afterwards became Roman Africa, which were of special importance, that of Syphax, the capital of which was Cirta, and that of Gela.[10] Naturally,

---

Berbers united under the command of that heroic queen, called the Kahena, in order to resist the invasion of the Arabs; but this is a history of which we know almost nothing.

these two great chiefs could not endure each other; these violent kinds of jealousy are in the blood of the Berbers, who hate nothing so much as their neighbours. Their whole policy consisted in doing one another the greatest possible injury. It was sufficient for one to declare himself for one side, for the other to support the opposite. Syphax,[11] for a long time an ally of Rome, having been drawn over to the side of the Carthaginians by his marriage with Sophonisba, daughter of Hasdrubal, Masinissa, son of Gela, who had come to Spain to war against the Romans, immediately declared himself for them.[12]

This alliance made his fortune. Through the friendship of Scipio and the gratitude of Rome,[13] he became a very powerful king. It must be said that, by his natural qualities, he was thoroughly deserving of the high position which the Romans gave him. Although educated at Carthage, he had remained a Berber, and this fact explains the power he retained over those of his race. In all Numidia there was no more intrepid horseman; no one who endured fatigue better, or took as long rides in the desert without eating or drinking. His liberality to his friends was without limit. He retained for himself none of the booty of the battle-field, but distributed it among those who had conducted themselves well; on the other hand, he was without pity for cowards and traitors. One day he ordered two deserters whom he had captured, to be put to death before his eyes. This severity was of as much service to him as was his liberality; the Berber has ever confused forgiveness with weakness, and he feels a particular respect for those who know fully how to avenge themselves. But the dominating characteristic of Masinissa was an unconquerable perseverance against misfortune; never did he lose courage; never, after the greatest defeats, did he acknowledge himself vanquished. In this, the Berber differs from the Arab, with whom we are too apt to confound him; while the true Mussulman accepts defeat as a decree of Heaven and resigns himself to it, Masinissa, in whatever position fate placed him, always counted on the chance of the future, and, as soon as he was able, began the fight anew. One should read in Titus Livius * the account of his heroic campaigns against Syphax, at the very moment that Scipio was preparing his expedition into Africa. The army of Syphax was superior, larger, better drilled; in almost every encounter it was victorious; but Masinissa found the means to steal away after his defeats, and at a time when he was least expected, returned with fresh troops. Once, however, he was so completely routed that of all his army there remained to him only four horsemen. Wounded, almost dying, he would have been captured, had he not flung himself into a river swollen by the rains, whither the conquerors dared not follow him. Of the four horsemen who accompanied him, two were drowned; the other two had great difficulty in saving him. They hid him among the grasses of the

* xxix., 32.

river bank, then in a neighbouring cave, where they
nursed him as well as they could. As soon as he
was able to sit a horse, he set out again, and in a
few weeks, from among the riders of the Aurès
and the Nomads of the desert, he had recruited
another army. It was in such ways, by dint of
courage and perseverance, that he held out until the
arrival of Scipio in Africa. As soon as he knew
that the latter had disembarked at Utica (Porto-
Farina),[14] he went to rejoin him, and contributed
greatly to his successes. As a reward, Scipio gave
him the dominions of Syphax, which adjoined his
own. Thus there was in Numidia a great kingdom,
the capital of which was Cirta.[15]

Cirta still exists under the name of Constantine,[16]
which name has flattered it and which it has retained.
Its position corresponds exactly to the idea that
Sallust gives us of the Berber cities. There is the
steep, inaccessible mountain, that those petty kings
chose in order to shelter their treasures and their
lives from a sudden attack. The acclivity on which
it is built forms a sort of peninsula, which is joined
to the rest of the continent only by a narrow neck
of land; on all other sides it is inaccessible. Toward
the north, an abrupt escarpment protects it; on the
east and on the south, it is surrounded by the Rummel (the ancient *Ampsaga*, or Wady el Kebir).[17] This
flows at the bottom of a narrow gorge, a deep rent,
which is formed as the result of some unknown
cataclysm, and which reaches to the height of one
hundred and seventy metres.[18] Along these two

lofty, vertical walls, on which the shining black rock is lightened now and then by a touch of green, on looking down, great birds of prey may be seen, their shrill cries mingling in a sinister manner with the noise of the Rummel. The torrent now disappears beneath natural archways, now bounds from rock to rock, white with foam, until it breaks from that barrier which restrains and binds it. Reaching the plain, it assumes a different aspect. Its course becomes wider and calmer; the torrent of a moment ago has expanded into a river that flows peacefully along between orange and pomegranate trees. Thus Constantine is accessible on one side only; therefore it is on this that it has always been attacked; but even on this side it was not easy to capture. During these last few years, in which there has been much building and tearing down, the accumulation of rubbish has rendered access more easy. We can, however, readily imagine that in olden times the cliffs were more abrupt, and even after they had been scaled, when the wall had been vaulted and the public square reached, all was not over; each street had to be besieged, each house taken, one after another. The Berber city was not cut up into straight, wide streets, as is the French city of to-day. I fancy that one can form an idea of what it must have been, by visiting the remains of the Arab quarters. This labyrinth of narrow, winding alleys,[19] which ascend and descend almost perpendicularly, which now pass beneath arches, now lose themselves in narrow passages, can make us understand what the ancient Cirta was like in the time of the Numidian kings.

That, however, which has not changed, and which must always have made Constantine a privileged city, is the incomparable beauty of the surrounding country. Although the city itself is built on a sort of uncultivated islet, its environs are charming, and appear still more so by contrast. I visited it in the spring, when the trees were beginning to clothe themselves with leaves. The foliage reached to the crest of the hills, which frame a landscape full of grandeur and of beauty. From the summit of the wall, one sees spread out a beautiful green plain, watered by the Rummel; in front, the mountains of Kabylia taper one above the other, with marvellous gradations of colour, up to the highest, which are lost in the distant haze.

I suppose that, following the ancient customs, the palace of Syphax must have occupied the highest part of the city, the easiest to defend, towards the Casbah.[20] Here there occurred, the very day that Masinissa took possession of it, a scene that remained celebrated throughout antiquity, and by which the modern theatre has often profited. The Berber king had entered Cirta without opposition, and had set out immediately towards his enemy's palace. At the gate stood Sophonisba,[21] the daughter of Hasdrubal, she, for love of whom, Syphax had been driven to declare for Carthage. She threw herself at the feet of the conqueror, and besought him not to let her fall alive into the hands of the Romans.

She was beautiful, says Titus Livius, she was young, she kissed his hands, and her prayers were full of tears; and, as the Numidian race is naturally susceptible to love, Masinissa felt for her something more than pity.* In order to save her, he found but one means: he married her that very day, thinking that the Romans would not dare to take her from him, from the moment she had become his wife. He was but little acquainted with them.

A few days later, Scipio ordered Syphax to appear before him, and rebuked him for having betrayed Rome. The prisoner, devoured by jealousy, replied that it was the fault of Sophonisba. "She has ruined me," he added; "take care lest she ruin others." Scipio, who realised the danger, demanded the Carthaginian from Masinissa. The wretched man, who dared not protect her, and who would not surrender her, sent her a cup of poison by a faithful slave, and the brave woman drank the potion without faltering.†

* xxx., 12. Appian claims that Masinissa had known her a long time, and that he was already in love with her when Syphax married her. But this story seems very romantic.

† The death of Sophonisba is the subject of one of the rare frescoes of Pompeii which are taken from Roman history. In a richly decorated room, supported by columns and ornamented with statues placed between them, a beautiful woman, a queen, with a sparkling complexion, covered with a purple tunic and holding a cup in one hand, is reclining on a couch. Behind her, a dark-skinned man wearing a white diadem on his head, in the fashion of Numidian kings, stands resting his hand on the woman's shoulder, as though to encourage her. His anxious gaze is fixed on a figure at the foot of the couch, who is looking sternly at him. The latter is a portrait, and

This act of obedience deserved to be rewarded. Masinissa received from the Roman people the title of king. They made him sit in a curule chair, like a consul; they allowed him to wear a toga embroidered in palms; they placed a golden crown on his head, and an ivory sceptre in his hand." What was still more pleasing to him, was the fact that they permitted him to annoy the Carthaginians, to whom they wished to leave but a precarious existence. He made wide use of the permission, and during the fifty years that remained to him to live he did not cease to take from his enemies, now and then, several strips of territory. At the age of eighty-eight he still rode without a saddle, and during the warm season waged war under the very walls of Carthage. The remainder of the time he lived in his *seraglio* at Cirta, in the midst of a family that was constantly increasing, and that trembled before him. He died at the age of ninety, without ever having been ill; his youngest son, the historians tell us with admiration, was only four years old.

III

The long reign of Masinissa was an epoch of great prosperity for Numidia; thanks to the peace which

Visconti, seeing it, recognised it at once as that of Scipio Africanus. As a matter of fact, neither Scipio nor Masinissa was present at the death of Sophonisba; the artist introduced them in order to render the scene more dramatic. I wonder if this method of conception and treatment did not come to him directly from the theatre, and if this tragic episode, which inspired Mairet and Corneille, had not already been the subject of some Roman tragedy (*prætexta*), from which the painter took it.

the aged monarch strictly preserved among the rival tribes, the cities along the seaboard became more flourishing; the plains of the Tell (or Ferikia ") were filled with cultivators; strangers began to throng the great market-places of the interior, where, as is the case to-day, all the business of the natives was carried on. Italian merchants, very clever and very enterprising, glided about everywhere. Utica, Sallust tells us, was filled with them *; at Cirta, Micipsa, who succeeded his father, Masinissa, had gathered a whole colony of Greeks,† and built a sumptuous palace, which his descendants could scarcely maintain. It makes us think of the beautiful home that Ahmed Bey had erected for himself, and which was scarcely finished in 1837, when the French took possession of Constantine.

And yet this prosperity was only superficial. The Berber dynasty was about to be the victim of its very successes; in striving with a sort of frenzy for the ruin of Carthage, it was unconsciously preparing its own. As long as Carthage existed, Rome had need of Numidian kings; they were its allies, necessary allies, who were flattered and made use of. When Rome had nothing further to fear, it was at rest concerning them. The former allies became *protégés;* they ruled the subjects, but on condition that they should obey Rome; they had to govern for Rome not for themselves. It was difficult for

---

* *Jug.*, 64. In paragraph 21 he says that there was at Cirta "a multitude of people who wore the toga."

† Strabo, xvii., 13.

them not to perceive this fact; the honours that were accorded them with such good-will, the crown which was laid on their head, the sceptre which was placed in their hand, could not deceive them. They fully realised that they were not wholly masters at home, and they acknowledged this when they were sincere. "I know," said the son of Micipsa to the Roman Senate, "that I have but the government of this kingdom and that the kingdom itself belongs to you."* From like situations arise mighty storms. One day or another the *protégé* and the patron cease to understand each other; war breaks out between them, and the *protégé*, who is not the stronger, disappears.

This was precisely the fate of the Berber dynasty. I need not relate how, discord having arisen among the heirs of Micipsa, the Romans were compelled to interpose in the affairs of Numidia, or tell of the long war that they sustained against Jugurtha, the most valiant of these princes. It is a history that is perfectly well known, thanks to the talent of him who undertook to write it. The work of Sallust is not only a literary masterpiece; it has for us a special interest in that it tells us of ancient Africa, and, as the author was in a position to become thoroughly acquainted with it, as he had visited and even governed it for some time, we open his volume with the liveliest curiosity. Does this curiosity find there the wherewithal to satisfy itself? Some think so, and we see those who go into raptures over the

* Sallust, *Jug.*, 14

wealth and the accuracy of the information he gives us. It seems to me that they are satisfied with little, and it is the contrary impression that I felt in reading it. However, I will not go so far as to share the opinion of those who, dissatisfied at not finding in him more details on Africa and the Africans, accuse him of being an incomplete historian, of treating the events superficially, of not going deep enough either into facts or men.* There is some injustice in these criticisms; if the volume of Sallust does not wholly satisfy us, it is not upon him alone that we must lay the blame of our disappointment,—it is upon ourselves as well. Why do we ask of him what he had no intention of doing?

This book, let us not forget, is a political pamphlet at least as much as a history. The author is frank enough to inform us of this in the very beginning; he has decided, he tells us, " to give an account of this war, in the first place, because it was important, perplexing, full of triumphs and defeats; then, because for the first time, it gave the people the opportunity of opposing the insolence of the nobles " †; and we may be sure that this latter reason was for him the chief one. When he wrote his book, the civil wars had just been brought to a close, and society, violently shaken, was beginning to reassert itself. Sallust, like everyone else, had completely recovered from the desires and the illusions of his early years.

* This is what Ihne especially criticises him for in his *Histoire romaine*.
† *Jug.*, 5.

He found that the democracy for which he had taken so much trouble, had rewarded him but poorly for his services; therefore he censured it without reserve. But the severity with which he treats the democrats has made him no more favourable toward the nobles. In this general disgust that he feels for all parties and for all leaders, and which is the basis of his politics, there is a special bitterness against those great nobles from whom he suffered all his life; and as he sees public opinion, brought by present misfortunes to look with regret upon the past, becoming more indulgent toward them, he desires to thwart this tendency by exposing every mistake they made while they were masters; and never were these mistakes more apparent, never did the nobles show themselves so avaricious, so corrupt, so incapable, as during the war against Jugurtha; and that is precisely why he set out to relate it.

If such was his intention, one can understand that he may have taken less care in describing places than in judging men. The events that he chronicled were for him only an opportunity for making us acquainted with the mediocrity or the venality of those who governed. In reality, Rome engrossed him more than Africa; from Vaga (or *Vacca*, now Beja), Suthul (afterwards Calama, now Guelma), or *Sicca Veneria* (now Kêf), he had his eyes fixed on the Senate and the Forum; what was happening there is his real subject.

Therefore he did not take the trouble to describe the places in which the events occurred, except when he thought it indispensable to do so; he even appears to apologise, and each time he takes great care to assure us that he will say only what is necessary, and he promises to be as brief as possible (*breviter, quam paucissimis verbis*). The way in which he describes them shows us how foreign to the ideas of his time was the love of the picturesque with which we are charmed, and attention to local colour. It was very necessary in the beginning of his work for him to describe the settings within which was to occur the action which he undertook to relate. This is essential to his subject, *res postulare videtur*. But in a sentence he has said all: " The sea there is dangerous, the shores have few good ports; the soil is fertile for cereals, favourable for herds, but not for trees; rain and springs being rare, water is lacking there." * That is all, and it may readily be seen that it is scarcely anything. Even when he refers to the phenomena which are unknown outside of Africa, and which must have roused his curiosity, he takes no more pains to describe them. It is probable that in his journeyings he became acquainted with the simoon, and that he suffered from it. One would not say so, however, from the way in which he speaks of it: " It rises in the desert like a veritable tempest at sea. The plain being unbroken and without vegetation, the wind, which nothing impedes, raises the sand, violent clouds of which cover the face and fill the eyes, so that the blinded traveller cannot continue

* *Jug.*, 17.

on his way."* It would be difficult to say less about it and in less poetic terms.

We must resign ourselves, therefore, to finding in Sallust, when he speaks of the places and the people of Africa, only very meagre and very dry accounts; but we are sure that, at least, they are perfectly exact; an experience of fifty years has proved this to us. Those hills which he pictures "covered with wild olives, myrtles, and other varieties of trees, such as grow in a dry and sandy soil," we are thoroughly acquainted with. Those cities, surrounded by great uninhabitable plains, where nothing grows, and where one drinks only the water from cisterns, still exist; our soldiers have often met them on their march. Those Numidians, without faith, eager for change, ever ready to throw themselves into new adventures, we have had to fight. How many times, after treaties and promises, have we been obliged to renew the struggle which we thought at an end! The army of Jugurtha, in every detail, reminds us of that of Abd-el-Kader; he has his regular soldiers, foot-soldiers, and chosen cavalry which he has equipped like the soldiers of the legions; and, in addition to them, the goums," which are furnished by every neighbouring tribe. The regular soldiers follow him faithfully everywhere and throughout all his fortunes; the others desert at the slightest accident; they hurl themselves upon the enemy like a storm-cloud, but, the first burst over, if they have not broken through the opposing lines they retreat

* *Jug.*, 79.

in greater haste than they came, and leave their leader to get out of the affair as best he can. All that has changed but little. And the Roman army, how its reverses and successes recall the history of our army! At the start, it knows neither the enemy that it is fighting, nor the country it wishes to conquer. It attempts in midwinter to carry Suthul by a bold *coup-de-main*, as we did on the first expedition against Constantine. It lets itself be surprised by that dauntless cavalry that awaits it at every hazardous pass, hidden behind brushwood or clusters of olive-trees. How is it possible not to be disconcerted by those unlooked-for alarms? The enemy attack before they are seen; are gone before any defence can be offered; and as they have tireless steeds that take at a gallop the steepest acclivities, it is impossible to follow them. Fortunately, it is decided, somewhat late, to send against the Numidian king a man of judgment and experience, Metellus, who realises that it is necessary to instruct his soldiers in other tactics. He teaches them, when the cavalry of the enemy approaches, to form quickly in a circle (*orbes facere;* we would say to-day in a square battalion), and to meet it on the point of their spears. He gives up those great marches which lead to nothing even when they succeed, and substitutes for them bold attacks, *razzias* (raids) as we call them, in which he overthrows the huts, burns the crops, and leads off the herds. The heavy Roman legion, so careful, so measured in its movements, so true to its ancient tactics, he makes supple and flexible. He accustoms the soldier to make forced marches by night in the desert, carrying, besides his arms, skins filled with water, and to appear suddenly before towns like Thala (afterwards Thelepte, near Husch-el-Cheme) and Capsa (or *Kafsa*, modern Gafsa), which considered themselves sufficiently fortified by their solitary position and lack of water in the surrounding country. All that, we too have seen, we have experienced. It is to be regretted that we do not find more frequently in the history of Sallust those vivid pictures which, in a word, give the impression of a country and bring before the eyes the lasting image of a people; but by his clear, condensed descriptions, he shows us that things are not changed, that the enemy is the same, and that in order to vanquish and govern him, the same method has always been used.

IV

It would have seemed natural that after the defeat of Jugurtha, Rome should change its policy; that it should decide to make Numidia a province of its Empire and govern it directly. But such was not the case; doubtless it had not found that the experiment was conclusive, and it sought for other descendants of Masinissa, to whom it gave the greatest part of the countries just conquered. It had not much to boast of. Juba, one of those princes who had succeeded in almost rebuilding the kingdom of his grandfather, thought himself capable of mingling in the civil wars; he threw himself on the side of Pompey, made himself conspicuous by his insolence, and was completely routed by Cæsar at Thapsus (Mahadda). Perhaps Masinissa and Jugurtha, his illustrious predecessors, even after a similar defeat, would not wholly have lost heart. There remained the desert, which offered a refuge to the vanquished, and those wandering and warlike peoples, fond of adventures, and hungry for plunder, from whom a new army could always be raised. But suicide was the fashion at that time. Juba found it easier to die. He and his friend Petreius, the old Pompeian general, ordered a great banquet in one of the King's country-houses, and when it was over they handed each other swords. Then in a strange and terrible duel, a duel of friendship, not of hatred, they strove to kill each other in order to escape the conqueror. Petreius, who was feeble with age, fell first; Juba had himself finished by his slave.

This catastrophe did not yet put an end to the Berber dynasty. Juba left a son, a child, who was taken to Rome by Cæsar, at whose triumph he was led, a captive, behind the chariot. Augustus, who strove to heal every wound of the civil wars, affected kindness toward this young man. He had him well educated, took him with him on his campaigns, became fond of him, and finally restored to him, in part, the kingdom of his father. But before long, as it seemed to him important to keep Numidia under the control of Rome, he transferred him to

Mauretania, that is, to the western region of Northern Africa. Mauretania comprised a part of the Algeria of to-day and that part of Morocco which the Romans possessed."⁵ It was a country but slightly known, scarcely subdued, almost barbarous, which was given to the young prince to civilise.

The task presented many difficulties, but Juba II. was perfectly well fitted to accomplish it. By nature he was curious; education made him a man of letters. He composed, in Greek, works which in his time enjoyed great celebrity. Every scholar in the Empire, delighted at having such a noted person for a colleague, covered him with praises. " He is," said one, " the finest historian there has ever been among kings," which perhaps was not much of a compliment. We have the titles of a great number of works which he wrote on many different subjects; among them were a Roman history, which is often quoted by Plutarch; treatises on geography; a description of Libya, which probably would have taught us many things; another of Arabia, dedicated to C. Cæsar, the grandson of Augustus, whom these distant countries allured; and works on the drama, in which he had occasion to treat of music, painting, and all the Greek arts in general. His works, as may be seen, formed a veritable encyclopedia. We should be greatly tempted to admire this general knowledge, did we not perceive, in looking closely at the fragments which remain of these books, that they must have been simple compilations. It is probable that the principal talent of Juba consisted in possessing a good library, made up of well chosen volumes, with intelligent secretaries, who knew how to find in those books bright thoughts and choice anecdotes. The result was a number of pleasing and useful works, by which historians were spared minute research, and, as they profited by them, they were apt to exaggerate their worth. After all, it was a curious sight and one to make literature proud, to see the descendant of a race of barbarians devoting himself to literature, writing in the most elegant language of the world treatises on history and erudition, and giving lessons to his masters. When one considers that these volumes bore the name of a king of Mauretania, it was natural that they should have been regarded indulgently, and even considered with some complaisance as masterpieces.

The love that Juba felt for Greek arts and letters, and which was the result of his education, was augmented still more by his marriage. Augustus had united him to the daughter of Antony and Cleopatra, she whom her mother called *The Moon* (Cleopatra Selene). It seems, indeed, that fate had made them one for the other; before knowing each other they had had similar fortunes. Stolen from her mother's palace after the battle of Actium, and taken captive to Rome like Juba, she had had the good fortune to find another mother in Octavia, the sister of Augustus. This noble woman, the most beautiful figure of that time, married by her brother to Antony, in order to serve as a bond between the two rivals, set herself to love the husband whom politics had given her, and who was little worthy of her. Several times she forgave him his infidelities; she mourned for him when he died; she received the daughters he had had by the Egyptian, and made it her duty to educate and establish them. Selene must have carried into Mauretania the customs of the Court of the Ptolemies. The Moorish King was very proud of having a wife from such a noble house, and it is probable that he let her exercise great influence over him. He proved the affection he bore her by stamping on his coins the delicate and gracious likeness of the Queen, and by accompanying it with attributes which recalled Egypt, her fatherland.

Doubtless to her influence are due some of the beautiful works that, happily, have been discovered in the city in which Juba II. had his residence. On leaving the kingdom of his fathers for Mauretania, he had been forced to abandon Cirta and choose for himself another capital. He decided on Iol, a Phœnician settlement, which, until then, does not seem to have had great importance, and in honour of his illustrious patron, he gave it the name of Cæsarea. To-day it is Shershell. It would have been difficult to make a happier choice. The surrounding country is fertile and smiling; in order to reach it one travels along at the foot of verdant hills, journeys through forests, and over prairies, a landscape which is a complete contrast to the barrenness of the African plains. On approaching, one comes upon the ruins of a great aqueduct, which carried healthful waters to Cæsarea. Between two hills the aqueduct is carried over several stages in order to maintain its level. In the distance, on one of the farthest mountains of the Sahel,[20] rises the tomb that the Arabs call *Kbour-el-Roumia*, and the Europeans, *The Tomb of the Christians*. It is a round building, enclosed by Ionic columns. The upper part consists of a series of circular gradings, which grow narrow in such a way as to form a sort of truncated cone or pyramid. When it was in a perfect state of preservation, with its covering of marble, its bronze ornaments, and crowned by some colossal statue, it must have presented a grand appearance. Even to-day, in spite of the ravages of time and man, when seen from El-Afroun, carved against the sky, it is difficult to take one's eyes from it. It was the sepulchre of the kings of Mauretania. In making excavations in the interior, series of passages have been found which intersect one another and terminate in burial chambers. It was there no doubt that Juba and Cleopatra rested, and they wished that their tomb, by its form and ornamentation, might recall the two countries that they loved more than all others, Egypt and Greece.

To-day, Shershell is a tiny bit of a town, enclosed within an embattled enceinte, and clustering about its harbour; it occupies scarcely a corner of ancient Cæsarea. The old wall is almost everywhere visible; it leaves the shore, rises straight to the highest part, now and then crowning its loftiest crags, and then descends again toward the sea. The vast space that it encloses must have been filled with monuments of every description, as the plough is constantly bringing to light fragments of them; but everything is in ruins. Of the theatre nothing is shown but a great hole in a field; a depression in the ground represents the circus; some fallen blocks of mortar" indicate the site of the amphitheatre. Almost everywhere the stone has disappeared.* However, some broken bits that chance has preserved, show us what must have been the splendour of the ancient capital of Mauretania. On the principal square of Shershell, planted with vigorous carob-trees, stands a column, surrounded by fragments that are wonderfully rich in capitals and friezes. Here and there enormous blocks of marble serve as benches to the few pedestrians of the country who come to breathe the sea air. A beautiful mosque, now turned into a hospital, is supported by a forest of antique columns of green granite, which give a very good idea of the monuments from which they have been taken. Finally, near the port, some thermæ have been excavated by Monsieur Waille, Professor in the School of Letters at Algiers (ancient *Icosium*), who seems to have devoted himself to the

* It must be said that Shershell is one of the cities of Algeria in which antiquities have been the least respected. Our domination has been much more fatal to the Roman monuments than that of the Turks. When I visited the Thermæ we could scarcely set foot there, the mosaic pavements were so covered with rubbish. It is probable that they will soon be demolished, if there be need of stones to build a house or to repair a road.

study of ancient Cæsarea; there have been brought to light beautiful rooms, elegantly decorated. But that which makes Shershell especially original is the great number and the beauty of the statues that have been found there. Some have been deemed worthy of a place in the Louvre; others ornament the Museum of Algiers. Those that remain—and there are very many of them—are piled up without order in a tiny garden, and, with the exception of a few which have been placed under a shed, are exposed to every whim of the African sun.

Antique statues are not very common in Algeria; there must be a particular reason for so great a number of them, and such beautiful ones, to be found in a single city. This cause is not difficult to discover; evidently it was Juba and his wife, the charming Egyptian, who made the collection. They wished to import into their improvised capital art treasures from Greece. At that epoch, Greek artists invented scarcely any new types; they seemed to have lost the gift of creating; but they always possessed great skill of touch, and could cleverly reproduce antique masterpieces. They did not lack for orders, and they did not cease to produce, after well known models, those Bacchuses crowned with vine-leaves, those massive statues of Hercules, especially those mocking satyrs, about which lovers of art dispute and with which every museum of Europe is filled. There were some at Cæsarea as elsewhere; but more noted works also have been found there, which do great credit to the artists employed by the King of Mauretania. Such an one is the Venus of which Monsieur Monceaux says that "by its plastic elegance it bears comparison with the Venus de Medici"*; such also is the Artemis, unfortunately mutilated and headless, but which "by the simplicity and the dignity of the pose, and by the exquisite lightness of the draperies, seems worthy of the chisel of a Greek artist." The museum at Shershell contains works of a very varied character, which show us that Juba prided himself on not having an exclusive taste. Beside a caryatid of the Erechtheum, is seen a torso which apparently belongs to the school of Lysippus, and a little farther on, suppliant figures stamped with an expressive though somewhat theatrical grief, which recalls the style of the artists of Pergamus. If it is true, as Beulé thought, that the marble from which the statues of Shershell are cut comes from the quarries of Africa, it must be admitted that they were modelled in Cæsarea itself, by sculptors brought from Greece by the King at great expense. He had therefore near him, besides scholars to aid him in writing his books, architects to build palaces, temples, thermæ, and theatres, and sculptors to decorate them. Is it not strange that in an incredibly short time the court of a petty Berber king should have seemed to continue that of the successors of Alexander, and that at the foot of the Atlas moun-

---

*See the article by Monsieur Paul Monceaux on the statues of Shershell, in the *Gazette archéologique* of 1886. **The Venus of Shershell is now in the Museum of Algiers.**

tains,²⁸ an African city should have assumed the airs of Pergamus, Antioch, or Alexandria?

But this prosperity could not be of long duration. The successor of Juba II., Ptolemy, to whom his father left the throne after a reign of fifty years, was, to his misfortune, called to Rome by Caligula. The Emperor, who pretended great affection for him, and who delighted in recalling the fact that they were both descended from the triumvir Antony, desired, he said, to keep his dear cousin near him. In reality this vain fool was flattered at showing himself before the people with a following of kings. But it was necessary that, in this *cortège*, no one should attract attention but himself. He possessed every conceivable vanity, and wished not only to be the greatest orator but the handsomest and the best dressed man in Rome. It happened one day, however, that the young King of Mauretania, entering the theatre in a superb purple cloak, excited the admiration of the populace. Caligula was furious. He threw Ptolemy into prison, but instead of killing him at once, took pleasure in torturing him. "He was refused a morsel of bread," says Seneca, "and in order to drink, he was forced to hold his mouth under the gutters."* Thus perished the last descendant of Masinissa.

This time the test was complete; the Romans

---

* *De Tranquill. Animi*, xi. This kind of punishment was not new. A few years before, Tiberius had compelled his nephew, Drusus, whom he wished to starve to death, to eat the stuffing from his mattress.

decided that they would no longer give the natives a king from their own people. They took possession of Mauretania, as they had already done of Numidia, under Augustus, and the whole of Africa was reunited under their domination.

TRANSLATOR'S NOTES TO CHAPTER I

1. There were several Herculeses; any great warrior, merchant, or traveller received this name.

2. "The scholiasts on Sallust think he was mistaken, owing to the errors of the translator of the Punic works of Hiempsal. They suppose that the Amorites or Arameans were confounded by him with the Armenians, and the Pharaseans with the Persians. The Moors themselves state that their origin may be traced to a district in Arabia called Sabæi, whence their ancestors under King Ifricki were driven by a superior force and compelled to emigrate to the west."—G. L. Ditson, *North Coast of Africa*.

Strabo says that, "according to some authors, Hercules brought the Moors from India."

Bochart derives the name *Moor* from the Phœnician *mauharim*, signifying the last, or those at the extremity of the earth. De Broses thinks it comes from the Berber *more*, a merchant. Dr. Shaw is inclined to the opinion that *Moor* is from a Hebrew word signifying a ferry, and applicable to this people because they lived near a ferry or strait (Straits of Gibraltar); Passow believes it is from the Greek *mauros*, black. "There is," says Ditson, "a more simple solution; . . . it is in the word that would naturally be applied to those inhabiting this region, . . . the western people, from the Arabic word *el morhab*, the setting, or the place where the sun goes down to the Orientals. From *el morhab* or *el moghreb*, doubtless comes the *rhrb* (written with three letters), the Arabic name of Morocco, for it is precisely like the preceding, with the exception of one letter, the first, which the latter lacks—the *mim*, corresponding with our *m*."

"It is, too, not improbable that from the same Arabic root, *rhrb*, or *gharb*, comes the name *Algarve*, applied to the most western province in Portugal, of which the Moors were for a long time masters."—J. J. Marcel's *Tunis.*

3. There was the "Arab of the village," the "Arab of the tents," the "Arab of the small tents," and the "Arab of the great tents." The latter lived in encampments formed of from twenty to one hundred tents, each encampment consisting of a particular tribe.
Compare G. L. Ditson in *North Coast of Africa:*
"To make an Arab into a Frenchman—put on him a slouched cap, blue pantaloons, and a blouse—is a design as *outré* as that of harnessing an ostrich of the desert into a stage of the town."

4. *Djemâa* or *djemmâ*, a council, composed of the sheiks or *amins* of the villages (which comprise a *ferka*, spelled also *farka*, or fraction of a tribe, *arch* or *kuebila*). *Djemmâ* is also the name given to a mosque and to Friday.

5. "There is as much difference of opinion regarding the etymology of the word Kabyle as there is concerning the origin of the Moor. Some derive it from the Phœnician. Baal is a generic name of Syrian divinities, and K, in the Hebrew, serves to unite the two terms of comparison (*K-Baal*, as the adorers of Baal)."—General Daumas' *Mœurs,* etc.

Herodotus applies the name Kabyle to some tribes of Cyrenaica, but in no other of the ancient writers is the word to be found; it is therefore inferred that this people were not called Kabyles till after the Arab invasion.

Some writers think the word comes from *kuebila* (tribe), in *kabel* (he has accepted), referring in this case to Islam—and in *kobel* (before), meaning that they preceded other peoples.

"A simpler and more natural explanation is that Kabyle is derived from *gebel* (a mountain), Gebels or Kabyles meaning mountaineers."
—G. L. Ditson.

G. L. Ditson in the *North Coast of Africa,* p. 152, says:
"The Kabyles all speak the *Berber* tongue, or a dialect of it, which is a pretty conclusive proof of the unity of their origin; but they have no books, no manuscripts, and the very alphabet of their language has been lost. In 1651, Thos. Darcos discovered near Tunis, in the ruins of Dugga, an epigraph containing seven lines of Phœnician and seven of an unknown language. In 1722, Walter Oudney

found at Djerma, in the country of the Touareg, and at El Kat, seventeen strange letters or characters, which so closely resembled those of Dugga, that a common parentage was claimed for them."

6. "The Djujura, a spur of the Atlas (the *Mons Ferratus* of the Romans), is a world of almost inaccessible cliffs—another Caucasus." —G. L. Ditson, *North Coast of Africa*, p. 152.

7. The Sersous is a succession of hills which border the Atlas Mountains and serve as a connecting link between them and the more depressed plateaus.

8. "The Balearic islands were Majorca, Minorca, and Ivica. The reader must not be tempted by the plausible derivation from the Greek βάλλω (ballo), to throw or strike. The name seems to be derived from some form of Baal."—Alfred J. Church, *The Story of Carthage.*

9. Pliny, *Hist. Nat.*, xviii., 5, "Regulis Africæ."

10. Gela, Gala, or Gula, probably the second king of Numidia; he succeeded Naravasus.

11. For Syphax, see Livy, xxviii., 17, 18; Appian, *Hisp.*, 30; Zonaras, ix., 10, 11.

12. For Masinissa, see Livy, xxv., 34; xxvii., 19; xxviii., 13, 16, 35; Appian, *Pun.*, 10.

13. Polyb., xiv., 1, 2; Livy, xxix., 28, 34, 35; Appian, *Pun.*, 16, 25.

14. Utica is supposed to be near the mouth of the river now called the Mejerda (ancient *Medjerdah*).

15. "Cirta, in the Numidian language, designated an isolated rock; it is synonymous with *Kaf* or *Kef*, an Arabic word which has become the name of the ancient *Sicca Veneria*."—*Annuaire de la Société Archéologique*, année 1853, p. 102. See also M. E. Carette's "Algérie," in *L'Univers Pittoresque*. Also Livy, xxx., 11, 12.

16. "Constantine, like Jerusalem, slopes toward the east and . . . does not look unlike the ancient 'City of David' from the 'Mount of Olives.' It is invested with a historical interest hardly surpassed by any place in Africa, after Carthage."—G. L. Ditson, *North Coast of Africa*, p. 255.

17. It rises in the mountains near Setif (ancient *Sitifi*), and empties near Djenna.

18. "At one point the walls rise 300 metres or 983 feet above the basin."—G. L. Ditson, *North Coast of Africa.*

19. Mr. Ditson calls them the "break-neck streets."

20. *Casbah* means literally "reed." I have not discovered its appropriateness.

21. See Bosworth Smith's *Carthage and the Carthaginians*, p. 298. Also Chateaubriand, *Itinéraire*.

22. See Livy, xxix., 33 ; xxx., 12–15 ; Appian, *Pun.*, 27, 28 ; Zonaras, ix., 13.
The honours bestowed upon Masinissa had never before been granted to one who was not a Roman citizen.

23. A peculiar feature of the Tell is the three plains or savannas, known as the plain of Bona, the plain of Metidja, and the plain of Oran.

24. The *Goums* were the irregular native cavalry, the bodyguard of the chiefs.

25. Algeria corresponds to Numidia, part of Mauretania and Gætulia. It is the name applied to all the French possessions in North-western Africa.

26. "*Sahel* is an Arabic word meaning coast or shore, and is more properly applied to the range of hills between the Haratch and Scherchell (Shershell) than the name *Boujareah* occasionally given them. The latter is a *part* of the Sahel back of Algiers."—G. L. Ditson, *North Coast of Africa.*

27. The mortar used in the building of Roman amphitheatres was called travertin.

28. The double chain of mountains which traverses Algeria is known as the Great and the Little Altas. The latter is the more northerly.

CHAPTER II

CARTHAGE

I

THE Berbers, as we have seen, formed the largest and the most ancient population of Northern Africa; but at an early date, strangers, Phœnicians, settled upon this groundwork of natives. Whence had they come and what cause had driven them to emigrate? This is what we must endeavour to learn before attempting to know what was their fortune there.

I do not wish to wander too far into these questions of origin which are so obscure. Let us, as much as possible, avoid hypotheses and confine ourselves to facts. What is known with certainty of the Phœnicians is that they spoke a language which is very closely related to that of the Hebrews; they were therefore, like them, a Semitic people, and they possessed many of their qualities, both good and bad. Prudent and cautious by nature, but bold and enterprising when they saw something to be gained, unscrupulous, indifferent to opinion, strong or weak according to circumstances, quick to profit by every chance, they were, prior to the Greeks, the great commercial race of the ancient world. It seems, indeed, that with them commenced that business interchange among nations which is the beginning and the dimmest dawn of civilisation.*

They accomplished great things, but it must be added that they did not always act from instinct or natural genius; they were often impelled by necessity. As they occupied but a very narrow strip of territory between Libya and the sea, and as their population soon began to increase, it became difficult for them to live in this contracted area. It was not possible to extend their territory toward the mountains, which are sharp and rocky; but the sea was open to them, and they took their flight on this side. Thus it was their position that made them a seafaring people. Shrewd as they were, they grew bold only by degrees. It is probable that they began by cruising along the neighbouring coasts; from there it was easy for them to venture into the archipelago, dotted with islets, by sailing from one strand to another; finally, experience having made them more skilful and more daring, they entrusted themselves to the open sea.

In venturing a little they were sure of gaining much, and this is what made them enterprising. At an epoch when nations scarcely knew one another

* In all that I am about to say concerning the Phœnicians, I shall scarcely do more than give a *résumé* of the third volume of *L'histoire de l'art dans l'antiquité* by Messieurs Perrot and Chipiez. One can follow no better guide.

and were without intercommunication, the business of those who acted as agents among them must have been very lucrative; handsome profits could be made in thus carrying the products of one people to another. But what is interesting to us in the commerce of the Phœnicians is that they did not limit themselves to providing actual necessities, which must be had at any cost, such as food and clothing, or to furnishing useful metals, such as silver, tin, and iron, to those who were without them; they trafficked in other requirements which are scarcely less necessary,—those which arise from curiosity and coquetry. They divined that passion, which is found even among barbarians, for adorning their persons and beautifying their homes, for possessing articles rendered precious by rare material and difficult workmanship, and they strove to gratify it.

In their neighbourhood were the two countries which were the first in the world to become civilised, Egypt and Assyria; nothing was easier for them than to seek there the objects of art which they thought would please, and to retail them throughout the whole world. In a short time they found it easier, and probably more profitable as well, instead of taking them from their neighbours, to manufacture them themselves. Usually they were satisfied with making exact copies of them; sometimes they combined the processes of the two peoples whose products they copied. This was the height of their audacity, and they never wholly succeeded in creating an original work of art. They were not artists; they were artisans, merchants, and for them art was never anything but a means of revenue. Nevertheless they possessed a wonderfully skilful touch which well fitted them for certain kinds of work. We have from them, for instance, metal *patera*, with figures traced by means of a needle, or hammered in, which have been found within Italian tombs. This shows how highly they were prized, for only the most precious possessions were buried with the dead. And indeed they deserved to be thus sacredly preserved. If, after so many centuries, we cannot help but be impressed, upon examining them, by the accuracy of the design and the delicacy of certain details, we may judge of the admiration that they must have aroused among those primitive peoples, who were not accustomed to the luxuries of life. They awoke in them a confused sense of beauty, and gave them the first enjoyment of the arts.

The Greeks themselves, who were soon to rival the Phœnicians, and take from them the trade of the world, were at first, like the other peoples, tributary to their industry. When the heroes of Homer wish to make a gift of importance, they give " a silver urn which Sidonian artists have executed with care," and in order that it may be understood that there is nothing more precious, they say that it is " a work of Hephæstus.' The Phœnicians were very skilful and very keen-sighted merchants. They strove to please not only warriors, but had also, among their goods, those little trinkets which are the delight of women—flagons of coloured glass, jewels of gold and silver, rings and bracelets, necklaces of pearls or precious stones, stuffs embroidered by Tyrian slaves, " who knew how to do such beautiful work," and those purple dyes obtained from their native shells, the monopoly of which they held for so long.

It is natural that people who came from such a distance, and so seldom, and who brought such beautiful articles, should have been awaited with great impatience. We can readily fancy the welcome they received; and even though the ancient writers had told us nothing of it, it would be enough for us, in order to imagine it, to see how things are done in our day; in this old Orient, where nothing changes, the present explains the past. We picture to ourselves the merchants of Tyre, arriving clothed in the long caftans and covered with the pointed hoods still worn by the Armenians and the Syrians * of to-day. Scarcely have they disembarked before the curious crowd surrounds them; they begin by calmly laying out their goods on the wharf. Above all, they do not seem to be in haste. We are told that occasionally they remain more than one season in the same place; they wait patiently for the buyer, as in the *souks* of Tunis and Cairo, letting him little by little become dazzled at the sight of the objects which they set before his eyes. A remarkable feature

* This is the costume that is represented on certain *steles*, notably on that of Lilybæum (see Perrot, p. 309). The following details are taken from ancient writers.

that makes them resemble the Jew of our day in the countries of the Orient, is the fact that they are at once necessary, yet detested; that they are longed for, yet feared; sought after, yet fled from. Not only in the business they carry on do they aim to make the greatest possible profit, which, after all, is their trade, but they do not hesitate to become pirates, in order to add to their emoluments. At the moment of setting sail, when the vast sea is about to protect them from all vengeance, if by chance a young boy or a beautiful girl, detained by curiosity, lingers too long watching the wonders they are stowing away, they fall upon the child and carry it off to sell at some neighbouring port.

It is known that, as they were not ignorant of the hatred they inspired, they were careful to take precautions for their safety. When their trade extended into distant lands, they felt the need of establishing solid trading-posts, in which they could rest without fear, store their merchandise, and wait for the mild season in order again to set out. These places of refuge were usually chosen among such favourable surroundings that they almost always became important towns. Naturally these towns were most numerous in the most barbarous countries and those that offered the least security to the traveller. Scarcely a trace of them is found in Greece or Italy; on the other hand, there were some in Sicily, in Sardinia, and along the shores of Gaul, Spain, and Africa. Africa, especially, early tempted the covetousness of the Phœnicians; much was to be gained there, but, at the same time, there were many dangers to run, on account of the barbarous inhabitants; therefore, whenever they found a coast that offered a natural harbour to their ships, or that could be made safe at small cost, they did not fail to establish one of their factories on it and to fortify it. It was thus that Carthage (Gr. Καρχηδών, Phœn. *Karta-khadasha*) was founded.

Carthage was not the earliest of the Phœnician colonies in Africa, although it became the most celebrated; Utica was considered older. The name that it bore (*Carthago*, " New Town ") seems to prove either that there had been older colonies along the shore, and that they wished to distinguish this from them, or that, on the very site that it occupied, it succeeded other factories which existed before it.[2] However this may be, it was not slow in becoming very influential and very rich. What especially gave it an individual and powerful position is the fact that it entered upon a new course, and that, in order to strengthen its domination, it dared to break with the customary policy of the merchants of Tyre.[3] When they established a factory on the shore of the sea, they generally were satisfied with a very small territory; they did not try to penetrate into the interior of the country. Far from making incursions upon their neighbours, they desired to attach them to themselves by their complaisance. As they had scarcely any prejudices, they had no objection to paying tribute[4] to those whose attacks they feared. This is what the Carthaginians did in

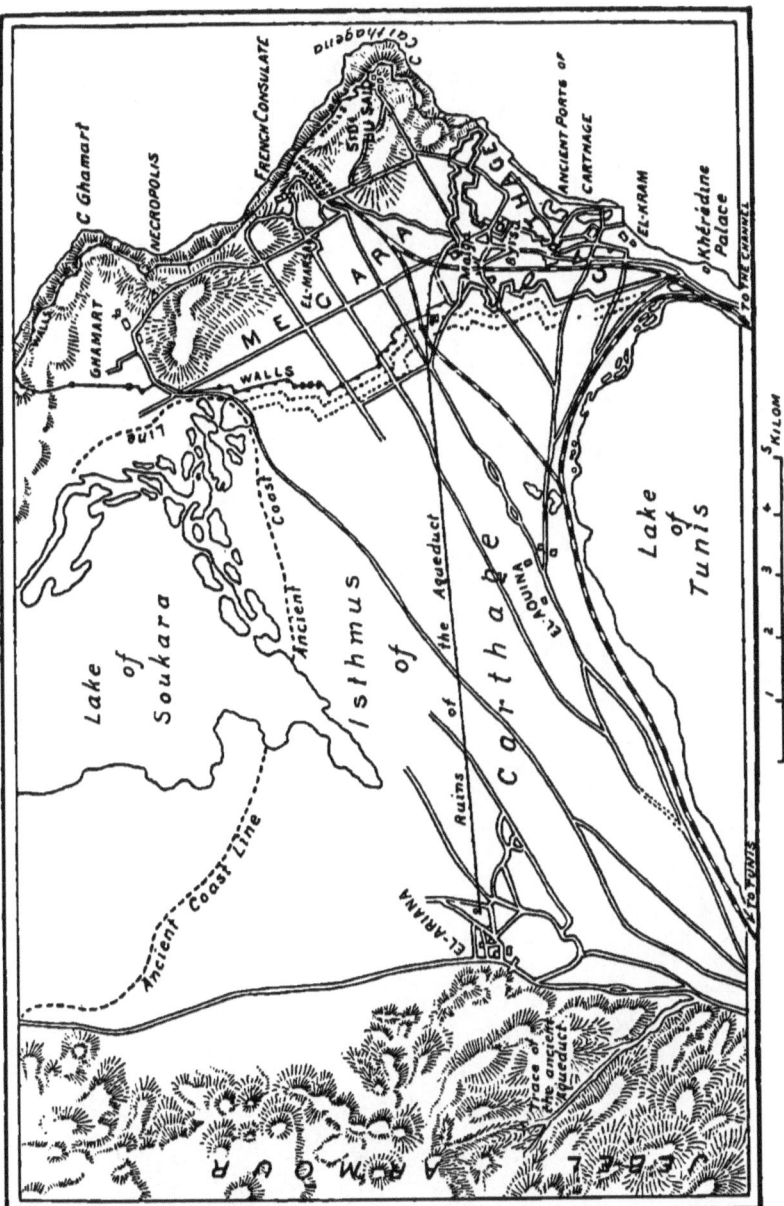

TERRITORY OF CARTHAGE.

early times. There must be a great deal of truth in the legend that tells of the manner in which they bought the soil on which their city was built, and how, like true Phœnicians, they found the means to cheat those who trafficked with them.[5] The time came, however, when they were led to change their policy. Here, again, necessity forced them to act contrary to their character. It is probable that they would have asked nothing better than to remain at peace with the natives, but the latter, warriors and plunderers as they have always been, gave them no rest. Not being able to subdue them by means of treaties, they were obliged to overcome them by force of arms, and thus it was that, in spite of themselves, they became conquerors. However, they were such as little as possible. At first they did not extend their possessions beyond the limits necessary to protect their factories along the shores; then they exposed themselves to combat as little as possible, and levied mercenaries who fought for them.[6] But once compelled to wage war, they did so resolutely and with success. As they were very rich, they could procure excellent soldiers; skilled officers came to them from foreign countries, and some Carthaginian families, who had grown accustomed to this new occupation, even furnished them with skilful generals.[7] Thus, the love of conquest having come to them with time and success, they took possession of almost the whole of Spain, and Sardinia,[8] and a part of Sicily. Then their ships, passing through the Straits of Hercules, skirted the length of Africa on the one side, and on the other, sailed, it is said, as far as Britain.⁹ Thus it was that, solidly established on every coast, possessing the most numerous and the best-equipped ships that had ever been seen, they were for some time masters of the sea. Theirs certainly was a great destiny, and there are very few peoples who have left as glorious a name in history.

Of this greatness, of this power, of this glory, let us see what remains.

II

Between the Lake of Tunis and that of Soukara, along the sea and but a short distance from the shore, rises a small hill, about sixty-five metres high.* For more than fifty years it has been almost French territory, Ahmed Bey having ceded a part of it to King Louis Philippe, who had the chapel of St. Louis built on the summit. Behind the chapel, opposite Tunis, Cardinal Lavigerie erected his immense cathedral, which dominates the whole country. This hill, which is to-day occupied only by churches and inhabited by a few monks, bears an illustrious name. It is called the Byrsa ¹⁰; it was the Acropolis, that is to say, the centre and the heart of ancient Carthage.

* The two maps which we give of the territory and of the city of Carthage are borrowed from Tissot's *Géographie de la province romaine d'Afrique*. We have indicated on them only the localities on which, as a rule, students agree. Still, we are far from being assured that we are not mistaken.

The view that is enjoyed from the Byrsa is marvellous; it has always aroused the admiration of travellers. Chateaubriand has described it in one of the most brilliant pages of his *Itinéraire*." Beulé declares that " neither Rome, nor Athens, nor Constantinople has anything which surpasses it, and that nowhere has he seen so magnificent a view." To rid oneself of this thought requires an effort of will; it is difficult to forget the scene before us and return to the past.

We may be sure that the Phœnicians were very little engrossed with the beauty of the site, in settling upon this shore. These merchants were not poets; in order to establish themselves somewhere, they had to find more solid advantages. Polybius, who knew them well, explains to us the motives which decided them. I re-read, from the summit of the Byrsa, his description of Carthage, and took pleasure in verifying its exactness on the spot. He tells us first of the gulf, at the farther end of which lies the city. This gulf, which is formed on one side by the ancient Promontory of Apollo and on the other by high mountains, the majestic lines of which are outlined against the sky, grows gradually broader and broader, as though to conduct the navigators by degrees from the tranquil waters of the lake to the open sea. Within this beautiful frame, the Mediterranean seems to me more beautiful, especially more attractive than I have seen it anywhere. Never did I understand better what a Latin poet calls " the treacherous challenges of the tranquil sea," * than when I stood before this blue sheet of water that caressingly laps the shore. It seems to me that, having this tempting sight before their eyes, the Carthaginians must have been constantly incited to undertake new expeditions. But if their attention was especially turned toward the sea, which was their domain and their natural element, as it were, they did not fail to protect themselves on the landward side. "Carthage," says Polybius, "forms a sort of peninsula, and is connected with Libya only by an isthmus of about twenty-five stadia [one kilometre] in breadth; this isthmus is closed in by hills difficult to cross, into which the hand of man has made inroads." † To-day the aspect of the places is changed; and when, turning our back to the sea, we look before us, we have at first some difficulty in recognising the peninsula of which Polybius speaks. The reason is that the Mejerda (the ancient *Bagradas*[12]), which empties into the Mediterranean a little above Carthage, has completely altered this ground. As it brings with it quantities of silt and sand, it has, little by little, filled up the Gulf of Utica, and washed away four or five kilometres of the shore; but traces of the ancient coast are still visible,‡ and carry us back to the time when the waves came to bathe the foot of

* *Placidi pellacia ponti*, Lucretius, v., 1001.
† Polybius, i., 73.
‡ We have indicated them, according to Tissot, on the accompanying map, between the Lake of Soukara and the end of the wall of the suburb of Megara.

the hills; the latter served in those days as a fortification to Carthage, which it guarded from any sudden attack on the land side, and Polybius was right in saying that the space between the sea, the lake, and the mountain formed a veritable peninsula.

Protected by these natural defences, and having, thanks to its position opposite Italy, Gaul, and Spain, become the centre of the commerce of the Occident, Carthage was before long one of the largest cities in the world. From the Byrsa, I can picture to myself its form and size. All the quarters were grouped around the hill, some facing the sea, others the plain. The city in its length extended from the Lake of Tunis to the environs of Sidi Bu Said (Cape Cartagena[13]). There began the immense suburb of the Megara (or *Magalia*, modern El Mersa[14]), a sort of new city which extended along the coast as far as Ghamart (now Cape Ghamart). On the side opposite the sea, between the wall of Carthage and the line of hills that separate it from the mainland, the country was covered with gardens and villas noted for their beauty. This part of the peninsula cannot have changed greatly, and I imagine that I see it almost as it was in the time of Hannibal. The country is still fertile and smiling. "It is," says Beulé, "the richness of the African soil combined with the poetry of the Greek and Sicilian nature." In the midst of barley- and corn-fields, little villages and beautiful country-houses hide beneath groves of fig[15] and olive-trees and form islets of verdure. It is there that the wealthy Tunisians come to spend the warm season, as did the merchants of Carthage in former ages."

But that is all which remains of the past; nature alone is unchanged; as to the city, there is no longer anything of it left. In vain have I turned on every side; I preceive nothing which attracts and holds my attention; scarcely, from time to time, do I see shining at my feet that marble dust which remains from the great ruined monuments." Here and there some sides of walls are pointed out to me, ancient cisterns that have been restored, remains of aqueducts, great holes in places where they have attempted to make excavations, but nothing, or almost nothing, which attracts my notice, nothing which resembles that mass of ruins which throughout all Africa has been left from vanished cities.

This would not be surprising if it were only a question of a single city, but we must remember that on the same site there have been two, built one over the other; and what cities! Punic Carthage [18] is said, to have had seven hundred thousand inhabitants; the other could not have been much less populous, since it was looked upon as the third city of the Empire.[19] Strictly speaking, there remain few traces of the older of the two; the Romans, who always feared it, vowed that they would destroy it when they should become masters of it, and this vow they conscientiously fulfilled. Moreover, the city that replaced it made use of the débris of the former, as always happens, and nothing was left of the first; but how could Roman Carthage have disappeared

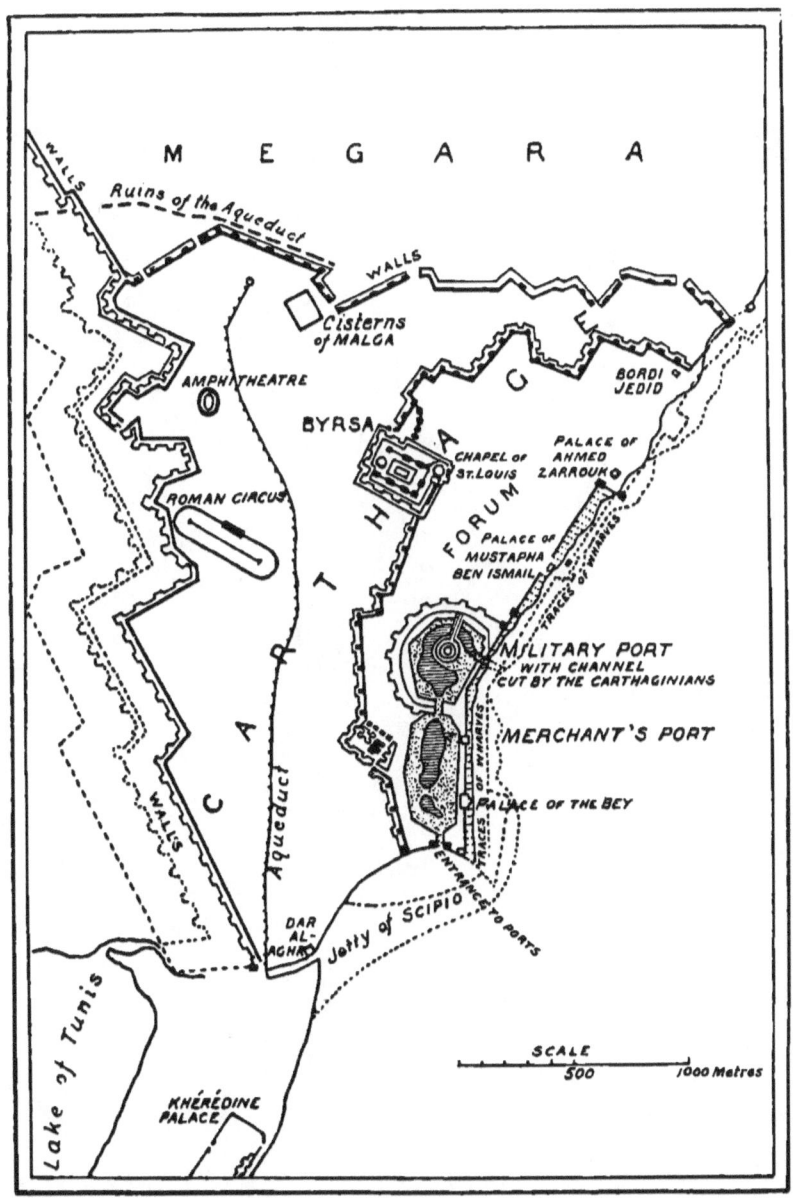

RUINS OF CARTHAGE.

so completely?[10] This is what we can scarcely imagine. Usually the Arabs do not destroy the towns which they have captured; they are content to let them die by degrees, and of this slow destruction there always remains something. Here, in the words of the poet, " the very ruins have perished." They tell us, in explanation of this devastation, that the inhabitants of that country and of the neighbouring countries early acquired the habit of using the deserted city as a quarry. It is true that at Tunis one finds at every step, embedded in the Moorish houses, fragments of marble or columns, which can come only from here. Even to-day the depredation continues, and every time that chance brings to light an antique stone, it is immediately carried away by those who are erecting some building in the vicinity.* Whether this is the only cause of destruction, or whether there are others, it is unfortunately too true that nothing or almost nothing remains of either Carthage.

The traveller whom this great name had attracted feels, one can readily understand, some disappointment at seeing before him only an arid plain, overturned by the plough, and scarcely a visible ruin. Perhaps he had made up his mind that he would no longer find Roman Carthage, which

* Father Delattre tells that he had great trouble in keeping the stones of the Punic tombs which he had discovered, from the greedy Arabs, who came to take them in order to utilise or sell them. As early as the thirteenth century the historian Edrisi mentions this exploitation of the ruins of Carthage, and says that it had been going on for a long time.

probably would have had nothing new to teach him; but of the Punic city there is no longer a part; it is here that he might expect to discover something, and it is hard for him to find his hope disappointed. That is why the student-world has taken so much interest in the excavations which have been made on the site of Carthage. As yet they have not been very successful; few ruins of undoubted Punic origin have been disinterred from the soil. However, during the past few years, some traces of ancient Carthage have been discovered which are not without importance.

These are, first, the tombs. In every human community, the tombs, to which a certain respect is always attached, have a greater chance of surviving than anything else.

The discovery of the tombs of Carthage is due to the intelligent explorations of Father Delattre, chaplain of St. Louis. He found them buried deep in the soil, some metres below the bed of ashes which remained of the fire lighted by Scipio." They consist, for the most part, of great blocks of masonry, without mortar or cement. Above each of them, slabs, leaning one against another, form a sort of triangle, either to protect the tomb against the pushing of the earth or to preserve it from dampness. Sometimes the bodies were laid directly on the bare stone, sometimes they were placed in cedar-wood boxes. They were found in their original position, after two thousand years; but at a touch they fell to dust. Some were in a better state of preservation; they were removed with care, and the remains of these old Carthaginians may be seen in glass cases in the Museum of St. Louis; and there also, what is still more important, may be found the collection of all that those tombs contained. There were but few weapons,—the Phœnicians by nature were not warriors,—but a certain number of articles of jewelry, rings, necklaces, earrings, some masks of burned clay, lamps with two burners, of a peculiar shape, which the Arabs still use to-day, besides vases of every kind and size. There is scarcely an ancient tomb that does not contain some of them; those from Carthage seem intended to hold provisions, and we imagine that there is still found in them some trace of the milk or the fruit that was put into them. This was the food for the dead which was placed thus by his side. As they could not believe that all feeling had left the body, it was buried with a lighted lamp, food, articles of toilet or amusement and everything that could entertain or please that part of life which was supposed still to remain was placed within reach.

The tombs discovered by Father Delattre must be very old; it has been conjectured that they date back to the earliest settlements of the Phœnicians, to the time when the latter still occupied only a strip of land about the harbour, and when the Byrsa had neither palaces nor temples, and was but a necropolis. Another discovery that has been made during these past years brings us down to more recent times; I refer to the *steles* of Tanit. They have been found between what is called the Hill of Juno and the Byrsa, along a deep-cut road that runs from the sea to the great cisterns and that seems to follow the line of an ancient roadway. They are small slabs of stone about fifty centimetres high, terminating in a sort of pyramidal fronton, with an acroterium on each side. As they resemble the small monuments which surmount the tombs in the Mussulman cemeteries, it was at first believed that they were used for the same purpose; but the inscriptions they bear and the places in which they have been found clearly show that they must have had another use. It is certain that they were votive tablets,[12] and it is very likely that they were placed in some Phœnician temple. These temples, Monsieur Perrot has very clearly shown, resembled but little those of Greece or Rome. While the Greeks attach the greatest importance to the *cella*, that is to say, the dwelling-place itself of the god, the chamber which contains his image, and subordinate to it the rest of the building, the Phœnician architect thinks first of all of building a vast court, or, as it were, a great open room, surrounded by porticoes, in one corner of which he puts up, in the best manner possible, the little shrine containing the idol.*

* Even to-day the great mosque at Mecca shows us that the Semitic peoples of all ages have remained faithful to the style of temple which their fathers left them. There may be seen a very interesting reproduction of it in the work by Monsieur Perrot, from which I have already so largely borrowed. It is an immense court enclosed within a portico, and contains the square oratory called *Caaba*, in which is found the famous black stone, the object of Mussulman worship.

It is in these courts, opposite the altar, that our *steles* must have been found, some affixed to the wall, others set up in the ground. They are all alike; they contain almost the same symbols,—a rough representation in the likeness of a human form, whereon the body is represented by a sort of triangle, the arms by a straight line, the head by a disk, one hand uplifted to heaven, the attitude of invocation and prayer. A little below is an inscription in Punic characters, in which the formula is always the same. Here is one of them, which will give an idea of all the others: " To the divinity Tanit,[23] face of Baal,[24] and to the Lord Baal-Hammon, a votive offering made by Hasdrubal, son of Hanno, because he has heard the voice of the goddess. Blessed be she!"

This Tanit was the great deity of Carthage. Virgil calls her Juno, others identify her with Diana; most frequently, in order not to compromise oneself, she was invoked under the name of *Virgo Cœlestis*. She was a lunar deity, and that is why it is said that she is the face or the likeness of Baal, who is the sun. Those who erected these *steles* belonged to every class of Carthaginian society; there are found among them Suffetes, that is to say, the highest magistrates of the city,[25] and the humblest workmen,—carpenters, locksmiths, and weavers. The hangman himself was anxious to express his gratitude to the goddess, " who deigned to make him hear her voice," as well as to all the others.[26] It is probable that the court of the Temple of

Tanit" contained a whole forest of these little monuments. Monsieur de Sainte-Marie has himself collected more than four thousand of them, and the harvest is not yet gathered. They must belong to very different epochs, but all date prior to the taking of the city by Scipio, since they are written in Punic. On looking over the interminable series in the *Corpus* of Semitic inscriptions, one finds that they are of very little importance and that they are tediously monotonous. However, as we are sure that they come directly from ancient Carthage, they again put us in communication with it; if they do not help us to penetrate deeply into this unknown civilisation, they at least aid us in catching a glimpse of it, which is a great advantage.

III

Monsieur Perrot remarks that the Phœnicians, who invented the art of writing, profited very little by it. Carthage did not produce any great writers like Greece or Rome, to record its history, therefore we are but slightly acquainted with it. Of its long life, which must have been greatly agitated and troubled by various fortunes, barely a few incidents have been retained; for instance, we know, or rather we think we know, how it came into existence and how it perished.*

---

* I might add to this the War of the Mercenaries, which Polybius has described to us, and which is the subject of Flaubert's novel. (*Salammbô.*—Tr.) As to the Punic Wars, the part of them with

The founding of Carthage by Dido is nothing but a legend, in which very little interest would be taken had it not been handed down to us by Virgil. The popularity which the *Æneid* brought him shows how forcibly the verses of a great poet obtrude themselves upon the memory. Thanks to Virgil, we look for Dido at Carthage almost as much as for Hannibal. Even students and archæologists who pretend to be strictly on their guard against the illusions of poetry, have escaped from this recollection no more than others. On a map of Carthage which I have before me, and which is taken from the works of two able scholars, Falbe and Dureau de la Malle, do I not see indicated in a corner of the Byrsa the site of Dido's home?

I should not be believed were I to say that my visit to Carthage did not awaken in my mind thoughts of the *Æneid*. At every step, as I travelled through it, I recalled unconsciously some lines of Virgil. He has described the scenes so vividly, he has presented them with so much naturalness and truth, that I forgot, as they came back to my mind, that they were creations of his imagination. I treated them as though they were the accounts of an authentic historian, and I could not help looking for the place where the events must have occurred. On this hill, on which it is said the Temple of Juno once stood, I see the Queen, " as beautiful as

which we are best acquainted is that in which the Romans had a share, and which belongs more directly to Roman history than to Carthaginian.

Diana, seated on a raised throne, surrounded by her soldiers," as she was when the shipwrecked Trojans were brought before her."²⁸ A little farther on, toward the point where the peninsula touches the continent, along the inclined planes of the Jebel-Armour, more woody then than now, the Carthaginian and Phrygian horsemen gave themselves up to the pleasures of the chase, which the poet has so magnificently described, and pursued the roe as it bounded over the rocks."²⁹ It seems to me that I should have no trouble in finding the perfidious cave in which Æneas and Dido, drawing apart from their followers, took refuge in order to escape the storm.

> " Speluncam Dido dux et Trojanus eamdem
> Deveniunt." ³⁰

As to the funeral pyre on which Dido lay down to die, I have no doubt but that it was erected on the heights of the Byrsa. It was the Queen's wish that the fire might be seen from the high sea, and that the burial flame might be a presage of evil to the ungrateful man who was deserting her.

Perhaps the reader has not forgotten that once I took pleasure in following Æneas into Sicily and to the shores of Latium.* I would indeed that it were possible for me to accompany him also to Carthage. This journey would have a great charm with such a guide as Virgil, but it would lead me too far from my subject. Since the opportunity presents itself,

---

* " Nouvelles Promenades Archéologiques," ch. iii., *Le Pays de l'Énéide*.

that we are in the land of Dido, and cannot help but re-read the Fourth Book of the *Æneid*, I ask permission merely to give in a few words the impression that this marvellous poem makes upon us, and the idea that the poet wished to give of the founding of Carthage.

Lamartine says that in his journey to the Orient he passed the coast of Africa, and saluted Carthage from afar. He, too, like everyone else, could not help thinking of Dido; but—can one believe it?—it was to pity her and to avenge her for the injury that she had received from Virgil.

"Virgil," he says, "like every poet who wishes to improve on truth, history, and nature, has marred rather than improved the story of Dido. The historical Dido, widow of Sicheus and faithful to the *manes* of her first husband, has her funeral pyre erected on the Cape of Carthage, and ascends it, a noble and voluntary victim of a pure love and of a faithfulness even unto death! That is somewhat more beautiful, somewhat more sacred, somewhat more pathetic than the cold coquetry which the poet attributes to her, with her ridiculous and pious Æneas and her loving despair, with which the reader cannot sympathise."

It is amusing to hear this serious writer speak of the historical truth of a legend, and it is a strange error of taste to apply the expression, "cold coquetry" to so true, so simple, and so profound a picture of love. However, Lamartine's idea brings up an interesting question: Why has Virgil represented Dido in love?

We may be sure that he was the first, or one of the first, to think of doing so. In the early literature of the Greeks, love held but a very small place, and it was not until much later that it gained the importance it has retained. This innovation must have aroused violent anger among the followers of the old school." Aristophanes ridicules Euripides very sharply on account of his love for " immodest Phædras," while he congratulates Æschylus " for never having sung the loves of a woman." But these protestations must have been very little heeded. Besides the pleasure that the public derived from the delineation of this sentiment, there was none that furnished a richer, more varied, or more flexible material for the art of the poet. Upon this attraction of one sex for the other, which is a simple instinct and almost the same with everyone, man grafts so many things, that he gives to it each time a new and individual character. This passion, which seems the most natural of all, is the one perhaps into which there enters the most conventionality and worldliness; for although the fundamental element scarcely changes, it is susceptible of undergoing the most varied aspects according to the times and the characters. It is easily understood that with this facility of constantly renewing itself, it quickly became the soul of literature. It had always ruled in elegy; Euripides gave it an important place in tragedy [32]; the followers of the Alexandrian school introuced it into the epic. It is this that made the success of the *Argonautica* of Apollonius

Rhodius, and it is probable that, without the love of Jason and Medea, this poem would be wholly forgotten to-day.

Virgil professed to imitate Homer, but it was difficult to imitate him only. As he wished to produce a realistic work, which would interest not only men of letters, but the entire public, he had to take account of what had been done since the Homeric poems and of what had entered into the habits and the tastes of everyone. The delineation of love had become so common, and so much pleasure was derived from it, that it was difficult for Virgil to deprive his poem of this attraction. But it was introducing a foreign element into the work of his great predecessor, and it was necessary to harmonise this innovation with the rest, in order that it might not shock by contrast.

Virgil's effort consisted chiefly in rendering love more serious, more dignified, more worthy of the epic. He had before him two masterpieces of Alexandrian art, the *Argonautica* of Apollonius and the *Epithalamium Thetidis* by Catullus; he profited by them, but in bringing them closer to the Homeric art.* In the first place he has changed the age of

* There is in the Fourth Book of the *Æneid* a passage in which this effort of Virgil to give a little more dignity to the Alexandrian art is especially apparent. In Apollonius, Venus, who has need of the aid of Love, goes to seek it and finds it in Ganymede, who is playing at dice and who cheats her. The picture is greatly softened in Virgil. To be sure, Love still preserves some of his playfulness. He is delighted with the disguise which makes him resemble the young Ascanius, and amuses himself by imitating his gait; but nevertheless

the woman whose love he is about to describe; she is no longer a young girl like Medea, still less a child like Ariadne, " who grew up beneath the kisses of her mother, in her little bed perfumed with sweet odours." * She is a woman who has known the trials of life, and who has been softened by misfortune. Her husband, whom she loved tenderly, has been murdered by her brother; in order to avenge him, she has placed herself at the head of a discontented people, equipped vessels, left her country, and led her companions as far as Africa, where she is occupied in building them a city; that is a true heroine for an epic. But, nevertheless, a difficulty arises for the poet. How could this energetic woman, wholly given up to the cares of government and generalship, succumb to the weakness of love? Virgil puts into her heart a sentiment which is the connecting link; she is kind and generous; she is well disposed towards strangers; as she has known trouble, she is full of pity for the unfortunate. This is what shows that in this virile heart there is room for the softer emotions, and prepares us to see Dido in love without too much surprise.

The way in which love comes to her is consistent with her age and character. It is not exactly one

he is a great god. Virgil reminds us of this fact when the imprudent Dido takes him on her lap and presses him unreservedly to her heart:

". . . Interdum gremio fovet, inscia Dido,
    Insidat quantus miseræ deus."

In this way the divine dignity is almost saved.

* Catullus, lxiv., 87.

of those sudden and irresistible impressions that the beauty of a man produces on a youthful heart. However, Venus has taken care to throw over the features of Æneas the glamour of youth, and as she realises the importance of first meetings, she causes him to appear unexpectedly; she quickly snatches away the cloud that conceals him, and places him suddenly before the Queen, glowing with a divine beauty. This unlooked-for appearance does not leave Dido unmoved; she is a woman, she has noticed the beautiful mien of Æneas (*quem sese ore ferens!*), and the poet tells us that his features remain deeply engraved on her heart.* But, in reality, it is his courage and his misfortunes that have fascinated her. When she hears him relate the story of the last night of Troy and the wonderful adventures which drove him from Phrygia to Africa, she can no longer resist:

". . .Heu! quibus ille
Jactatus fatis quæ bella exhausta canebat!"

She would have him begin the tale over and over again, she is carried away by this story which enchants her, and each time " the poisoned dart sinks deeper into her heart."

Her passion is violent. Virgil says that there is a secret wound in her heart, that a flame consumes her very bones †; all these expressions, in passing into the language of gallantry, have lost their force,

* *Æneid*, iv., 4 : *hærent infixi pectore vultus.*
† *Ibid.*, iv., 2: *cæco carpitur igni;* 67: *tacitum vivit sub pectore vulnus.*

and have become metaphors; here they must be taken literally; and although she hesitates, she defends herself against herself and nothing less is necessary for her to yield than the intervention of two goddesses. Why then does she make such firm resistance? She has not the same reasons as Medea and Ariadne, who, in listening to the beautiful stranger, betray their father and their country. She is responsible to no one; she is her own mistress; she is not afraid of injuring her growing city, since, on the contrary, her sister, Anna, has just proved to her that the aid of the Trojans will bring her security and glory. That which deters her, and causes her anxiety and remorse, is the remembrance of her first husband, to whom she wishes to remain true.

"May the earth," she cries, "yawn to its very foundations! may Jupiter, with a blow of his thunderbolt, hurl me into the shades, the pale shades of Erebus, and into infernal darkness, before I outrage modesty and fail in my duty! He to whom I gave my first love bore it away with him; may he retain it forever; I wish to bury it within his tomb." *

Does this imply that her love for Sicheus has remained as great as it was at first? Time, no doubt, has done its work. The poet gives us to understand this when he speaks " of that early, burned-out flame of which only the ashes remain;" when he says that " Dido's heart has grown calmer, and that it is less restless in its love." † The time is ripe for a

* *Æneid*, iv., 24. † *Ibid.*, iv., 23; i., 722.

new passion when there is left of the old only just what is necessary to arouse in us the desire to replace it. Dido realises it in a confused way and rebels against it. In that first hour of grief, when it seemed as though she could never become reconciled, she had promised herself that Sicheus should not have a successor, and she is determined to keep her word. Such a resolve greatly surprises her sister, who finds it strange " that one should resist a love which brings pleasure, and that one should be stern enough to deny oneself the delights of Venus and the joys of maternity."* The society in the midst of which Virgil lived was also of this opinion. It understood but little that respect for the marriage tie that survives death, for it was seldom that marriage lasted as long as life. Toward the end of the Republic, divorce had become so common that the most virtuous and the most serious-minded could not escape it. Cato himself was divorced; Cicero divorced two of his wives, the second at the age of sixty. The marriage tie, so often broken and renewed, was at that time, in the words of the poet, no longer anything but legal adultery. But, as always happens, from the excess of the evil came the remedy. Protesting against this immoral elasticity of the divorce laws, public opinion, from the time of Augustus, affected to accord a particular esteem to women who had had but one husband. The women themselves boasted of the fact in their epitaphs, and proudly assumed the

* *Æneid*, iv., 37.

title of *univira, unicuba, unijuga*. At the very time that Virgil was writing his *Æneid*, his friend, the poet Propertius,[33] composed an elegy for a great man, Æmilius Paulus, who had just lost his wife, a descendant of the *Cornelii*. The lover of Cynthia and of many others had, with time, become virtuous; he had let himself be persuaded by Mæcenas, another converted *roué*, to consecrate his Muse to serious and patriotic themes. He who had never wished to marry was this time thoroughly inspired by the idea of marriage. The stanza in which he makes the young wife about to die utter words of consolation to her husband, is without a doubt the most beautiful of any he wrote. He depicts her as less proud of her birth and fortune than of the fact that she is able to inscribe on her tomb that she has had but one husband, and as giving no other counsel to her daughter than that she shall some day merit the same praise [34]:

"Fac teneas unum, nos imitata virum." *

Dido might well have wished that the same could be said of her also. But, although she has not known how to resist the passion that is sweeping her away, she does not forgive herself for it. She accuses herself, as of a crime, for having broken her promise, she is determined to punish herself for it, and finds that her mistake can be expiated only by her death:

"Quin morere, ut merita es!" †

* Propertius, iv., 11, 68.   † *Æneid*, iv., 547.

Carthage 69

A century later, the question of second marriages was to be brought up in the infant Church; there would be inflexible doctors who would mercilessly interdict them, and who would not fail to recall to those who wished to sanction them, in order to make them ashamed of their complaisance, that there had been pagans who were stricter than they. Here again, as on many other occasions, Virgil proved to be one of the forerunners of Christianity.

In short, when the character of Dido is analysed carefully, it seems to be made up of contradictory elements. We have seen that the Homeric and the Alexandrian art are combined in it. Now she is a heroine who conducts with energy a great enterprise, *dux fœmina facti;* now she is a woman like others, lonely in the solitude of her home, regretting with charming tenderness that she has not with her a child, " a little Æneas," to remind her of his father; here, she commands, a queen; there, she humbles herself before the man she loves, ready to ask him, if she were not sure that he would not consent, to let her follow him, in any capacity whatsoever, as companion or slave.* In many respects

---

* There has been surprise that Virgil did not profit by the touching sentiments of Ariadne when she begs with such humble resignation to follow Theseus as his servant, if he does not want her for his wife:
> " At tamen in vestras potuisti ducere sedes,
> Quæ tibi jucundo famularer serva labore,
> Candida permulcens liquidis vestigia lymphis
> Purpureave tuum consternens veste cubile."
>   (Catullus, lxiv., 160.)

It is evident that Virgil did not feel that the dignity of the epic

she belongs to antiquity; but there are also in her many sentiments which seem modern: that high conception of marriage, that struggle between passion and duty, that delicacy, those scruples which seem inspired by Christianity, bring her close to us. Those are indeed diverse elements to be found in the same person; but she is a woman, and with women contradictions do not always contradict. Out of all these various elements there is produced one of the broadest and truest characters ever portrayed by an ancient writer, and as the individual characteristics of every epoch and almost every type of person are unfolded in it, it may be said that the fact of its not having aged is due to its very complexity.

Æneas, on the other hand, at least in this Fourth Book, is wholly a character of Homer; he deserts Dido as Ulysses does Circe and Calypso. How, then, does it happen that one is so indignant at Æneas, while forgiving Ulysses so readily? We are told that it is the fault of Dido, and the answer is perfectly just.* Calypso and Circe interest us but little; they are scarcely brought before us; we

---

would allow him to go as far as that, but he indicates that Dido had thought of it, when he makes her say:

> "Iliacas igitur classes atque ultima Teucrum
> Jussa sequar?"

and when she adds that they would not receive her.

(*Æneid*, iv., 537.)

* This opinion is set forth in the charming thesis by Monsieur Rébelliau on the character of women in the *Æneid*.

know perfectly well " that they are goddesses who have no greater pleasure than to unite themselves by love to mortals," and who make as much of the opportunity as possible. But as soon as Jupiter commands them to set free the wretched one whom they force to share their couch, they obey with very good grace, and even help him to build the vessel which is to bear him far from them. Since they resign themselves so quickly we have no reason to pity them; all we can wish them is that a propitious breeze may soon waft to their isle another mortal in place of him whom they have lost. It is not the same with Dido; we love her too well not to suffer from her injury. It is the affection we have for her that makes us so severe toward Æneas. Perhaps if Virgil had kept us wholly in the world of the *Iliad* and the *Odyssey*, we should be less shocked to see Æneas conduct himself like Ulysses; but Dido, who is of our blood, transports us from the epic of Homer; she brings us down to our epoch; she is the cause of our judging Æneas with the sentiments and the opinions of to-day, and this judgment is very unfavourable to him. It is an ordinary occurrence in love stories, as they are told by novelists and poets, for the principal rôle to be given to woman, and for man to play a very mediocre part; it is poor Æneas who heads the list of these absurd lovers.

Here, this defect assumes from the circumstances a particular dignity. It is evident that Virgil has brought Æneas and Dido together merely to pit against each other from the first day and in the very persons of their founders, the two cities which contended for the empire of the world. It seems therefore that patriotism made it a stern duty for him to assign the principal rôle to the champion of the Roman race. We may be sure that the aged poet Nævius [35] would not have failed in this; had he treated the same subject as he might have done, he would have been obliged to give to Æneas a prouder bearing. But they were at that time in the thick of a pitiless war, and the Carthaginians were an object of horror. In the time of Virgil, the Punic Wars were but a far-off memory; Carthage, no longer inspiring the same alarm, no longer roused the same hatred. Rome had but lately raised it from its ruins, and the gentle poet had to applaud this reparation. He could, therefore, give himself up without scruple, as without danger, to his tenderness of heart which naturally attracted him toward the unhappy and the vanquished. It is no less strange that in a poem destined to glorify the Romans, the one who represents the greatest enemy of Rome should be the very one to whom we accord all our sympathy.

IV

Let us leave these fabulous times, where perhaps the beautiful verses of Virgil have detained us too long, and come back from legend to history. I have said that one of the events with which we are best acquainted in the life of Carthage, is its final struggle and fall."⁶ Appian, who has narrated it, is far from being an historian of the first rank; but he had before him one greater than himself, probably Polybius. His account is a valuable help, especially to those of us who visit Carthage; it is marvellously exact, so that when we are on the spot we follow all the details and fit them into their places.

When Scipio, who wished to stand for the office of ædile,³⁷ was elected consul³⁸ by the people, and called upon to take command of the army in Africa, the siege of Carthage had been going on for two years; Rome wished to bring it to a close. It seems that the new general, in order to carry out the wish of those who had just elected him, strove at first to end the war by force. But where could he direct the attack in order that it might succeed in a few days? It was impossible to think of making the assault on the side of the plain, as there the defence was strongest. "On that side," Appian tells us, "the city was protected by a triple wall." ³⁹ It evidently must be understood, although he seems to say the contrary, that the three walls which surrounded it were not of equal importance.⁴⁰ The outer one must have been a simple intrenchment, the next a somewhat stronger rampart; finally rose the wall proper,* which was from fifteen to eighteen

---

* Traces of the triple wall are supposed to have been found almost as far as the headland of Ghamart. They are indicated on our Map of Carthage. The rest of the suburb of the Megara, as far as the sea, was shut in by a simple wall. Perhaps it was by this that Scipio entered the suburb.

metres high and ten metres thick. Ancient writers speak of it with great admiration. They say that casemates for three hundred elephants had been constructed on its lower floor; that above, stalls had been built for four thousand horses, with storehouses filled with fodder and barley, and barracks and food for twenty-four thousand men, infantry and cavalry.* " These were formidable defences, and the Roman generals who endeavoured to carry them by surprise did not succeed. Scipio turned to another side. The suburb of the Megara was less defended than the rest, and a successful assault enabled him to make his way into it. But he soon perceived that this dearly bought success led to nothing. The Megara was full of gardens separated from one another by walls of hard stone or hedges alive with prickly thorn-bushes and intersected by deep watercourses. Scipio dared not risk his army further on this difficult ground, and hastened to leave it. He was forced, therefore, to renounce all idea of a speedy assault and to resign himself to the delays of a regular siege.

He realised thoroughly that from the moment they wished to proceed in regular order, it was first necessary to isolate the city, deprive it of the aid that it was receiving from the neighbouring countries,

---

* Daux has found the same arrangement in what remains of the walls of other Punic cities. The result of his researches may be seen in the work of Tissot on the geography of the African province. I have followed Tissot exactly in all this description of the taking of Carthage.

and cut it off from further supplies of food. Opposite the triple wall to which I have just referred, he caused to be constructed one of those works of fortifications of which the Romans were masters. It consisted of a double line of intrenchments about five kilometres long, closed at both ends by two other transverse intrenchments in such a manner as to form a sort of soldiers' drilling-ground, which he filled with troops. On the side facing Carthage he flanked the intrenchment with walls and towers in order to prevent the inhabitants from leaving the city; he contented himself with covering the other side with palisades, which sufficed to close the approach to those on the outside if they attempted to come near. This enormous work, within bowshot of the enemy, who more than once must have impeded its progress by their attacks, was completed in twenty days. Carthage was thus effectually cut off on the land side, but the sea was left to it. It was necessary to render the ports useless, and, as will be seen, this was no small task.

Appian has left us a detailed and interesting description of the harbours of Carthage.[12] They were cut out by human hands from the clayey sandstone, like those at Thapsus, Utica, and Hadrumetum (modern Susa*). There were two of them, a Merchants' Harbour and a Military Harbour.[13] They had but one entrance, which was closed by iron chains, and one harbour opened into the other.

* We are told that the harbours thus dug out by human hands received the name of *Cothons*.

The Merchants' Harbour, which was the outer one, was filled with numerous cables for anchoring the ships. Around the other were great quays in which had been built a series of two hundred and twenty docks, each of which was large enough to hold a warship; and above were storehouses for the rigging. Thus beauty was joined to utility. " In front of each dock were two Ionic pillars which gave to the whole the appearance of a colonnade." An original feature was a circular island in the centre of the second harbour, which was connected with the mainland by a tongue of land. On this island was built the admiralty. It was a structure high enough to dominate both land and sea; from it one could not only keep watch over the harbours, but also note what was taking place on the open sea. On the other hand, from the sea the harbours were invisible, and even from the Merchants' Harbour, separated from the other by a double wall, it was not possible to perceive what was taking place within the Military Harbour."

All this has not wholly disappeared; there remains enough of it for one to verify to-day the accuracy of Appian's description. The entrance to the harbours must have been on the side of the lazaretto, a little beyond El-Kram, but the buildings that have been erected in this place no longer allow traces of it to be found. Of the Merchants' Harbour there remains in the centre of a field only a small pool of stagnant water, which is still confined by a jetty that leads to the country-house of the Bey; but the shape of the harbour is visible, and its size may be imagined. Another body of water indicates the site of the Military Harbour; it washes an almost circular piece of land, which we recognise at first glance as the island on which the admiralty was built. These, then, are the harbours of Carthage!* What memories the places recall! But it must be admitted that at first they do not seem wholly to come up to our expectations. Gazing upon the spectacle that lies below, it seems a mere nothing when one thinks of the great events of which it was once the theatre. Even when in imagination we give to the harbours their ancient proportions and clear them from the debris that covers them, we cannot help but find them small, and we ask ourselves how they could have been large enough to hold the commerce of the world. In looking at them I again experience the impression made upon me by the Port of Trajan at Ostia which was the object of such lively admiration among the ancients: now that the sea has receded and it is left in the midst of a desolate waste, it seems no longer anything but an ordinary pool. However, the harbours at Carthage are somewhat larger than they appear at first sight. It has been

* Some new plans have recently been made of the site of the Harbours of Carthage. Monsieur Cecil Torr was anxious to establish the fact that they were situated in the open sea and that they are to-day submerged (see *Revue archéol.*, 1894, p. 34 *et seq.*). I am of the opinion of Tissot and Beulé, which, on this question, seems to me probable. An effort has been made in reproducing the position of the ports on the Map of Carthage to indicate approximately their ancient site.

estimated that their size almost equals that of the ancient harbour of Marseilles and that they could shelter more than a thousand ships; this is indeed something. Moreover, we must not forget that the vessels which came to this shore had other anchoring places. Without speaking of the Lake of Tunis,[15] which must have been of greater depth than to-day, all along the coast as far as Bu Said, a distance of several kilometres, one can follow a line of quays, the stones of which have rolled into the sea. From time to time there can be discerned receding lines like little coves, where the ships might have been unloaded, to be afterwards drawn on shore. It is there especially that the commercial movement of Carthage has left its impress. After all, when one imagines those two hundred and twenty warships lying at their docks, below arsenals filled with everything necessary for repairing them; those hundreds of great vessels anchored in the Merchants' Harbour; along the quays the thousands of coasters unloading their cargoes in order to store them in the warehouses, the ruins of which are still visible on the shore, or to carry them to the markets of the city, while, from the centre of his invisible island, the admiral, attentive to everything, commands all the movements by the voice of his trumpeters,— it can then be understood that this activity, all the more striking when one considers the limited space in which it manifested itself, that this meeting on a few square miles of the sailors of all nations, and the products of all countries, must have been the admiration of a people unaccustomed to the size of our vessels and the immensity of our harbours.

At the time of the siege of Carthage, all this prosperity was at an end. The quays were deserted, the harbours almost empty. The warships had been removed from the docks in order to be given up to the conqueror. But the besieged still possessed a few light boats which did much damage to the heavy Roman galleys. When the wind blew from the land, the small Carthaginian ships sailed out of port, towing boats filled with oakum, vine-shoots, and other inflammable materials. When they came up opposite the enemy, they covered the boats with pitch or sulphur, set fire to them, and abandoned them to the wind. These fire-ships more than once almost destroyed the whole Roman fleet. To put an end to these attacks, and to deprive Carthage of the resources of every kind that came by sea, Scipio determined to build a mole which completely closed the entrance to the harbours; it is supposed that the heavy stones found on the shore on the side of El-Kram, or visible on the bed of the sea when it is calm, belong to Scipio's mole."[46]

It was then that the Carthaginians gave one of those proofs of energy which do honour to the last moments of a people. They had surrendered their galleys to the Romans, but their storehouses contained the necessary materials out of which to build others. Approach by sea was cut off, but they could dig a watercourse across the tongue of land which separated the harbours from the shore.

They set themselves bravely to the task, men, women, and children working without intermission. From their ships the besiegers heard the alarming sounds which came from behind the walls; they anxiously questioned the captives and deserters, but no one could tell what was going on. When all was ready the cause was suddenly revealed, and there were seen issuing from the watercourse, the existence of which they did not suspect, fifty triremes, with other ships of less importance. The war began anew. Even to-day there is pointed out along the shore a depression in the land which the sand has almost filled up, in which we think we recognise the watercourse dug by the Carthaginians.*

During one of the fights between the new fleet and the Roman galleys, an incident occurred which perhaps suggested to Scipio his new plan of attack. One day, after severe fighting, when the Carthaginian galleys wished to return to port, they found the entrance, which could not have been very wide, filled with small boats. Closely pursued by the Romans, they brought up against the quays, and, aided by the archers from the shore, they kept the enemy at a distance." Was it this combat that turned the attention of the Roman general to this side of the fortifications? He had always been aware that this part of the wall would be easier to carry than the rest. Carthage, mistress of the sea, feared only

*See Map of Carthage. Naturally, this supposition can only be hypothetical.

the dangers that might come from the land side; therefore the wall was much less strongly fortified along the quays than elsewhere. Here, then, Scipio disembarked his machines and his soldiers; he made a breach in the wall,[18] and succeeded in taking the whole quarter of the harbours as far as the Forum, which was near by,[19] driving before him the frightened populace, which sought refuge in the Byrsa.

There the last and the most terrible struggle of all must have taken place. Three long streets led up from the Forum to the citadel, close-lined with houses six stories high. The Romans were forced to storm them one after another. They fought on the roof-tops and in the street; the inmates, who had no means of saving themselves, were hurled from the windows and caught on pikes. The house taken, it was fired, and if it did not burn quickly enough, it was levelled to the ground by means of machines.

"One should read in Appian," says Tissot, "the whole account of those last days of Carthage. This description is without doubt that of Polybius, and the eye-witness of that frightful massacre has related every detail with his usual exactness, we were going to say with his cold and pitiless precision. Those houses which crumble to the ground with their defenders; the survivors, women, children, and old men, dragged along by hooks, thrown pell-mell with the dead, and buried alive beneath the debris which the besiegers hastily level off; the still quivering limbs protruding from the ruins, and which are trampled down by the hoofs of the cavalry; the coming and going of the cohorts as they relieve one another in this work of destruction ; the blasts of the trumpets, the orders carried by the aides-de-camp, the hurried commands of the tribunes and the centurions ; no detail is forgotten, and this account is one of the truest and most touching pictures that antiquity has bequeathed to us. We say 'the truest,' for the thick bed of ashes, of blackened stones, of charred wood, and of fragments of metals twisted or melted by the fire, that is still found at a depth of five or six metres beneath the ruins of Roman Carthage, is sufficient proof of what that horrible destruction must have been." [50]

The struggle lasted six days; on the seventh, the Carthaginians imprisoned in the citadel asked for mercy. Scipio spared their lives and allowed them to go forth; they numbered, it is said, fifty thousand. After them, Hasdrubal, who had directed the defence, lost courage in turn, and presented himself before Scipio with the fillets of a suppliant.[51] His wife, braver than he, was unwilling to follow him, and with nine hundred deserters, who well knew that there was no pardon for them, sought refuge in the temple of Æsculapius.

This temple, one of the most beautiful and celebrated in Carthage, was probably situated on the very spot on which the chapel of St. Louis has been built. Its vast area occupied the corner of the Byrsa and faced the sea and the harbours. From it a superb flight of sixty steps descended to the public square. This flight of steps, which was one of the ornaments of the city in times of peace, and which the sailors could see from afar as they approached the land, could easily be destroyed at the first sign of danger. Then the hill resumed its ruggedness, and the temple, which rose on a perpendicular cliff, added to the fortifications of the citadel. When the last defenders of Carthage, who had sought refuge there, saw that resistance was becoming impossible, they set fire to the temple; the wife of Hasdrubal was seen standing on the roof, heaping reproaches on her husband for his cowardice; then she hurled her children into the flames and threw herself in after them. Such was the final act of the tragedy.[52]

TRANSLATOR'S NOTES TO CHAPTER II

1. Regarding Phœnician workmanship, *cf.* Homer, *Odyssey*, iv., 613-619; xv., 115-119; *Iliad*, vi., 289, 291; xxiii., 743. Also 1 Kings v., 6; *cf.* Homer, *Od.*, xv., 425. Also Herod., vii., 23, 34.

2. "The date of the founding of Carthage is uncertain; but the current tradition refers it to a period about a hundred years before the founding of Rome."—R. Bosworth Smith.

Justin., xviii., 6, 9: "Condita est urbs hæc septuaginta duobus annis antequam Roma."

Appian (*Pun.*, 1) places its foundation fifty years before the fall of Troy.

"The wide discrepancy may perhaps be accounted for by the existence of an earlier Phœnician settlement on or about the same spot, said to have been called *Cambe* or *Cacabe*."

"The word Carthage—in Latin, *Carthago*, and in Greek, *Karchedon* —contains in another form the word Kirjath, a name familiar to us in the Bible in the compounds. Kirjath-Arba and Kirjath-Jearim. Kirjath means "Town," and the name by which Carthage was known to its own inhabitants was Kirjath-Hadeschath, or the "New Town"; *new*, to distinguish it either from the old town of Tyre, from which its settlers had come forth, or from the older settlement of Utica."—*The Story of Carthage*, by Alfred J. Church.

3. For change of policy see Herod., i., 165, 166, and Sallust, *Jugurtha*, 79; also R. Bosworth Smith's *Carthage and the Carthaginians*, p. 14, and Mommsen's *History of Rome*, vol. ii.

4. Justin., xviii., 5, 14; Justin., xix., 1, 3; ii., 4; Appian, *Pun.*, 2.

5. R. Bosworth Smith says, in *Carthage and the Carthaginians*, p. 11: "It is more than probable that the story of the ox-hide (Virg., *Æn.*, i., 367, 368; Justin., xviii., 5, 9) is nothing but a Greek legend based on the superficial resemblance of the Phœnician word *Bozra*, a fortress, to the Greek *Byrsa*, an ox-hide."

6. "It was not from high moral motives but from a shrewd and calculating policy, that the Phœnicians . . . long forbore to aim at foreign conquest or at territorial aggrandisement."—R. Bosworth Smith, in *Carthage and the Carthaginians*, p. 4.

"Careless they dwelt, quiet and secure, after the manner of the Zidonians, and had no dealings with any man."—Judges xviii., 7.

Ezekiel xxvii., 10: "They of Persia and of Lud and of Phut were in thine army; thy men of war; they hanged the shield and helmet in thee; they set forth thy comeliness."

See also Plutarch, *Timoleon*, 20.

7. The so-called "Sacred Band" consisted of 2500 Carthaginian citizens. See Diodorus Siculus, xvi., 80; xx., 10–12. *Cf.* also Plutarch, *Timoleon*, 27; also Arist., *Pol.*, iv., 2, 10.

8. That "greatest of all islands."—Herod., i., 170; v., 106; Polyb., iii., 22, 25.

9. For preëminence of Phœnician commerce, see R. Bosworth Smith, *Carthage and the Carthaginians*, p. 7. Also Thucyd., i., 8; *cf.* Herod., iv., 147; vi., 47; Thucyd., vi., 2; Polyb., i., 10, 5; Virg., *Æn.*, x., 174. *Cf.* Livy, xxi., 51; Diod., v., 12; Cicero, *Verres*, ii., 72; iv., 46, and *Hannibal*, by Wm. O'Connor Morris, p. 32 *et seq.*

10. The Byrsa or Upper City. A Greek word corrupted from the Canaanitish *Bozra* or *Bostra*, that is, a fort.

"It is known in the country only by the name *Bersach*, which seems to be a corruption of Byrsa."—Chateaubriand.

Carthage

"It lies," Appian says, "toward the isthmus which connected Carthage with the mainland."—Appian, *Pun.*, 95.

Strabo, in his clear, concise way, describes it as being "a brow sufficiently steep, lying in the middle of the city, with houses on all sides of it."—Strabo, xx., 9.

Dr. Davis, the excavator and explorer, places the Byrsa on Burj-Jedeed, a hill near the sea, considerably to the south-east of the hill of St. Louis.

Ritter identifies the Byrsa with Djebel Khawi or the Catacomb Hill, on the north-west of the city.

For plan of wall at the Byrsa, see Church's *Story of Carthage*, p. 293.

11. "From the summit of the Byrsa the eye embraces the ruins of Carthage, which are more numerous than is generally supposed; they resemble those of Sparta, being but poorly preserved, but occupying a considerable space. I saw them in the month of February. The fig- (see note below), olive-, and carob-trees were already putting forth their first leaves; great angelicas and acanthus-trees formed clusters of verdure among the ruins of marble of every hue. In the distance my gaze wandered to the isthmus, to a double sea, to far-off islands, to a smiling landscape, to bluish lakes, to azure mountains. I saw forests, vessels, aqueducts, Moorish villages, Mahometan hermitages, minarets, and the white houses of Tunis."—Chateaubriand, *Itinéraire*, part vi.

12. "The river Bagradas, Bagrada, or Backara, perhaps the Meliana of to-day, entered the Gulf of Tunis on the north side of the city. Its mouth was at Utica."—G. L. Ditson, *North Coast of Africa*.

13. Ras Sidi Bu Said,—so called from the saint's tomb found there,—or Cape Cartagena (Carthage), is of red sandstone and is the most commanding eminence within the precincts of the ancient city. Its highest point rises to 393 feet above sea level. It is crowned at present by an Arab village of peculiar sanctity. See R. B. Smith, *Carthage and the Carthaginians;* also Mommsen's *History of Rome*, vol. iii., chap. i.

14. The Megara (Hebrew Magurim). See Polybius, i., 73-75; Livy, *Epit.*, 41; Strabo, xvii., 3, 14.

15. "The Barbary fig (*cactus opuntia*), whose sharp, fleshy leaves afford sure protection against every animal except the camel. Hedges are often made of it. The fruit constitutes the sole nourishment of many of the natives."—G. L. Ditson, *North Coast of Africa*.

16. "Here dwelt the richest of the Carthaginians, and vied with each other in pomp and luxury."—R. Bosworth Smith. See also Diodorus Siculus, xx., 8.

17. "Bits of tessellated pavement, of porphyry, of the famous Numidian marble, green, white, and red, everywhere are found. But they belong to periods later than that of the Phœnician city, not a stone of which, after its fire of seventeen days, was left standing." —R. Bosworth Smith, *Carthage and the Carthaginians*, p. 379.

18. "A Phœnician, Roman, Vandal, and Byzantine city had been founded on the same site, had risen to opulence and power, and had vanished again, leaving barely a trace of their existence behind."— R. Bosworth Smith, *Carthage and the Carthaginians*, p. 376.

19. "It is a proof of its natural advantages that within two centuries of its total destruction, Carthage became the third city of the Empire."—*The Story of Carthage*, by Alfred J. Church.

20. R. Bosworth Smith, *Carthage and the Carthaginians*, p. 361, says: "Augustus . . . attempted, it is said, to evade the letter of Scipio's curse by building his city not on but near the site of the Phœnician city" (Appian, *Pun.*, 136). Pliny, however (*Hist. Nat.*, v., 3), says that the Roman city was built on the exact site of the Phœnician: "Colonia Carthago magnæ in vestigiis Carthaginis."

"The remains of Roman Carthage, still called Kartajina by the Arabians, are very scanty, owing to the destruction by the new capital, Tunis."—Heinrich Kiepert, *Manual of Ancient Geography*..

21. For destruction of Carthage by Scipio, see Florus, ii., 15, 18. Also Chateaubriand's *Itinéraire*, part vi.

22. For votive tablets disinterred at Carthage, see Davis, *Carthage and her Remains*, p. 256 *seq.*, and plates; *cf.* also Beulé, *Fouilles à Carthage*, plate 3; also Africa, in vol. ii., *L'Univers Pittoresque*. For illustrations of Carthaginian *steles*, see pp. 16, 98, 107, 110, 111, 113, 121, 124, Church's *Story of Carthage;* also p. 17 for Carthaginian tombs.

23. The horned Ashtaroth, or Astarte (her Carthaginian name was Tanit, or Tanith), the crescent Moon, was the consort of Baal-Moloch, the sun- or fire-god. She was identified with Ceres, Juno, Diana, and the Venus Cœlestis. Her worship, like that of the Babylonian Mylitta, sanctioned immorality.

See Herod., i., 199, for worship of Mylitta at Babylon ; for that of Venus at Sicca, see Val. Max., ii., 6, 15 ext., and *cf.* Justin., xviii., 5, 4.

24. Baal-Moloch was a malignant deity, rejoicing "in human sacrifices and in parents' tears." See Diodorus Siculus, xx., 14, 65 ; Silius Italicus, iv., 765–773 ; Polyb., i., 34, 12 ; 36, 1 ; Diod., xx., 14, 65.

25. Suffete, the same as the Hebrew *Shofetim*, or Shophetim, mistranslated in the Bible as *Judges*. See Aristotle, *loc. cit.*, 3 ; Polyb., vi., 51, 2 ; Livy, xxx., 7 : "Senatum itaque Suffetes (quod velut consulare imperium apud eos erat) vocaverunt."

There were two Suffetes at Gades, as probably in all the Phœnician colonies. Livy, xxviii., 37 : "Suffetes eorum, qui summus Pœnis est magistratus . . . cruci adfigi jussit."

They were appointed for life. See also Herod., viii., 167, *et. seq.*

"Possibly 'Suffetes' was a reminiscence of the Latin word *suffectus*, which was used when a magistrate was elected to fill a vacancy occurring at some casual time."—Alfred J. Church, *The Story of Carthage.*

26. "Other gods, such as Esmun, or Æsculapius, to whom the temple on the Byrsa was dedicated ; Apollo, whose temple, adorned with plates of gold, excited the cupidity of the Roman soldiers, even amidst the horrors of the final assault, and whose colossal statue was afterwards carried to Rome (see Plutarch, *Flamininus*, i. ; Appian, *Pun.*, 127); Demeter and Persephone, whose worship was imported from Sicily after a pestilence which had broken out in the Carthaginian army as a punishment for the desecration of their temples (see Diod. Sic., xiv., 77) ;—were originally looked upon only as manifestations of the two superior deities, but in time they assumed a separate existence of their own."—R. B. Smith, *Carthage and the Carthaginians*, p. 33.

Another inferior god was Melkart, or Melcarth, that is, Melech-

Kirjath, or, the king of the city. The Greeks call him " the Phœnician Hercules." In Greek mythology he is Melicertes. The city he particularly presided over was Tyre, where he had a magnificent temple. He had one also at Thasos and Gades. At Carthage, the whole city was his temple. His worship was more spiritual than that of the other gods.

27. The Temple of Tanit lay at the foot of the Byrsa. It was a collection of monuments and of gardens, courts and fore-courts, hemmed in by a little wall of uncemented stones.

28. *Æneid*, i., 505.
   " Tum foribus divæ, media testudine templi,
   Septa armis, solioque alte subnixa, resedit."

29. *Æneid*, iv., 150–155.

30. *Æneid*, iv., 165.

31. The so-called Old Comedy of Athens.

32. " He knew men and women thoroughly, loved them, found them heroic, generous, noble,—and he so painted them."—Wm. Cranston Lawton, in *Library of the World's Best Literature*, vol. x., p. 5571.

33. " With all his defects, Propertius is undoubtedly the master of the Latin elegy."—G. M. Whicker.

34.
   " I doffed the maiden's dress ;—I was a bride,
      The matron's coif confined my braided hair.
   Too soon, O Paulus ! doomed to leave thy side,
      I was but thine, my tombstone shall declare.
         .   .   .   .   .   .
   " Twice had my brother filled the curule chair,
      A consul ere his sister's days were run.
   Thy censor-sire in mind, sweet daughter, bear ;
      Uphold his honour : wed, like me, but one."
                              Cornelia, stanzas and 7.
Translated from Propertius by Dr. James Cranstoun (Edinburgh, 1875).

35. Nævius, a soldier-poet, "the last of the native minstrels."

36. See Henty's *Carthage and the Carthaginians* for a description of Carthage in the time of Hannibal.

37. See Livy, xxv., 2; Appian, *Hisp.*, 18.

38. Livy, xxvi., 18; Appian, *Hisp.*, *loc. cit.*; Zonaras, ix., 7; Polyb., xi., 33, 7, 8; Livy, xxviii., 38; Appian, *Hisp.*, 33.

39. "The remains of this triple line of fortifications have very recently been brought to light. See Beulé, *Fouilles à Carthage*, iii. and iv. He gives dimensions as follows in metres and in Greek feet (1 = 0.309 metre):

Outer wall..................	2	metres	=	$6\frac{1}{2}$ feet
Corridor...................	1.9	"	=	6 "
Front wall of casemates......	1	"	=	$3\frac{1}{4}$ "
Casemate rooms.............	4.2	"	=	14 "
Back wall of casemates.......	1	"	=	$3\frac{1}{4}$ "

Whole breadth of the walls, 10.1 metres = 33 feet.

Or, as Diodorus (p. 522) states it, 22 cubits (1 Greek cubit = $1\frac{1}{2}$ feet), while Livy (*ap.* Oros., iv., 22) and Appian (*Pun.*, 95), who seem to have had before them another less accurate passage of Polybius, state the breadth of the walls at thirty feet. The triple wall of Appian—as to which a false idea has hitherto been diffused by Florus (i., 31)—denotes the outer wall, and the front and back walls of the casemates. That this coincidence is not accidental, and that we have here in reality the remains of the famed walls of Carthage before us, will be evident to everyone: the objections of Davis (*Carthage and her Remains*, p. 370 *et seq.*) only show how little even the utmost zeal can adduce in opposition to the main results of Beulé. Only we must maintain that all the ancient authorities give the statements of which we are now speaking with reference, not to the citadel-wall, but to the city-wall on the landward side, of which the wall along the south side of the citadel-hill was an integral part (Oros., iv., 22). In accordance with this view, the excavations at the citadel-hill on the east, north, and west, have shown no traces of fortifications, whereas on the south side they have brought to light the very remains of this great wall. There is no reason for regarding these as the remains of a separate fortification of the citadel distinct from the city-wall; it may be presumed that further excavations at a corresponding depth —the foundation of the city wall discovered at the Byrsa lies fifty-six feet beneath the present surface—will bring to light like, or at any rate analogous, foundations along the whole landward side, although it is probable that at the point where the walled suburb of Magalia adjoined the main wall the fortification was either weaker from the first or was early neglected. The length of the wall as a whole cannot be stated with precision, but it must have been very considerable, for three hundred elephants were stabled there, and the stores for their fodder and perhaps other spaces also, as well as the gates, are to be taken into account. It was very natural that the inner city, within whose walls the Byrsa was included, should, especially by way of contrast to the suburb of Magalia, which had its separate circumvallation, be sometimes itself called Byrsa (App., *Pun.*, 117; Nepos, *ap.* Serv., *Æn.*, i. 368)."—Mommsen, *Hist. of Rome*, vol. iii., bk. iv.

40. Appian tells that the three walls were of equal height and breadth. This is incredible, because such an arrangement would have been useless. No trace of any such kind of fortification can be discovered either at Carthage or in any ancient town. The real meaning of the author—possibly Polybius—from whom Appian quoted, seems to have been as above.

Appian gives the height of the wall as forty-five feet. Diodorus gives the height, probably inclusive of the battlements, at forty cubits, or sixty feet. The remnant preserved is still from thirteen to sixteen feet (four to five metres) high.

"The rooms of a horse-shoe shape brought to light in excavation have a depth of fourteen and a breadth of eleven Greek feet; the width of the entrances is not specified. Whether these dimensions and the proportions of the corridor suffice for our recognising them as elephants' stalls, remains to be settled by a more accurate investigation. The partition-walls, which separate the apartments, have a thickness of 1.1 metre = $3\frac{1}{2}$ feet."—Mommsen, vol. iii., bk. iv.

41. See Appian, *Pun.*, 95; Strabo, xvii., 3, 14. *Cf.* Appian, *Pun.*, 88; Diodorus Siculus, xxxii.; *Frag.*, p. 522.

42. For cuts of the harbours of Carthage according to Beulé, see Church's *Story of Carthage*, p. 290; according to Daux, p. 291;

for port of Carthage, p. 287. Also R. Bosworth Smith, *Carthage and the Carthaginians*, p. 345.

43. This is also called the "Harbour of the Warships, or *Cothon*."—Alfred J. Church, p. 296.

It was called *Cothon*, from its shape, which was circular, like a drinking cup.

"In the times of the Vandals the word *Cothon* is unknown, and that of *Mandracium* has taken its place."—R. B. Smith, in *Carthage and the Carthaginians*, see p. 344.

Procopius, *Bel. Vandal*, i., 19, 20, shows that it could be closed then, as in the Carthaginian times, by a chain.

"That this Phœnician word (*Cothon*) signifies a basin excavated in a circular shape is shown both by Diodorus (iii., 44) and by its being employed by the Greeks to denote a 'cup.' It thus suits only the inner harbour of Carthage, and in that sense it is used by Strabo (xvii., 2, 14, where it is strictly applied to the admiral's island) and Fest., *Ep. v. Cothones*, p. 37. Appian (*Pun.*, 127) is not quite accurate in describing the rectangular harbour in front of the *Cothon* as part of it."—Mommsen, vol. iii., bk. iv.

44. Appian, *Pun.*, 96 ; Strabo, xvii., 3, 14.

45. The Lake of Tunis was called the Stagnum.—Procopius, *Bel. Vandal*, i., 19, 20.

46. See Appian, *Pun.*, 120, 121.

47. See R. Bosworth Smith, *Carthage and the Carthaginians*, p. 354. Also Appian, *Pun.*, 123, 124.

48. Appian, *Pun.*, 124, 125.

49. Appian, *Pun.*, 127.

50. Appian, *Pun.*, 127-129 ; Zonaras, ix., 30 ; Chateaubriand, *Itinéraire*, part vii.

51. "On the following day a deputation came forth, with suppliant branches and fillets, taken from the temple of Æsculapius, in their hands, begging Scipio to spare their lives."—R. Bosworth Smith, *Carthage and the Carthaginians*, p. 357.

52. See Polyb., xxxix., 3. 1, 2 ; Appian, *Pun.*, 130, 131, 133-135.

CHAPTER III

THE GOVERNMENT AND THE ARMY

I

IT was not sufficient to destroy Carthage; it was necessary to prevent it from springing up again. Scipio, having razed it to the ground, had priests pronounce solemn imprecations against anyone who should attempt to rebuild it. But curses did not suffice. In order to blot out forever what remained of the Carthaginians in Africa, more efficacious measures were resorted to: Rome was obliged to make up its mind to occupy the country it had just conquered; it would be more correct to say that Rome resigned itself to this, for it seems that it did so without haste, and as though unwillingly. It did not take all that it might of the enemy's territory, but limited itself as much as possible. The new province extended only to *Tabraca* (*Tabarca*, now Bithecusæ[1]) and *Thenæ* (*Henchir-Tina*, now Taine[2]), and care was taken to dig a ditch between these two cities, as though to indicate that that was the definite boundary line of the Roman possessions and that they were determined never to go further; what remained was left to Masinissa. These half-measures arouse the anger of Mommsen; he sees in them "the absence of foresight, the narrowness and the absurdity of the Republican government," and he is glad to oppose to this timid conduct the bold policy of the Empire, which so resolutely accepted the task of conquering the whole of Northern Africa in order to civilise it.

However, it is easy to account for the reasons that the Republican government had for acting as it did. In the first place, let us admit that we do not always form a just idea of the Romans. We judge them according to the extent of their conquests; from the fact of their having succeeded in vanquishing almost every other nation, we think ourselves justified in concluding that they had an insatiable ambition, that they threw themselves upon the world with the fixed idea of becoming masters of it, that they acted according to a preconceived plan, and that they carried out this plan to the end, without hesitating or weakening. This is indeed what the devoted admirers of the Romans, like Polybius, give us to understand; in order to explain this success, these writers search for deep and subtle reasons. As a matter of fact, the Romans did not always have such high ideas nor such a clear insight into their future. They were a keen people, cautious and in nowise tempted by love of adventure; if they ran some risk, it was because they could not do otherwise. One war led to another; they were often brought to undertake a new conquest in order to make sure of an old. The key to their character and their strength lay in their not planning boundless projects, although they succeeded in coming into possession of an empire beyond all limit. Perhaps it was this moderation and prudence that rendered their domination so secure.

Africa seems to have tempted them even less than all the rest. It was a distant land, separated from them by the sea, a terrible sea, *mare sævum*,* swept alternately by the north and the west wind, which drove ships upon rocks. The inhabitants, too, inspired them with but little confidence. They had suffered too much from the Carthaginians not to detest them; it was a proverb with them that Punic faith could never be trusted.³ As for the natives, they had merely caught a glimpse of them, but from the first they had formed a very bad opinion of them; they believed them to be capricious, fickle, enemies of peace, and ever ready to fall upon the lands of their neighbour and to live at his expense. Nor does the country itself seem to have attracted them. Doubtless the environs of Carthage appeared to them very fertile and thoroughly cultivated; but it is probable that as far as anything else was concerned, they felt as Sallust did later when he expressed his sentiments at sight of those arid plains and those mountains bare of trees. Appian imagines that a discussion arose in the Senate, after the defeat of Hannibal, as to what should be done with the Africa that had just been conquered; and whether, as they despaired of gaining any sure profit from it,

* Sallust, *Jug.*, 18.

they should let Carthage live.* When it had been destroyed, they had to resign themselves to rebuilding it; but politicians were not lacking to whom this necessity seemed unfortunate, and who were very anxious to renounce the heritage. This opinion lasted a long time, and even under Trajan, a Latin historian who considered himself a sage questioned seriously whether it would not have been better if Rome had never occupied either Sicily or Africa, but had been satisfied with ruling over Italy.†

To-day these ideas seem very strange to us, and yet we should comprehend them better than anyone. We must remember the uncertainty, the hesitation, and the confusion which with us followed the capture of Algiers. What was to be done with this conquest which overthrew every prevision of our ancient policy? Opinion was strongly divided, and the subject was discussed in the French Chamber of Deputies as it had been formerly in the Roman Senate. Every year, *à propos* of the address or the budget, orators were heard who held the most conflicting opinions; while some were astonished that the whole of Algeria had not yet been conquered, others could not comprehend why there should be any hesitation in giving it up. Placed between factions, one of which wished to seize everything, the other, to retain nothing, the government, which strove to offend no one, came to a standstill. It dared not assume the direct government of the

* Appian, *De Reb. Punicis*, 57 *et seq.*
† Florus, iii., 12.

subjugated country, and spent its time looking about for kindly disposed natives who would like to be Beys of Oran or Constantine under the protection of France. For fear of being accused of wishing to extend its conquests too far, it established itself firmly in no part, which fact forced it to retake Blidah (*Velisci*) and Medeah (*Tuliusii*) every year. All that lasted until the day when Bugeaud gave the whole world to understand " that the definitive peace of Algeria was in the Great Sahara," and that in order to possess in quiet the towns along the seacoast, it was necessary to be master of the rest.

The Romans before us had made the same mistakes, with the same results. In order to avoid the responsibility and the expense which the government of a country entails, they found it convenient to establish there a chief or a king who belonged to some ancient race, and whom they charged to maintain the peace and to govern under their authority. This is the system of the protectorate. They very frequently used it in the countries they had conquered, and often, too, with good results. It has been seen that in Africa they gave to Masinissa and his successors not only the kingdom of Syphax, but that part of the territory of Carthage which lay along the desert. Numidia, thus constituted, must have formed a sort of belt around the province of Africa, which protected it against the invasions of the Nomads and allowed the subjects of Rome to cultivate their fertile plains in peace. The disadvantage of this form of government lies in the fact that the subject royalties are of no use if weak, and if, on the other hand, they are strong, they may be tempted to assert their independence and become a danger instead of a protection. In Africa they caused great annoyance to the Romans, and yet it has been seen that they had great trouble in giving them up; it was not until the time of Caligula that the last of these petty kings disappeared, and that, throughout the whole country, the protectorate was replaced by direct government.

· The system of limited occupation had no more success with the Romans than with us. Experience soon showed that it was not possible for them to confine themselves to the narrow boundaries that they had laid down. In the time of Augustus, the Gætuli attacked the province and were vigorously driven back into their mountains *; but then it was found that they were aided by the Garamantes, who dwelt behind them; whether willing or not, the Romans had to conquer the Garamantes, in order to be sure that the Gætuli would remain quiet. Cornelius Balbus, nephew of that Spaniard whose friendship for Cæsar had made his fortune, crossed the frontier, penetrated as far as *Cidamus* (Ghadames), and travelled through the oasis of the Fezzan (or Fazzen, *Phazania*). At his triumph he ordered the names of twenty-six tribes, towns, rivers, and unknown mountains that he had visited and con-

* Dionysius, lv., 28.

quered, to be carried about on posters before the astonished populace. Among them was Mount *Garas*, " where the pearls are born." * Under Claudius, the Moors of the West having revolted, a general was sent against them who thoroughly understood his business,—Suetonius Paulinus, who later conquered Britain. He was not the man to be satisfied with half-success. He set out in pursuit of the Moors, who fled before him, dared to follow them into unknown countries in order to prevent them from recommencing hostilities, and pushed on as far as that river of Morocco called the *Oued-Ghir*.'† His successor, Hosidius Geta, renewed the campaign, and penetrated so far into the desert that he and his entire army nearly perished there of thirst, but were saved as by a miracle.‡ It is evident that the Romans made up their minds valiantly, and that once convinced of the necessity of breaking away from the timid policy of the early conquerors, they went forward without hesitation.

Moreover, this decision did not mean merely a few bold attacks in order to frighten plunderers or some expeditions lasting a few weeks or months, after which they would hasten to return home; they intended to remain permanent masters of those countries to which war had led them, and they built solid posts there. Each time that they pushed

---

* Pliny, *Hist. Nat.*, v., 5.
† Pliny, v., 14.
‡ Dionysius, lx., 9.

The Government and the Army

forward their conquests, a line of fortifications guaranteed their possession. Even to-day, remains of these forts are found. They were satisfied, in the first century, to occupy the northern slope of the Aurès, from *Theveste* (Tebessa)⁸ to *Lambese* (*Lambæsis*, now Tezzût, which has lately been rebuilt and renamed Lambèse), by passing through *Mascula* (Krenchela) and *Thamugade* (Timegad), and they there founded towns which protected the defiles of the mountain. In the following century, by a bold step forward, the border was carried to the other side. It was resolutely extended southward, and was guarded by strong citadels wherever natural irregularities did not shelter it from sudden attacks. Leaving Gafsa,⁹ that is to say, the place where the shotts of Tunis end, we remove the débris from stations which were called *Ad Speculum*, *Ad Turres*, *Ad Majores* (Tadert, near the oasis of *Negrin*), then *Thabudei* (Sidi Okbah) *Piscina* (Biskra). All these posts, which are still easily recognised, guarded the approach from the Aurès. Others, the trace of which is less apparent, and which were built at the foot of the *Zabi* Mountains and along the *Oued-Djedi*, protected Hodna. Thus the frontier extended from east to west like a belt, behind which the tribes subject to Roman domination breathed in peace. From there, when necessary, they could go forth by every path of the desert.

Where did they definitively stop? What, in those regions of the South, was the exact limit of their domination? It will be known when further explorations are made. In the meantime it may be said that there is scarcely any country in our African possessions, however distant, however barbarous it may be, in which there is proof that they did not settle before us. Wherever our soldiers have ventured they have found, not without surprise, some trace of their valiant predecessors. General Saint-Armand wrote to his brother, on June 7, 1850, that he had just penetrated into one of the most inaccessible passes of the Aurès, " a sort of funnel surrounded by perpendicular rocks five hundred metres high, which might be called the end of the world." He fully intended to inscribe on the side of one of the mountains the number of regiments, the name of the commanders-in-chief, and the date when, for the first time no doubt, an army had appeared in that wild place. But a few days later he was obliged to alter his words:

"We flattered ourselves, dear brother," said he, "that we were the first to pass through the defile of Kanga, but this was a mistake. In the very middle, cut into the rock, we discovered an inscription, perfectly preserved, which informs us that under Antonius Pius the sixth Roman legion made the route over which we are struggling sixteen hundred and fifty years later. We were dumbfounded."*

Thus it was that Roman domination, after continuing for some time in the territory of Carthage,

* I quote this interesting paragraph from the memoir of Monsieur Masqueray on *Mont Aurès*.

had on all sides gone beyond Scipio's narrow ditch. At the most flourishing epoch of the Empire, under the *Antonini* and the *Severi*, it extended the whole length of Northern Africa, from the sands of Cyrene to the Atlantic; in breadth it had advanced into the desert as far as one could go. Thus it occupied the Tripolitana Provincia, Tunis, Algeria, and a part of Morocco.

II

So vast a territory, inhabited by warlike races but poorly subjugated and often but little civilised, was not easy to administer; therefore the Romans failed at first to find the best means of governing it. Like us, they groped about, and hesitated a long time as to various systems. It was not until the close of the reign of Claudius that the problem was solved, and the government of Africa permanently organised. Scipio, we have just seen, made a Roman province of what he had taken from the Carthaginians. Later, it was called Ancient Africa (*Africa Vetus*); it comprised nearly the Tunis of to-day. Cæsar, after the victory of Thapsus, joined to it Numidia, which became a sort of New Africa (*Africa Nova*), by the side of the ancient. As the country was still agitated, troops were left there, who naturally lived in the least tranquil part, that is, in Numidia. It is known that a few years later, Augustus, in reorganising the Empire, thought of sharing with the Senate the government of the territories which Rome had conquered. He gave to

the Senate the provinces that were wholly subdued, and reserved for himself those in which the presence of legions was rendered indispensable by the turbulence of the inhabitants and the proximity of the frontiers. In this way he kept the whole army under his control, which was a matter of great importance to him. But Africa, where one legion was stationed, was none the less counted among the senatorial provinces. It is difficult to understand the motive for this exception, which was so contrary to the policy of the Emperor; yet the arrangement continued for more than half a century, until Caligula finally put an end to it. He directed that the African legion should no longer be under the orders of the proconsul, but that it should be commanded directly by the Emperor. This was still only a half-measure, which was completed when it was decided that Numidia, where the legion was encamped, should be separated from proconsular Africa. It was made an imperial province, and was governed, under the direct authority of the prince, by the standing chief of the legion, who was called *legatus.**
The legate thus held in his hand the administration of the country and the command of the troops.

In this way the Romans settled a problem which greatly troubled us. In our case, the question of Algeria was discussed for a long time, in order to discover which was better, civil or military government. As late as 1870, the whole authority was in the hands of one general, and this caused much com-

* Or, as he was formerly called with us, lieutenant-general.

plaint. Therefore the first act of the Revolution was to remove the sovereign power from the commander of the army, and to place a civil governor over him. The Romans settled the difficulty in another manner. As they feared that if the authority were divided it would be weakened, they decided to separate the civil territory from the military; but with each the entire authority was left in the same hand. Proconsular Africa, rich, flourishing, peaceful, and lying around Carthage, which had just been rebuilt, was governed by a prominent noble, a man of the world, who to maintain order had need only of a few soldiers; Numidia, on the other hand, which on all sides faced hostile tribes, was placed under the authority of the general who commanded the legion. In this way all trouble was avoided, and, what greatly pleased the Romans, the two governors, the civil magistrate and the military, remained master each in his own province. For proconsul of Africa a person of importance was chosen, who usually possessed a large fortune and bore a well known name. He had to reside at Carthage, which was rapidly becoming one of the most beautiful cities in the world, and to hold there a sort of court. He was elected by the senate, taken from among the consulars, and according to an ancient custom was chosen by lot. He never remained in office longer than one year. Augustus having decreed that all office-holders outside of Rome should receive a salary in silver, in place of those payments in kind which gave opportunity for so many exactions, the salary of the proconsul of Africa was fixed at a million sesterces, that is, a little more than two hundred thousand francs. Without having as much apparent importance, the legate of Numidia also held a very prominent position. He was taken from the senate, and was of the rank of the ancient *prætor*, sometimes called consul. The Emperor himself chose him, and he had to remain at his post as long as it pleased the prince to leave him there. He was not elected under the same conditions as the proconsul; his task was less brilliant, perhaps, but more difficult. The safety of the two provinces rested upon him, and it was his duty to check the enemies on the border. Thus he could not be chosen at random like the other, and it would have been dangerous to remove him too soon from his duties when he fulfilled them well.

Beyond Numidia, from the river *Ampsaga* (*Oued-Kebir*) to the Atlantic, extended Mauretania. When Ptolemy, king of the country, was killed by Caligula, his dominions were again joined to the Empire. Two provinces were made of them.' The one, *Mauretania Cæsariensis* (Cæsarean Mauretania), which comprised our department of Oran and the largest part of that of Algiers, with Cæsarea,' the city of Juba II., for a capital; the other, *Mauretania Tingitana*, which took its name from *Tingis* (now Tanja, vulg., Tangiers), its most important city. Both of these were imperial provinces, that is, the Emperor reserved to himself the right of appointing the governors; only, as they were but slightly known and very little civilised, he did not send legates to govern them, but simple intendants (*procuratores*), and this term shows that he looked upon them as his own possessions, and that he meant to keep them wholly under his control. These procurators were selected from among the knights; they bore the title of *vir egregius*, and received a salary of two hundred thousand sesterces (forty thousand francs). As in the case of the legates, they were charged with both the civil government and the military command; but unlike them they did not command legionary soldiers, that is, Roman citizens; they had under their orders only auxiliary troops, levied among the conquered nations.

Thus, during the greater part of the Empire, the Roman possessions in Northern Africa formed four provinces: Proconsular Africa, Numidia, and the two Mauretanias. It must be added that the importance and the civilisation of these provinces diminished as one advanced toward the ocean. The proconsular province rivalled Italy in wealth, brilliancy, and literary culture; Numidia was as yet more uncivilised and less peaceful; as to the Mauretanias, especially Tingitana, they were partly barbarous.

III

The first duty of one who governs a country is to maintain peace. This was not easy to do in Africa, in the midst of warlike peoples who were but slightly disciplined, and in the face of those wandering tribes that roamed about the desert and the high plateaus. The Romans thoroughly understood this, and that, no doubt, is why they showed so little haste to settle there. They were not ignorant of the fact that it was necessary to keep an army there, and that a military occupation is expensive. The emperors, thorough masters of the world though they were, always had great difficulty in paying their legions, or, as would be said to-day, in poising their war budget; therefore they were very much occupied in reducing the number of soldiers who guarded the provinces. They managed in Africa as elsewhere, and it is interesting and instructive to try to discover how with so few troops and with the least possible outlay, they succeeded in assuring their domination there.* But in order the better to comprehend their policy in that province, it is necessary to give first a few more general explanations.

We must remember that at the death of Augustus

* I borrow almost all that I am about to say from the volume by Monsieur Cagnat, Professor of Roman Archæology in the College of France, entitled *L'Armée romaine d'Afrique* (1 vol., in 4°, chez Leroux). This work is assuredly one of the best to which the scientific exploration of Algeria has given rise up to the present time. We refer to it all those who are curious to learn the smallest details of the organisation of those armies which conquered the world, and who wish to see them living before them. Monsieur Cagnat has a wonderful knowledge of Africa. He travelled several times through Tunis, when there was was some danger in doing so, and brought back such a rich harvest of new inscriptions that the Academy of Berlin engaged him to publish, with Monsieur Schmidt, the supplement of the eighth volume of the *Corpus inscriptionum latinarum*.

the Roman army proper, that which might be called the regular standing army, consisted of twenty-five legions; there had been thirty under Vespasian and thirty-three under Septimius Severus,⁹ that is to say, almost two hundred thousand men.¹⁰ That was a small thing when one thinks of the extent of the Empire; but, in reality, the legions formed scarcely more than the half of the army; they contained only Roman citizens, and in addition to them other bodies of troops were organised, the ranks of which were open to those who did not yet enjoy the rights of citizens. Among the peoples that Rome had conquered were found some energetic ones, who had not suffered themselves to be vanquished without resistance, and whom she had learned to respect in fighting against them. As Rome possessed the knowledge of making use of everything, it was impossible for her to neglect an element of strength which victory placed in her hand; therefore she took into her pay the bravest of the vanquished. Left free, they might have become enemies; she made them her soldiers. Some formed the troops of cavalry, called the wings (*alæ*); others, the cohorts¹¹ of foot-soldiers.* Generally they were given the name of the countries in which they had been levied (*ala Thracum, cohors Lusitanorum*), or that of the particular army to which they belonged (*sagittarii, funditores*). In the early ages their native commanders-in-chief had been left to them, but

---

* Some of these cohorts contained horsemen as well; these were called *cohortes equitatæ*.

after the revolt of the Batavi, under Vespasian, Roman officers were generally placed at their head, as is done with our native soldiers. The wings especially were useful to the Romans; as their legions consisted almost exclusively of foot-soldiers, they had no real cavalry except that which the provinces furnished them. The wings and the cohorts formed what were called the auxiliary troops (*auxilia*). They were sometimes used alone, but as a rule they served by the side of the legions, and in the latter case care was taken that their number was not larger than that of the legionaries.

Let us now return to Africa and see what were the troops charged to defend it and how they were distributed. The inscriptions make it perfectly clear to us; there is no question on which we have more light. Proconsular Africa, being a senatorial province, had no soldiers except the garrison of Carthage.[12] * Numidia had one legion, the third Augustan, which encamped at Lambèse, and the auxiliary troops which were usually added to the legion, making in all about twelve thousand men. The two Mauretanias, which were governed by procurators of equestrian rank, could not have had legionaries in their garrisons, as the legions were always commanded by legates of senatorial rank;

---

* Mommsen thinks that this garrison, in addition to a certain number of soldiers detached from the legion of Numidia, comprised one of those *city cohorts* which had been formed to guard Rome, and which were used later to maintain order in a few large provincial towns like Carthage or Lyons.

The Government and the Army 109

they were therefore guarded by the auxiliary troops alone. In making the most accurate possible calculation of the wings and the cohorts which seem to have been stationed there at the same time, Mommsen reaches a total of fifteen thousand men. Thus it was an army of almost twenty-seven thousand that the Romans maintained in Africa, and this figure will appear but slightly exaggerated when it is remembered that we possess neither the Tripolitana Provincia nor Morocco, and that we need forty-eight thousand men in time of peace in order to protect Algeria and Tunis.

How, then, did the Romans set about accomplishing a heavier task than ours with fewer forces? It is worth while to know.

In the first place, they thoroughly understood how to make good use of their troops; they distributed them very skilfully over that vast territory, a merit that all of our officers who have served in Africa are unanimous in according them. Each troop was placed at the post which best suited it, and where it could render the best service. When once it was firmly established, it was left there; it grew accustomed to living there and became better and better acquainted with the country and with the inhabitants. The oasis of El Kantara (ancient *Wadi El-Kantara* [13]) is well known to tourists. It is the place where, having for a long time followed a gloomy and monotonous route between barren mountains, one suddenly perceives through a gap in the rocks the immensity of the desert; at this unexpected sight the traveller experiences a fascination of which his eyes do not weary." The ancients relate how Hercules, by a kick, cleft the mountain in twain, and in remembrance of this exploit they called the place *Calceus Herculis;* it was the entrance to the Great Sahara, and in order to guard it they stationed there a company of auxiliary troops levied in Palmyra (*numerus Palmyrenorum*), who, accustomed to the heat of the desert of Syria, must have felt almost at home. They remained there, doubtless, some time, for traces are found of their sojourn, notably altars which they raised to Malagbal, their national god.* The proof that the site of the Roman stations was well chosen lies in the fact that we have usually been forced to establish ourselves also in the same places, or to construct other posts in their neighbourhood. Generally they command dangerous passes and guard the routes by which plunderers may debouch. These *castella*, or *burgi*, as they are called, are almost all built in the same style. They consist of a rectangular enceinte, pierced by four portals, like the Roman camps, and flanked by round or square towers. In any sudden danger, the peasants from the surrounding country took refuge there with their families. Under shelter of those solid walls, a few brave soldiers could hold out for several days, as did our 123d Zephyrs at Mazagran. The important thing was to

---

*C. I. L., 2497 *et seq.* (In this way I shall designate the eighth volume of the *Corpus inscriptionum latinarum*, of which I shall make great use.)

inform the commanders-in-chief of the army as quickly as possible of the situation in which they were placed. This was provided for by an ingenious invention, the secret of which we again discovered just one century later. Usually the *castella* were connected with one another by isolated towers, of which some débris remains. As a rule, these towers must have been rather narrow. Some had a door and a staircase leading to the top; others were reached only by a ladder, which was placed on the outside and drawn up after ascending. They were intended, according to Monsieur Cagnat, for carrying the news from one fort to the next. Frequently, in order to announce the approach of danger, a great fire was lighted, the flame of which by night and the smoke by day was perceived from afar; this kind of signal is still used by the Arabs. At other times recourse was had to a more complicated method, which Vegetius has described: " On the towers of the citadels or of the cities," he says, " beams are raised or lowered, and in this way they transmit to the neighbouring station what they wish to make known." It was the aërial telegraph, sixteen centuries before the epoch when we suppose we invented it.*

The generals thus warned, the troops immediately began to march. From one end of Africa to the other, superb roads had been made, with cisterns and inns, or, as is said there, *fondouks*. Several of these roads still exist; for some kilometres, at in-

* Cagnat, *L'Armée romaine*, 683.

tervals, the traveller treads on that bed of indestructible cement on which lay great arched slabs. In some places the Roman roads are almost intact. "They are found," says Tissot, "just as they were when the last couriers of the Byzantine governors of Carthage and the first scouts of the Arab invasion travelled over them." On these highways, marvellously preserved by the foresight of the emperors, wings of cavalry, light-armed troops, and archers and slingers were in the habit of rushing forth against an enemy whom it was even more difficult to seize than to conquer. His assaults, it is well known, were for the most part mere audacious feints. If he found the men on their guard, or if at the first onset he did not carry the station which protected them, he retreated to his home faster than he came. But, usually, the Romans did not leave him there in peace; it was necessary to teach him a lesson that would prevent him for some time from renewing his attacks. They set out in pursuit of him, they sought him among his mountains, as far as the end of his steppes. If need be, they fought in the desert behind him. It was a bold thing to do, for at that time they did not have the means that we have for crossing it. The Romans do not appear to have made use of the camel in Africa until very late. We do not see that they ever thought of forming there, as in Syria, companies of riders mounted on dromedaries (*dromedarii*); they were satisfied with those brave Numidian horses, which carried not only the man and his baggage, but leather bottles filled with water under their bellies; with them they faced the fiery wind and the sandstorms; they made forced marches, and succeeded in overtaking the plunderers and recovering the booty they had stolen.

Alarms of this kind, in a country but partly subdued, must have been very frequent; fortunately, they were usually nothing but alarms. The tribes of the natives have always been divided by local rivalries; it was still more difficult for them to be friends with the Romans; even the hatred of the stranger was not always able to reunite them. They made single attacks and fought separately. Thus it was that Rome scarcely ever had to withstand in Africa more than one enemy at a time, which fact made victory easier. If, however, it happened that a more successful and more popular commander put an end for a time to the quarrels and the enmities among the Nomads of the high plateaus and the Great Sahara, and re-united under his command those unruly hordes, if the frontiers were threatened on several sides, and if a long and difficult war was foreseen, they had the expedient of calling on the troops from the neighbouring countries. We have proof that under serious circumstances legions came to Africa, not only from Spain and Cyrenaica, but even from Syria and the borders of the Danube. This was with great effort and at great expense; but the Romans were convinced, and with reason, that this kind of insurrection must be promptly stopped, and that, in Africa especially, a vigorous and speedy repression alone could prevent it from extending and breaking out again. It was by these skilful measures, the clever management of their forces, the rapidity of their movements, their energy, their prompt action at critical moments, their knowledge of the country and of the peoples who inhabited it, and, last, by the support that the troops from the various provinces gave one another, that the Romans made up for the weakness of their effective forces, and that with armies which seem to us insufficient, they dominated and governed Africa for five centuries.

However, it must be added that the troops which I have just enumerated were probably not the only forces employed in their African provinces. Monsieur Cagnat thinks they had others which are seldom mentioned, but which must have rendered them important services. It has been remarked that among the cohorts and wings of the auxiliary troops stationed in Numidia and Mauretania there were but three or four which, judging from their names, were levied in the country.* This fact causes us some surprise. We have just seen that the Romans voluntarily enrolled in their army good soldiers whom they found in the dominions they had conquered; why should they have neglected to do so in Africa? It could furnish them with foot-soldiers, incapable of being overcome by fatigue, and above all, which was more useful to them, with incomparable cavalry. It must be believed, therefore, that, if they did not form wings and cohorts of them as they did else-

* Scarcely more are found in the other provinces of the Empire.

where, it was because they used them in another way. Tacitus, in speaking of a general who governed the two Mauretanias, tells us that he had under his command nineteen cohorts and five wings of cavalry, " with a company of Moors, whom hunting and love of plunder render well fitted for war." * This *numerus Maurorum* must have been a number of irregular soldiers, who represented more or less what to-day we call the " goums." Thus the Romans had them, as we have, and, like us, they recruited them among those adventurous peoples who had had a hand in their local quarrels by mercilessly pillaging the neighbouring tribes. We see that they left them their native commanders. One of them, who was called Lucius Quietus, succeeded by force of courage and talent in making a great name for himself. He came from afar, if we must believe Themistius, from those border countries on the limits of the desert which scarcely recognised the authority of Rome. He levied among his countrymen a body of cavalry, with which he made himself so useful to Trajan during the war of the Dacians that the Emperor had him chosen consul, and later, wishing to leave the Empire to the most worthy, he thought at one time, it is said, of appointing him his successor. It is believed that there has been found on the Trajan column the representation of the cavalry of Lucius."[15]

"They are in the act," says Monsieur Cagnat, " of

* *Hist.*, ii., 58.

charging upon the enemy on their small horses, which they ride without saddle or bridle, African fashion. They have for clothes a bit of cloth rolled about the body in such a way as to form a sort of short tunic, fastened to each shoulder by a clasp, and belted at the waist; this is the costume that the Arabs of the country still wear to-day. But that which especially characterises them are the curls that fall about the head.* For weapon, they have only a lance, perhaps at one time indicated on the marble of the column, but which is to-day obliterated, and a small shield."

Such were assuredly the " goums," that the Empire employed in Mauretania. †

IV

Among the companies of troops that were stationed in Africa there is one that interests us more than the others. This is the legion of Numidia, the camp of which we found at Lambèse.[16] In no country of the world has an army left so many souvenirs; the inscriptions and monuments which remain of it allow us to follow the history not only of the legion itself, but of the Roman army under the Empire. Let us sum up as briefly as possible the principal points that they teach us.

We know that Augustus completely changed the conditions of the service and the character of the

---

* Strabo says that the Moors considered it an ornament to wear the beard and the hair curled.

† Cagnat, *l'Armée romaine*, 332.

The Government and the Army

army. In the first place, he made it permanent. Before that, troops were levied for each campaign undertaken by the Romans; the campaign over, the soldiers returned to their homes, and settled down until the next war. Augustus retained them under the standards for a fixed length of time, whether in time of war or peace. The first result of this measure was to render permanent the legion, which until then had been reorganised for each new campaign and disbanded when it was over. It was formed anew each year by recruits who took the place of soldiers who had served their term or of those who had been lost, but it continued to exist. From that time each legion had its civil position, its history, and its name. That of Numidia was called " the third Augustan legion " (*legio tertia Augusta*), and this somewhat lengthy designation was necessary in order that it might be recognised. As Augustus had incorporated into his army the legions of his rivals, he found those among them that bore similar numbers; he let them retain these for fear of offending them. There were, for instance, three third legions, but each of them assumed a different surname in order to be distinguished from the others. The one which ours received seems to indicate that it had given special proofs of its devotion to the Emperor, and that he wished to show his gratitude.

But in organising permanent armies for the Romans, Augustus had no intention of undertaking new conquests; his Empire seemed to him large enough; he wished merely to maintain peace there and to make it respected by the neighbours. In the most of the provinces, local tranquillity seemed to him sufficiently assured by the militia, and still more by the confidence that the imperial government inspired. With the exception of a few important cities, like Lyons and Carthage, which received garrisons, he left no legions in the other towns, but distributed almost all of them along the borders in order to meet the enemy from without. They lived there in camp, where the military spirit is better preserved than in the midst of the corruption of large cities, and, as a rule, they scarcely ever went away from the country where their camp had first been pitched.

The third legion seems never to have left Africa. It was there at the death of Augustus; it remained there until the time when Diocletian reorganised the provinces and the army.* We find it at first stationed at *Theveste* (Tebessa); this was a wise arrangement, as it was necessary to protect the proconsular province against the Gætuli and the Garamantes, that is to say, against the barbarians of the south-east. When the Roman domination was extended toward the west, and it was necessary to put a stop to the invasions of the tribes from the Aurès and the Great Sahara, the legion was transferred to Lambèse. It had just arrived there and

---

* The third legion suffered in its service but one interruption. It was disbanded under Gordian III. for having taken the part of Maximin; but fifteen years later Valerian reorganised it, gave it back its name, and sent it to serve in Africa.

was beginning to build its camp, when it received the visit of Emperor Hadrian. This indefatigable traveller, who spent his life in journeying through his Empire, wished to see with his own eyes the condition of his army in Africa. He had the legionaries manœuvre before him; he saw them work at field fortifications, build walls, dig ditches; he was present at feigned attacks and defences of fortified places. He inspected the auxiliaries also, and was delighted at the ease with which the cavalry of the sixth cohort of the Commagenians wheeled, charged with closed ranks upon the enemy, and alternately handled the sling or hurled the dart. The inspection over, he showed his satisfaction to the troops in a sort of order of the day in the form of an address, of which the legion must have been very proud, and which we have preserved.*

The camp of the third legion, which was at that time in process of building, was not exactly the same as the one we have before us. It seems that some parts must have needed to be restored or rebuilt very soon. They were working on it from the reign of Marcus Aurelius, and at that time we see the legion occupied in strengthening the towers which, no doubt, threatened to crumble. It must have suffered greatly from the troubles that desolated every province in the third century and which caused so many ruins. And even outside of the detailed repairs, which the wear of time must often have made necessary, it cannot be doubted but that

* C. I. L., 2532. It is to-day in the Museum of the Louvre.

they were compelled more than once to rebuild the whole in order to adjust it to the changes that the army underwent during the Empire. These changes were not accomplished at one time. The reforms of Augustus, of which they were the natural outcome, took time to produce all their results, but, by degrees, they succeeded in completely modifying the character of the ancient Roman army.

Here, for instance, is an innovation which occurred rather late, and the results of which were very serious. The soldiers were forbidden to marry when serving for only one campaign, and it was even attempted to keep women from roaming about the camps, although it was not always easy to prevent this. Strict generals persisted in it as long as the Republic lasted. At Numantia, Scipio once sent away two thousand courtesans whose presence had greatly weakened the military discipline in his army. But when the service became permanent, and the soldiers remained with the standards during the best years of their life, it was very difficult to prevent them from having a family there, or something which resembled one. Then, women were allowed to settle in great numbers in those clusters of dwellings by which the camps were surrounded. This toleration soon brought another. From the moment that these irregular unions were licenced,* it was

---

* Was this union placed on the same footing as the legal marriage, or was it merely regarded as a quasi-marriage, to which certain privileges were accorded? This is a question which is discussed among lawyers.

The Government and the Army

scarcely possible to be strict regarding the consequences that they might entail." The children born of these unions were enrolled in a special tribe (the *Pollia* tribe), which was not that in which the illegitimate children were enrolled (the *Spuria* tribe), and we must indeed suppose that they received the title of citizens, since they were admitted to service in the legions. Septimius Severus extended the privilege still further. " He allowed the soldiers of his army," says Herodian, " to live with their wives." There has been much discussion as to the meaning of this text. Willmans thinks that it should be taken literally, and that from this time the soldiers had, outside of the camp of the legion, a dwelling-place which became their true home and that of their family.* This is what a visit to the camp of Lambèse succeeds in proving.

The camp was built according to the rules which the Romans ordinarily applied to works of this kind, on the brow of a hill, near a water-course, and in such a way as to command a complete view of the surrounding plain.[18] At some distance, its shape could be very clearly defined. It was a great rectangle, five hundred metres long by four hundred and twenty wide, enclosed by a wall with rounded corners, and flanked by towers, which are peculiar in that their projection is turned inward. When Léon Renier visited it for the first time, the walls still rose almost four metres above the earth; there no longer

* See the discussion of Willmans in the eighth volume of the *Corpus*, p. 283.

remains anything of them. In the interior of the camp, two wide roads intersect each other at right angles and terminate in four gates, one of which, the northern, is still visible. On the place where the two roads meet, stands a monument, which as one approaches attracts attention from every side; it is a massive shaft thirty metres high by twenty-three wide, the preservation of which is very remarkable. The northern façade, which is the principal one, is pierced by three portals,[19] one of which, monumental in appearance, is ornamented with Corinthian columns. On either side of the portal, great niches, empty to-day, must once have held statues; above we distinguish, or we imagine we do, figures of Victory, bearing in their hands palms, eagles, and military standards, all of which have been greatly impaired by time. On the southern side, in front of the wall, two isolated columns, one of which has remained standing in its place, doubtless supported statues or trophies. The structure belongs to a very early epoch; an inscription, only a few words of which remain, but which Willmans has very cleverly completed, shows that it was built in 268, under the Emperor Gallienus, after an earthquake which must have laid waste the country. At that time Roman art was clearly on the wane; the ruins of the shapeless pieces of sculpture which adorned the walls prove this only too well. But architecture was better preserved. To the last it retained some of its ancient characteristics; at an early date it lost its elegance, but its dignity remains. On the very eve of the invasions, Rome was still erecting buildings that were grand in appearance. This structure, although built in times of public misfortune, when the treasury was empty and the Empire half disjointed, produced none the less a fine effect, and it is impossible to rid oneself of a very vivid impression on perceiving this great and almost naked wall, that Time has clothed in a marvellous colour, rising in the midst of ruins. As to the name we must give it and the use to which it must have been put, there is no possible doubt: it was the *prætorium*, that is, the official residence of the chief of the legion. As the command (*imperium*) was considered by the Romans a sacred office, the *prætorium* was a sort of temple. Before the principal entrance are found the altar, on which the general offered sacrifices and took the auspices in the name of the Emperor, the tribunal, whence he rendered justice, and that grassy hillock from the summit of which he exhorted his soldiers.

There remain to-day only the four walls of the *prætorium* of Lambèse; the interior is filled with débris of every description. In traversing it we were impressed at perceiving that there are found in it none of those bits of tiles or bricks which are so often discovered elsewhere. This is what first aroused the suspicion that the building was open, and the examination of what remains of it has on every point fully confirmed this supposition. The conclusion is finally reached, therefore, that the interior of the structure consisted merely of a vast court, a sort of open *atrium* for meetings and military functions; the quarters and offices of the general must therefore have been elsewhere. They have been sought for in the other parts of the camp, but in vain. What is found there are monuments, the ruins of which aid us in imagining their use; bases bearing statues consecrated to the emperors or to their families, *thermæ* intended for the legionaries, which occupy a very considerable space; especially rooms in which the associations of officers or sub-officers met, and which were very numerous in the legion; but of private apartments there is not the slightest trace. It is not merely the quarters of the general which are lacking; in this mass of buildings of every sort there are found no barracks for the soldiers. Then one recalls the words of Herodian which I quoted above, and the opinion is confirmed that at the time when the camp was repaired for the last time and put into the condition in which we see it, neither the general nor his soldiers had their quarters there; they took advantage of the permission which had been accorded them to live elsewhere with their families.

"The condition of the legionaries," says Willmans, "after the decree of Severus, resembled that of the native militia of French Algeria on the border of Tunis; at a short distance from the fortified camp, the *spahis*[20] arrange their tents, or rather their huts, so as to form a village laid out into streets; there they live with their wives, their children, and their animals, appearing at the fort only to drill."

V

Since the soldiers did not live in the camp, can we discover where they did live ? Nothing is easier.*

If we leave the camp by the eastern gate, we have before us the delights of a Roman military road, which slopes toward the south-east. We know its name; it is the *Via Septiminiana*. At first it runs along beside a bald hill, which is all that remains of the amphitheatre; afterwards it loses itself under gardens, which hide it for almost a kilometre; then it reappears and terminates in a triumphal arch with three portals, which, wholly dilapidated as it is, preserves an air of elegance and grandeur. Beyond that, rubbish is heaped up on every side; as far as the eye can reach nothing is seen but ruins; at every step are mounds of earth, piles of broken stones, with fragments of columns, blocks of marble, and bits of mosaics. We are in the town of Lambèse ; it is here, two kilometres from the camp, that the officers and soldiers of the third legion lived with their families.

Like all towns which are founded under the same conditions, Lambèse no doubt had very modest beginnings. At the start it was probably nothing but

* Those who, travelling in Africa, wish to visit in detail the ruins at Lambèse will do well to supply themselves with the *Guide* that Monsieur Cagnat has just published. In a few pages he gives its history and conducts the tourists into the midst of the ruins of the camp and of the Roman city. In reading Monsieur Cagnat I imagined I was visiting them again.

one of those gatherings of sutlers' and tradesmen's huts to which is applied the term *canabæ legionis.* At the end of a few years these huts formed a village (*vicus*); under Marcus Aurelius it was a municipality, which had a regular administration and which magnificently styled itself *Respublica Lambæsitanorum.* Two forums were built there, surrounded by a colonnade, with a capital, of which some very beautiful fragments remain; like the one at Rome, they were consecrated to Jupiter, Juno, and Minerva. The city must have grown in size and beauty very rapidly; each generation was desirous of adding new ornaments to it. For instance, the fathers were content to force the spring which to-day is called Aïn-Drin, and to make a canal of it; the sons, at the spot where it issued from the earth, built a temple to Neptune; the grandsons, not satisfied with repairing it, surrounded it with a portico *;. it was an emulation of magnificence with them. Among the structures which are not wholly in ruins is the Temple of Æsculapius,[21] which seemed to me most curious. It does not resemble what is ordinarily seen, and this is a great achievement in Algeria, where almost all the monuments seem constructed after the same model. The temple proper, a small and coquettish structure, is built at the rear of a sort of court or parvis, on a terrace which rises a few feet above the ground. The inscription which covers the fronton and which to-day is fallen to the ground, tells us that it was built under Marcus Aurelius, and that it

* C. I. L., 2652.

was consecrated to Æsculapius and Health, or, as the Greeks said, to the goddess Hygeia.* But the temple itself is only a small part of the building. The terrace on which it is erected projects to the right and left in such a way as to form with the line of the rear a sort of trapezium; it has a colonnade, which frames in the parvis, and terminates on either side in two circular chapels supported also by columns and dedicated to Jupiter (*Jovi valenti*) and Sylvanus. Nothing could be more elegant or graceful than this mingling of straight lines and rounded forms, so harmoniously blended together. Unfortunately this beautiful monument is in a deplorable condition; time began its destruction, man is completing it—and man is much more terrible than time; it took centuries to injure the structure, yet in a few years man has left scarcely anything of it. I sought in one of the side chapels for the mosaic that Léon Renier saw there, and on which were written those words, so beautiful and so sacred that a Christian might place them on the threshold of a church: *Bonus intra, melior exi.* It has disappeared; it is probable that some contractor of public works destroyed it in order to pave a street of the neighbourhood.

Although Lambèse was apparently a city like others, governed by a council of *decurions*, by *ædiles, quæstors,* and *duumvirs,* it must have had

* In the débris statues of the two deities have been found. They may be seen to-day in the small museum which has been placed in the *prætorium.*

an individual character: it was a thoroughly military city, inhabited for the most part by soldiers, either in active service or on the retired list, and by officers of every rank. For a long time the Roman officers, proconsuls, legates, or imperial procurators had been forbidden to have their wives follow them into the countries they were about to govern; but with the Empire this severity was relaxed. Tacitus has preserved for us the account of a discussion which took place on this subject in the Senate, under Tiberius. Cecina, a senator of stern mien, demanded that a return be made to the ancient customs, under the pretext that women, when permitted, meddle with everything; that they are a great embarrassment, on account of their luxury in times of peace, and on account of their nervousness in times of war. The reply was that if it was somewhat inconvenient to take them into the provinces, it was much more so to leave them by themselves in Rome. " It is difficult," it was said, " even under the eyes of their husbands, for them always to conduct themselves properly; what would happen were they no longer watched? and how could they bear that kind of separation that lasts sometimes for several years?"* These reasons appeared convincing, and we do not see that the discussion was renewed from that time. What is certain is, that at Lambèse the wives of the legates of the legion accompanied their husbands, and that we find them occasionally associated in the honours which the

* Tacitus, *Ann.*, iii., 33.

soldiers rendered to their commanders. Naturally, the officers followed the example of their general, and the soldiers still more so. The inscriptions show them to us, with their wives and their children, in the act of offering prayers to the gods, and raising altars to them. These children, as a rule, followed the profession of their fathers; as one became a sailor at the seaports, so one wished to be a soldier at Lambèse. Long lists of legionaries have been found there who gathered together at various times for the purpose of testifying their gratitude to the prince or the legate. Usually they add to their names the mention of their native country,* and in the later ones it is seen that a good half of them were born in the vicinity of the camp. Thus the legion at that time was recruited among the children of the regiment; one was a soldier by tradition,

* These lists are of use to us in that they show us a very important result of the military reforms of Augustus. From the time when a body of troops did not change garrison and was always stationed in the same country, it must have come about that in the end it recruited there. This is what happened to the third legion as to the others. In the oldest of the lists found in the camp at Lambèse, we see that the soldiers composing the legion came from almost everywhere; the others were composed almost wholly of Africans, which is a very significant fact. Thus the Romans did not think it necessary to take precautions against the awakening of the provincial spirit. They did not feel the need, as is the case to-day in Italy, of taking the soldiers from the various provinces and distributing them throughout different companies of the army, for fear that if they were together there would come to their mind some remembrance of and some regret for their ancient independence. They had full confidence in the force of cohesion of their Empire; they knew that the Africans, like the Spaniards and the Gauls, had become Romans.

from father to son, and this led to the forming of a sort of military caste in which was recruited the best and the most healthy part of the army. The emperors saw it with pleasure, for it was their tendency to confine everyone to his profession. We know that they finally decided that the son of a soldier should be a soldier, like his father; but the inscriptions of Lambèse show us that such was the case before they had given the order, and their law only confirmed a custom which was still more ancient than the law itself.

We should derive great pleasure as well as profit from studying in detail these inscriptions with which the soil of Lambèse is covered; nothing would make us better acquainted with the Roman army in its organisation and government; but Monsieur Cagnat has done this work and there is no necessity for doing it over again. Another and perhaps a greater interest that they have for us is the fact that they aid us in discovering what, as a rule, is not known, and what books do not tell us, namely, the true sentiments of the soldiers: what they thought of their profession, and the sorrows and the joys they derived from it. The impression conveyed by the epitaphs on their tombs, or by the dedications which they inscribed on the monuments they erected, is that, on the whole, they were not dissatisfied with their lot. In what they tell us there is never found the bitter, threatening tone that Tacitus gives to the complaints of the legionaries of Germania in the early years of the Empire. Those of Lambèse

The Government and the Army

seemed to love their commanders; they spoke of them with respect, they were well pleased with their justice and their kindness; the service did not seem to them too severe; they bowed without a murmur to the exigencies of the discipline; there were even some of them who raised altars " to the military discipline." * When, after twenty-five years, the time came for retiring, they parted from their comrades with grief; before leaving, they liked to dedicate a little altar to the Genius of the legion or of the company in which they served, as though to give thanks for the happy days they owed to it. Then, when it was possible, they did not go far away from the camp in which they had passed the best years of their life; they settled at Lambèse itself or, if this were not practicable, at *Verecunda*, *Thamugade*, or *Mascula* (Krenchela), towns in the vicinity. Their old age was far from being penniless. In the first place they received, upon dismissal, a sum, which for simple soldiers was fixed at twelve thousand sesterces (twenty-four hundred francs); they added to this what they had been able to save while in service, and which often was not inconsiderable. In the first place, they set aside something from their salary, which amply sufficed for all their needs, as they themselves acknowledged with uncommon frankness.†

---

* C. I. L., 10,657.

† The lieutenants of the centurions, having had a room built for their meetings and having ornamented it with the images of their protecting deities and of the imperial family, tell us that they have

But the gifts that, under certain circumstances the emperors made them, were of still greater import to them. Augustus set this example to his successors; it was so important to win the attachment of the army that they ruined themselves in acts of liberality. Of these sums due to the imperial munificence the soldiers spent barely the half; the remainder was put into a sort of savings-bank and placed in the keeping of the standard-bearer. "That is why," says Vegetius, "men are chosen for ensign who not only are honest, but who have a knowledge of numbers, for they have both a savings-bank to guard, and account-books to keep." Each one's share was given back to him when he left the service, and was added to what he received as his retiring fund. This sometimes amounted to a small fortune.* At death he left it to his relatives or friends, and his grateful heirs built him a tomb on which they were careful, in a few words of affection, to mention the record he had made. Stones of this kind are found at every step along the military roads around Lambèse.

Among the ruins which cover the *prætorium*, a number of monuments of medium size have been noticed, which are in the form of a rectangle, one of the sides of which is rounded like an apsis. These were the apartments in which the lieutenants

---

been able to make this outlay as a result of their salary, which is very liberal: *ex largissimis stipendiis* (C. I. L., 2554). It is not common to find officers who do not complain of their appointments.

* See Cagnat, *l'Armée romaine*, p. 457, *et seq.*

(*optiones*), the trumpeters (*cornicines*), the sergeant-majors (*tesserarii*), and the scouts (*speculatores*), met together in their leisure moments; these rooms were called *scholæ*—we should say to-day, clubrooms. The emperors authorised various officers to organise associations, or, to use the proper term, *colleges*, and they let these colleges build their *scholæ* in the midst of the camp. This was a means of keeping a closer watch over them. The members deposited yearly in the common savings-bank a certain sum, a part of which was returned to them when they retired from service, or, in case of their dying before retiring, was used for their proper burial. The care of interment was, under the Empire, the motive or the pretext of every association of this kind; they seemed to exist merely in order to assure to their members a tomb and a decent burial; they were all, at least apparently, funeral associations (*collegia funeraticia*); but this was mere etiquette; our association seems to have had other objects, and to have been less occupied with death than with life. In every army of the world one looks for speedy promotion; it was the desire of the officers of the third legion as it was of others; and, first of all, they asked these military associations of which they were members to aid them in making their way. We see the association of lieutenants giving eight thousand sesterces (sixteen hundred francs) to one of its members who was working to become ensign or centurion. The sum is large and makes us think that the steps he had to take in order to " attain his hopes," as he says, must have been rather expensive. The fact is, that in order to become a centurion, it was not sufficient to send a petition to the emperor, as Juvenal seems to say *; it was more efficacious to go in person to Rome to proffer the request. The journey was long, and the sojourn in the capital of the Empire expensive, but the cost was risked in order to be surer of success. There has been found at Lambèse, in the centre of a beautiful mosaic, which, no doubt, ornamented the home of some wealthy man, a base which must have supported a statue of Bacchus. It was erected by a prefect of the camp (a sort of major of the legion), and as he was a poet as well as an officer, he engraved some verses on it which we have preserved. This is what he says to the god in conclusion: " In return for the gifts that I offer thee, preserve my children and their mother; grant that I may see Rome and return thence covered with the glory that I seek, and crowned with the favour of my masters." Let us hope that these prayers were answered, and that, thanks to the protection of Bacchus, this prefect of the camp came back to Lambèse a military tribune.†

VI

History shows us that of all the armies that Rome maintained in the provinces, there is none perhaps that served its country better and accomplished its

---

* *Aut vitem posce libello*, Juvenal, *Sat.*, xiv., 193.
† C. I. L., 2631.

task as well as the army in Africa. It was not very large, as we have just seen, and it had an immense territory to watch over; but it made up for its deficiency in numbers by its vigilance, bravery, and knowledge of places and of men. It had sometimes to sustain veritable wars, which demanded great efforts. Under Tiberius, the Numidian chief Tacfarinas held the Romans in check for seven years, and was conquered only through treachery. Like Jugurtha and Abd-el-Kader, he had his regular troops, equipped and organised after the manner of the Romans and which he enlisted only in important combats. Under his orders a valiant chief, Mazippa, led forward hosts of riders, who rushed down upon the plains, ravaged the farms, carried off the herds, penetrated even into the cities, pillaged them, and disappeared before the inhabitants could rally to defend themselves. When the Roman army succeeded in overtaking them, it easily gained a victory. The generals at that time were in the habit of sending false reports and receiving in return the triumphal ornaments. But while at Rome they were offering thanks to the gods for that success and proclaiming that the war was over, Tacfarinas, who had formed a new army, reappeared on the border, and the war began anew. It was necessary, in order to bring it to a close, to resort to the policy that later gave the victory to Bugeaud; to form flexible columns which surrounded the enemy on all sides and closed in successively upon him, to hem him into a narrower and narrower circle, and to pursue him into inaccessible countries, in which he had his reserve of men and provisions, until he was deserted and betrayed by his soldiers, who were growing weary of following him.

The great wars were not, however, what cost the army the greatest trouble and made it run the most risks. The petty incursions which were constantly recurring and which succeeded in exhausting the patience of the soldiers, were much more dangerous. The situation of Africa was not exactly like that of the other provinces of the Empire. Gaul, for example, once conquered, was wholly conquered. Roman domination very quickly expanded throughout the country; there was no mountain high enough, no river deep enough, no forest dense enough to arrest its progress. The legions which guarded the banks of the Rhine had only to look before them; if they prevented the barbarians from passing, all was tranquil; at the rear, they had no enemies. It was otherwise in Africa. The configuration of the country, which places barren regions in the midst of fertile ones, makes it very difficult to guard. Nature seems to have taken it upon herself to maintain barbarism by the side of civilisation, in procuring for it, even in the midst of the richest lands, almost inaccessible places of refuge. This is what made the subjugation of Algeria so difficult for our troops. The Romans had the same obstacles to overcome, and it does not seem to me that they surmounted them so quickly or so completely as we did.

After several centuries of domination, they were not so advanced as we are. It is now thirty-five years since we conquered Kabylia, and every day we penetrate farther into it. Toward the middle of the third century, under Decius, the Romans were not yet firmly established in the mountains of the Babor and the Jurjura. This mountain citadel contained a reserve of barbarous tribes, ever ready to hurl themselves upon the cities along the seaboard and upon the rich countries of the Shelliff. Soon these intrepid horsemen began to glide unseen between two Roman posts, to make a skirmish across country, and to return to their homes with their booty and prisoners. When once the captives were brought to those mountains, which were not well known, it was not easy to rescue them, and when, toward the third century, the fall of the Empire began, it was found more simple to ransom them. We have a touching letter from Saint Cyprian, who gave one hundred thousand sesterces (twenty thousand francs) to the priests of Numidia, to help pay the ransom for the Christian men and women who were taken off by the barbarians. It was the result of a collection taken up among the Christians of Carthage, and he sent their names with their money that prayers for them might not be forgotten.*

These depredations must have been very frequent for so many traces of them to remain in the inscriptions that we have preserved. Nothing is more

* St. Cyprian, *Epist.*, lxii., p. 698 (Hartel).

common than the mention of these thefts or murders. At *Simittu* (Schemtu), where they were in the habit of working quarries of beautiful African marble, and which must have been the centre of a great commercial movement, a veteran is one day traitorously assassinated on the highway, and his comrades can do no more than erect a tomb for him at their own expense.* In Mauretania, near Cæsarea, it is a child, the son of an officer of the auxiliary troops, who one fine day is found dead, with the two slaves who guarded him. At *Auzia* (Aumale) we read on the tomb of a young man these touching words: " Adieu, Secundus, flower of youth, whom barbarians have cut down! " † A veteran of the third legion, an architect and land-surveyor by profession (the legion, having to support itself, contained men of every profession), tells us that having been called to *Saldæ* (Bûjaya, vulg. Bougie) for the construction of an aqueduct, he was attacked by brigands on one of the most frequented roads of the province, in a region that had been conquered and subdued a long time before; that his companions and himself had great difficulty in escaping, and that he succeeded in getting away not without several wounds and minus his baggage.‡

Thus Rome, in spite of every effort, did not succeed in subduing all the independent tribes of Africa. There remained some, along the borders, and even

* C. I. L., 14,603.
† C. I. L., 9238.
‡ C. I. L., 2728.

in the heart of the country, which kept themselves outside of the " Roman peace." Absolute security has never been felt there; civilisation and barbarism have often dwelt side by side. It is a source of anxiety for the present and a danger for the future. However, we shall see that this condition of affairs did not prevent Africa from becoming one of the richest and most civilised countries in the world.

TRANSLATOR'S NOTES TO CHAPTER III

1. " *Thabrăca* or *Tabrăca*, at the mouth of the River Tusca, and the frontier town on the side of *Zeugitana*. According to Ptolemy, it was a Roman colony, and here the tyrant Gildo put an end to his life in A.D. 398. In the vicinity were forests thickly inhabited by apes, a circumstance to which Juvenal alludes. The ancient name may still be traced in that of the island of Tabarca, at the mouth of the river."—Charles Anthon, *Ancient Geography*.

2. " *Thenæ*, at first a Phœnician town, subsequently became a Roman colony, with the name of *Ælia Augusta Mercurialis*."—Charles Anthon, *Ancient Geography*.

3. " Punic faith " passed among the Romans into a proverb for dishonesty; and "faithless" or "perfidious" is the epithet which Horace applies to Hannibal. See Horace, *Ode IV.*, 4, 41-44. But see also Polybius, ix., 22-26; xi., 19. Also Livy, xxviii., 12; xxi., 4; and Silius Italicus, *Pun.*, i., 56 *et seq.*

4. " *Gir*, the common word in the Libyan language for flowing water."—Dr. H. Kiepert, *Manual of Ancient Geography*.

5. " Theveste (Tebessa), 'the city of a hundred gates,' is a French post on the frontiers of Tunis. It has a greater number of ruins than any place in Northern Africa."—G. L. Ditson, *North Coast of Africa*, p. 290.

6. *Gafsa* (or Cafsa) is said to have been founded by the Libyan Hercules. Jugurtha kept his treasures there.

7. This was in A.D. 42.

8. The Roman *Julia Cæsarea*. "There is a tradition that the ancient as well as the modern city was erected by Andalusian Moors."—Blofeld.

9. "Of other monuments here [Lambèse] particularly worthy of note, I have yet to mention a beautiful gate (of Septimus Severus) of three porches."—G. L. Ditson, *North Coast of Africa*, p. 293.

10. "Polybius, ii., 24, estimates the entire armed strength of Rome and of Italy before the Second Punic War at 777,000 men, including 70,000 horse. These figures have been adopted by Napoleon III., *Hist. de Jules César*, i., 153, and by Colonel Dodge, *Hannibal*, p. 95."—Wm. O'C. Morris, *Hannibal*.

11. Some writers have maintained that the cohort was a formation later than the Second Punic War.

12. For the civil and military institutions of Carthage, the great work of Hennébert should be studied, vol. i., books i., ii. A good sketch will be found in Mommsen's *History of Rome*, vol. ii., chap. i.

13. It is called by the Arabs of the eastern portion of the great desert, the *mouth* of the Sahara, for this is the only avenue by which they can pass and repass to and from Constantine.

14. For similar description see G. L. Ditson, *North Coast of Africa*, pp. 303, 304.

15. Virg., *Æn.*, iv., 41; Silius Italicus, i., 215.

16. "Lambèse, according to Ptolemy, whose statements are confirmed by numerous inscriptions found here, was a colony of the third Augustus. It was one of the most advanced posts, and a very important position in a chain of routes and defences established by the Romans in Numidia."—G. L. Ditson, *North Coast of Africa*.

17. See Mommsen, vol. iii., p. 4.

18. For *Roman Camp* see Napoleon, *Correspondence*, xxxi., 462, 467.

19. The *Univers Pittoresque* says: "Each side is pierced with three portals; that in the middle is of colossal dimensions."

G. L. Ditson in the *North Coast of Africa*, p. 291, says: "The sides, thirty-eight paces in length, have each four portals, differing very considerably in size; the second from the western end being of . . . colossal dimensions."

20. The *Spahis*, or irregular native cavalry, "wear their ordinary costume, and their only distinctive uniform is a red bornous instead of a white one. They mount their horses from the off side. . . . This probably arises from the fact that their right arm is free (the right side of their bornous being usually thrown back over their right shoulder) to grasp the bridle and the mane."—G. L. Ditson, *North Coast of Africa*, p. 143.

21. G. L. Ditson in the *North Coast of Africa*, p. 292, says: "The remains, however, of the building which exhibits the most originality and taste in design . . . appertains, it is said, to a temple dedicated to Esculapius and to Health. The portion of the door still standing, the steps leading up to it, the delicately fluted shafts that glisten around you like snow, the variegated and highly polished stone that encircles the sanctum of the deity it enshrined, all attest with what a gracious care and with what a lavish hand the whole was carried on to completion."

CHAPTER IV

THE SURROUNDING COUNTRY

I

IF one wishes to know the results of the Roman domination in Africa the surest means is not to consult books or historians; it is better to travel through the country. A journey, even a rapid one, into Algeria and Tunis will teach us more than a long sojourn in libraries.

There is no country in the world in which there is a greater number of ancient ruins. They are found everywhere, not only in the fertile plains, which from all time must have attracted the inhabitants, but on the most barren plateaus, where to-day could not be found the wherewithal to subsist. When one wishes to go from Kairwan (the ancient *Vicus Augusti*) either to Tebessa (*Theveste*), Gafsa (*Capsa*),[1] or Gabes (*Takape*),[2] it is necessary to cross great stretches of reddish sand where nothing grows, and which are almost uninhabited. Yet this territory is the ancient *Byzacium*,[3] whose wealth was formerly boasted of, and we have positive proof that the praise given it was merited. Monsieur Paul Bourde recalls the fact that in the midst of these wilds rise the ruins of cities, the importance of which can be estimated approximately by their monuments, some of which are standing, and by their position, which is still visible. First of all there was *Thysdrus* (El-Jemm),[1] whose amphitheatre, circus, and huge temple were colossal, and which must have contained more than one hundred thousand inhabitants; *Sufetula* (Subeitla or Sbîtla) no doubt had from twenty to twenty-five thousand; *Scillium* (Kasrun) from twelve to fifteen thousand; and *Thelepte* (Medinet Kadina),[5] one of the largest cities of ancient Tunis, from fifty to sixty thousand. "Besides these great centres," adds Monsieur Bourde,* "some large towns themselves counted several thousand inhabitants; and, in addition to these cities and towns, the country was covered with a great number of villages and isolated farms, the ruins of which are met with, so to speak, at every step."

The exact number of these farms and villages that peopled Roman Africa will never be known, for there are very many the last trace of which has been destroyed by time. But if what is gone cannot be restored, everyone realises how useful it would be to take the trouble to describe in detail all that remains; this is precisely what is being attempted at the present time, at least in regard to Tunis. The minister of public instruction has just begun the publication of an archæological atlas of this country, which,

*In his very interesting report addressed to Monsieur Rouvier, resident general of France at Tunis, *Sur les cultures fruitières, et en particulier sur la culture de l'olivier au centre de la Tunisie.*

when completed, will be of the greatest service.*
On the fine topographical map, drawn by the staff-
officers of our army of occupation, there is indicated,
without one omission, every trace of antique ruins
which still remains. It is a means of giving us some
idea of what the country must have been during the
beautiful epochs of the Roman domination. Let us
take, for instance, the environs of the little town of
Mateur (*Matero*), situated near Bizerta (or Benzerta,
Hippo Zarytus s. Diarrytus, Διάρρυτος).⁶ To-day this
country is still fertile, and, in comparison with the
rest of Tunis, well inhabited; but how much more
so must it have been in antiquity! In order to be
convinced of this, we need only to consult the maps
of the archæological atlas. On a territory scarcely
larger than one of our districts, the number of
Roman ruins which have been noted amounts to
more than three hundred; and think of all that has
forever disappeared during fourteen centuries! To-
day only one town is found in the country, that of
Mateur, the ancient *oppidum Mataurense*, which
contained about three thousand inhabitants. There
were several in the time of the Romans; in the first
place, two, the names of which we know, *Thugga*
and *Chiniava*, besides three or four that we can no

* *Atlas archéologique de la Tunisie*, with explanatory notes by
Messieurs Babelon, Cagnat, and Solomon Reinach. The first part in
this useful work is compiled by the officers composing the topographical brigades, under the direction of General Derrécagaix. This
means that here, as on every occasion, the army has rendered the
most important and the most intelligent services in the scientific
exploration of Africa.

longer distinguish save by the ruins that they have left. These ruins, which sometimes occupy more than a kilometre in space, are almost deserted; it is seldom that even a few miserable huts inhabited by some half a hundred Arabs stand on one of them. They must formerly have been flourishing and peopled. As to the other ruins, they have a certain importance; they consist of bits of crumbling wall, wells, cisterns, and slabs, which mark the site of ancient habitations now gone, and here and there columns, mosaics, and round or square towers, the remains of beautiful villas or fortified farms.

What we notice in the environs of Mateur, we may be sure that we shall find again almost everywhere; everything shows us that this country was formerly covered with cities, towns, villages, and houses for pleasure or for trading companies,' and that it was crowded with a rich and industrious population. In seeing what it is to-day, and in thinking of what the Romans made it, we feel at first a very lively admiration for them, but at the same time we cannot help being very greatly surprised.

In order to render Africa so flourishing, in order to gather together in the country and the towns such a crowded population, in order to make the soil produce fine harvests, in order everywhere to call forth abundance and life, it seems to us that Rome had to struggle against almost insurmountable difficulties; it had to conquer the resistance both of men and of nature.

In the first place, the men did not, as a rule, seem of a character to be easily attached to the soil. We see to-day that even among those who appear to have become permanent cultivators, there are many who move away with great readiness, and who, summer having come, are less willing to live in the hut than in the tent. A much greater number still is wholly nomadic and never settles down.

"At the approach of summer," says Monsieur Wahl, "the caravans set out on their route toward the Tell; they reach it after the harvest is over; the herds still find pasturage in the despoiled fields. In the autumn, when the first rains fall, they return to the high plateaus and the Great Sahara. It is a curious sight, that of a tribe on the march; the camels advance solemnly in single file, bearing the provisions, the tents, and the household utensils; then follow some oxen or lean cows, the goats, and the dense flock of sheep covered with a cloud of dust; the women walk on foot, their children on their backs; only the great ladies of the desert take their place in the *attatouch*, the palanquin, which is placed on the camel. The men, gun in hand, walk in advance, in order to keep an outlook on the road, or at the rear, in order to protect it; others run along by the side of the long column, watching the beasts and keeping them from wandering away or being stolen. When evening comes they halt and encamp." *

If the ancients had not the very same sight before their eyes, they had others similar to it. Virgil has

* *L'Algérie*, by Maurice Wahl, p. 187.

described in beautiful lines the African shepherd, "who takes with him his dog, his arms, his house, and his flocks, and dives into the wilds, where he wanders for entire months, without finding an hospitable dwelling, so vast is the desert!"

> "Sæpe diem noctemque et totum ex ordine mensem
> Pascitur, itque pecus longa in deserta sine ullis
> Hospitiis, tantum campi jacet!" *

It must not, therefore, be supposed, as is too often the case, that in Africa the love of a nomadic life dates only from the Mussulman invasion; it is probable that the Numidian or the Gætule resembled the Arab and the Berber of our day. Like them he little cared to shut himself up beneath a roof of tile or thatch, and it must always have been difficult to make a farmer or a labourer of him. But neither must we exaggerate; if the majority of the natives have always been nomadic, it would be going too far to pretend that they are so by nature, and that they can be nothing else. What proves this is the fact that there are those who, of their own accord, group themselves into villages, and who leave them only to till their fields; the Kabyle, for instance, is as energetic a labourer as the Tuareg is a confirmed nomad; and yet the Tuareg and the Kabyle belong to the same race, and speak almost the same language. It

* *Georg.*, iii., 343. One may read in Monsieur Boissière (*L'Algérie romaine*, i., 53) an interesting commentary on these lines of Virgil. It may be seen there how, even to-day, they have not ceased to be true.

has often been said, and with truth,* that what in the long run has made them so different from each other is the diversity of the countries which they inhabit, and the fact that they have submitted to the necessities imposed on them by nature. The one of the two peoples who found in his mountains a sure refuge wherein he could rest, and a few acres of fertile land on which to live, remained there; the other, to whom the desert offered only occasional pasture-lands, was indeed forced to wander constantly in order to escape dying of hunger. It was not therefore presumptuous to suppose that with an ensemble of wise measures which would alter the conditions of life among the people of the country, they might also change their habits. This is what Masinissa understood and what he strove to do; it is said that he attempted to wean the Numidians from their wandering life, to attach them to the soil, and force them to live together in villages or cities; and Polybius gives us to understand that he succeeded very well in this.† But his dynasty did not last long enough, and was agitated by too many storms for the work of the Berber king to produce lasting results. The credit of that great enterprise belongs, therefore, to the Romans; all that the historians tell us proves that the civilisation of Africa is indeed their work. To refer again at this point to Byzacium, which has already been mentioned above, we know

* See *The Sahara*, ch. xiv., by M. H. Schirmer, to cite only the most recent work on this subject.
† xxxvii., 3.

from Sallust that when Marius, in his march upon Gafsa, crossed that territory, it was uncultivated, barren, and deserted.* This condition is the one in which we still find it to-day; but the ruins which cover it show that in the meantime, and as long as the Roman domination lasted, it must have been rich and inhabited. It was, therefore, the Romans who little by little drew the natives to the fertile lands, and held them there by the security and the comfort of good living; then they incited them to the conquest of the neighbouring waste lands, so that the habitable country was constantly being enlarged, and there remained untilled scarcely any soil susceptible of cultivation. Everywhere nomad huts were clustered together in order to form villages, and a little later these villages, in which labourers and traders were crowded together, became towns.

It was an important result, which required several centuries of unceasing effort on their part; and yet the victory which they had to gain over nature presented still greater difficulties. Assuredly they must have had less trouble in converting into farmers those wandering shepherds than in enriching with corn, wine, or oil the soil in which to-day the alfa and the dwarf palm will scarcely grow. They succeeded so well in this, that in the presence of the remains of villas and farms, in places which seem to us uninhabitable, we are tempted to imagine that the climate must have undergone some change since the olden days, that the rains were formerly more

* *Jug.*, 89.

frequent, the springs more abundant, and the rivers less prone to drying up. It must be admitted that if this were the case we should have some reason for being discouraged, and that it would be necessary for us to give up much of the bright future that we dream of for our African colonies. But it seems to me difficult to prove that the climatic conditions differ greatly to-day from what they were in the time of the Romans. No doubt it is possible that the clearing away of the woods on the mountains has had an unfortunate influence on the rainfall and the flow of the rivers.* The springs, too, may have become less numerous and less copious; we see that in the time of the Romans it was always necessary to be careful of them, and that they ceased to flow the moment they were neglected.† How many must have been lost and dried

* We ask ourselves, without being wholly in accord, if Africa was very greatly wooded in the time of the Romans. It is important to know this, in order to be sure that it might become so again. Before their time, trees must have been very scarce there; Sallust says that the soil is not favourable to them. On the other hand, the most ancient Arabian writers claim that when once entered, it could be traversed throughout its whole length under a vault of foliage. If it were proved that this statement could be trusted, it would be necessary to believe that the forests multiplied greatly during the Roman domination. What is certain is that at the close of the Empire, Africa not only had enough for its own consumption, but exported to Italy considerable supplies of timber and kindling-wood. There still remain oaks and cedars in *Kroumirie* and on the *Aurès*. Moreover, it is not unusual to have a fine tree pointed out in the midst of a barren plain and to be told that it is the last survivor of a vanished forest.

† C. I. L., 8809.

up during the fourteen hundred years in which they were no longer used! And yet the ancients always referred to Africa as a dry and poorly watered country; we must not forget this. It is what first impressed the early Romans who settled there: *Cælo terraque penuria aquarum;* and these words of Sallust did not cease to be true in after years. In the time of Emperor Hadrian, that is to say, when the Romans had been masters of the country for three centuries, we are told that for five whole years there was no rain.* Nor is it probable that the rivers at that time were any different in appearance from those of to-day. The description that Silius Italicus gives of the Bagradas, the most important of all, is still true; it continues, as formerly, to drag its muddy waters across the sands of its bed, so slowly that it sometimes resembles a swamp:

"Turbidus arentes lento pede sulcat arenas." †

In fact, in default of other proof, I believe that the great hydraulic works that the Romans undertook, and of which such beautiful ruins remain, are the clearest evidence that the country, in those days, must have been almost as dry as it is now; people who calculated so well would not have taken so much trouble and expended so much money to procure water if enough fell from the sky.

Undoubtedly these marvellous works partly took the place, in Africa, of what was denied by nature.

* Spartian, *Vita Hadr.*, 22.
† Silius, *Punica*, vi., 140.

It is impossible to attempt to describe them in detail, for the soil is everywhere covered with them; we must be satisfied with giving a rapid sketch of them.

No one understood as did the Romans how to discover the resources of a country and how to make the most of its wealth. If it was necessary to water it in order to make it fertile, they knew how to utilise the smallest springs, how to increase their flow, to maintain, regulate, and distribute them according to their needs; and thus derive the greatest possible benefit from them. In Africa, the inscriptions everywhere show us the people occupied in clearing the cisterns, rebuilding the aqueducts, and repairing the harbours. They realised perfectly well that they could do nothing that would be of greater use in that country, constantly threatened with drought; thus there was nothing on which they were more disposed to pride themselves than works of this kind. It may be seen with what pleasure an inhabitant of *Calama* (Guelma) boasts of the repairs that he has made on a fish-pond. " In former years," he tells us, " barely a thin stream of water flowed; to-day it is a veritable river which makes a noise of thunder." * When the municipal magistrates wished to leave some souvenir of their administration, they often erected fountains, and some of these, the ruins of which remain, must have been elegant monuments, combining beauty with utility. There is one found at *Tipasa* (Tipech), near Shershell,

* C. I. L., 5335.

which formed a sort of hemicycle or water-works with statues and columns of blue marble. The water flowed from above into small superposed basins in such a way as to fall from one into the other and give out that gentle trickle that was so restful and refreshing during the hot hours of the day. From there it spread into a semicircular canal whence it was easy to draw it.* A very curious inscription has been discovered at Thysdrus, in which a magistrate congratulates himself on having brought thither water in such abundance that after it had been carried through the whole city by means of fountains which played in the public squares, it could, under certain conditions, be distributed among the homes of the citizens for their private use: *Aqua adducta . . . coloniæ sufficiens, et per plateas lacubus impertita, domibus etiam certa conditione concessa.*† Thus there were in the cities of Africa, at the entrances to the desert, seventeen hundred years ago, water-grants for the inhabitants, a feature which a century ago did not exist in any city of France.

When the water was not on a level with the ground, wells were dug to conduct it along subterranean beds,—many of these wells still exist, and, when they have not been allowed to become filled with mud, are still used by the Arabs,—or great

---

* See Gsell, *Tipasa*, p. 346 (in the XIVth volume of the *Mémoires d'archéologie et d'histoire* of the French school at Rome). Apropos of this, Monsieur Gsell recalls several other water-works, the remains of which have been found in Africa, and which must have been even more remarkable than those at *Tipasa*.

† C. I. L., 51.

care was taken to preserve all that fell from the sky; there was so little, that they could not afford to lose any. Cisterns were hollowed out under almost all houses of any importance; and, independent of those that were for private use, there were many larger ones for the benefit of the public. Those of Carthage,[9] which are probably of Phœnician origin, but which were repaired by the Romans, are the admiration of visitors. They were composed of two groups, one of which has been restored in our day and serves for supplying the neighbourhood; in the other, which is in ruins, a whole hamlet is housed, and the half-hollowed-out arches are used for rooms or stalls. At *Tupusuctu*,[10] which the Romans, fearing a war with the Berbers of the Jurjura, had converted into a storehouse, they dug cisterns which measure three thousand square metres.

But here are works still more considerable, perhaps, and which are of more importance in that they show clearly what we should do. The African rivers are little else than torrents; after a storm, they overflow their banks and inundate the country; the rest of the time they are almost dried up, and sometimes disappear in the sands. In order to keep these waters from passing and to prevent them from losing themselves in the sea, the Romans constructed systems of dikes and immense reservoirs.[11] There remain enough of these great works for us to admire the skill of the engineers who constructed them. Every precaution was taken to insure their lasting. We see, for instance, that they were careful to build them after a curve in the river, which lessened the shock that the walls of the dam had to bear.* As they wished to expend as little as possible, they generally used, in building them, the materials that they had on hand. But with pebbles mixed with cement, a kind of mortar (beton) was made, so strong that it was difficult to dig it away even with a pickaxe. These reservoirs or dams exist everywhere; in the Hodna, an almost savage country, there have been found as many as three of them, one over the other, and among the number is one which held twelve hundred thousand litres. The water thus preserved in vast basins flowed from the high regions to the plain, where small canals conducted it across the fields. The distribution of it was effected in a prescribed manner, and according to fixed regulations; every landlord, in turn, had a right to it, and for a certain number of hours, as is still the case in the oases. At Lamasba, a little town not far from Lambèse, a very minutely worded regulation has been found, which was posted up, no doubt, on the public square, and which indicates the share that was due to each one.† It is probable that these rules survived even the Roman domination. They still existed, no doubt,—Procopius seems to say so, —in the time of the Vandals, who, like all Germans, preserved the administration of the ancient masters

---

* See on these hydraulic works, *Société arch. de Constantine*, 1864–1868, and the Memoirs of Doctor Carton, in the *Bulletin arch. du minist. de l'inst. publ.*, 1888–1891.

† C. I. L., 4440.

of the country.* But the Arabs have let it all perish. Thanks to their apathy and improvidence, the springs have dried up, the dams have given way, the rivers have again carried all their waters to the sea; and this is why the plains, that seemed so beautiful to the companions of Sidi Okbah, and which they called " a flower-garden," have almost everywhere become a desert.

II

Naturally, very few traces are found to-day of the small estates; peasants do not build for eternity. Sallust tells us that in the early times the habitations of the Africans were very squalid, and that they resembled ships with their keels in the air.† They were called *mapalia*.[12] It is probable that, when from contact, first, with the Carthaginians, and then with the Romans, the natives grew somewhat civilised, their homes became less uncouth. They were still very rude, however. Monsieur de la Blanchère thought that he had discovered some ruins of them while crossing the *Sud-Oranais*, and he gives us a description of them.‡ They are heaps of fallen walls, the ruins of which reproduce almost exactly the form of the buildings from which they have come, which fact proves that they were not overthrown by violence, but that they fell of their own

---

* See Tissot, i., 53.
† *Jug.*, 18, *quasi navium carinæ sunt.*
‡ *Voyage d'Étude*, p. 27.

accord. These walls were made of uncut stones joined together with mortar, like that which the people of the country still use, and which is nothing but mud. " Let there come a somewhat severe rain, the so-called mortar softens, again becomes earth, and the wall crumbles." These constructions, in which as yet brick and tiles were but very seldom used, were often isolated; they occupied the centre of a small field which the landlord tilled for his private use. Frequently also, in places which were not safe, the agriculturists joined together in order to protect themselves. Their houses, crowded one close to another along the sides or on the crest of some abrupt cliff, where it was less easy to be surprised, formed inaccessible villages, which must have resembled those of the Kabyles.

In these villages or on these farms lived a sober and robust population. The country, in short, is healthful. Fevers, no doubt, are to be feared there *; but we know from our own experience that they are considerably mitigated, and even disappear completely, when the soil is drained and rendered wholesome by cultivation. Herodotus tells us that there are no people in the world who enjoy such good health as the Africans, and Sallust claims that they do not know what illness is, and die only from old age. Everyone who has made any study of African epigraphy has been impressed by the large

---

* In the epitaph of a woman of *Auzia* (Aumale), her husband states as a miracle that she lived forty years without having the fever: " Quæ vixit sine febrebus " (C. I. L., 9050).

number of centenarians mentioned in the inscriptions.* The fact was so common that the relatives of the dead, if the latter did not live to be very old, were amazed and indignant. A woman of *Haïdra*, who lost her husband at the age of eighty-two years and seven months, said to him: "You have died too soon, you should have lived to be one hundred; and why not?" † In *Scillium*, a city of Byzacium, an immense mausoleum has been discovered, built in the form of a pyramid, and surmounted by a rooster, like our town clocks; a long epitaph of more than two hundred lines tells us that it was the tomb of Flavius Sabinus, a well-known man of the place, and of his wife. The husband had lived one hundred and ten years and the wife one hundred and five; yet this does not prevent the author of the lines from sadly bewailing the fact that the life of man is so short:

"Sint licet exiguæ fugientia tempora vitæ." ‡

Some of these petty farmers, by force of order, work, and economy, made a fortune. There was one at *Mactaris* who took the trouble to tell it in a metrical inscription which he left us. Assuredly he did not compose it himself, for his education must

---

* "In the time of Ibn-Khaldoun," says Tissot, "the usual duration of life among the Tuaregs was eighty years. This is still the actual average; centenarians are numerous, and mention is made of some who lived to the age of one hundred and thirty and one hundred and fifty years."—*Géogr. de la prov. d'Afrique*, p. 479.

† C. I. L., 11,594.

‡ *Ibid.*, 211.

have been greatly neglected; but as it was the custom for people of importance voluntarily to place verses on their tombs, he himself or his heirs must have expressed the wish to one of the fine scholars of the province. They did not make a bad choice, and the epitaph has an accent of simplicity and sincerity very rare in bits of this kind. " I was born," says the rich peasant to us, " in a poor hut, of a miserable father, who left me neither money nor a home." Fortunately he possessed energy and courage, which make up for everything. He did nothing during his lifetime except till the soil, but there was no cultivator more active than he.

" As soon as the season had ripened the grain, I was the first to cut it; then, when the men who carry the scythe had gone to gather the harvest in the plains of Cirta or the Fields of Jupiter (Zaghouan), I walked at their head, the first at work, and I left piles of bound sheaves behind me. Thus, under a sun of fire, I cut twice six harvests, until the day when I myself became head of the workers. For eleven years more I cut with them the ripe corn in the Numidian countries."

That is how he made money and finally became the owner of a house and a farm " which lacked nothing." With wealth came honours; he was elected decurion—that is, municipal councillor—in his country, and he was even chosen by his colleagues, the decurions, to be the highest magistrate of his town. Thus from a poor labourer, he came one day to sit in the assembly as president, in the very midst of the curia. "So it is," he adds, "that my labour brought me brilliant years which no envious tongue ever dared assail"; and as a peasant does not lose the opportunity to point something of a moral, he assumes a more serious tone and concludes by saying: "Learn, mortals, by my example, to live a life above reproach, and, like me, to merit by an honest life a gentle death." *

But in Africa, as elsewhere, those who made a fortune could not have been very numerous. It was sufficient for the majority to have enough on which to subsist; still they succeeded in earning their living only by being very industrious. They made the most of everything. On the hills, as in the poorly watered plains, they planted the olive and the vine. It may clearly be seen from the number of presses found at every step among the ruins, that the olive must have been one of the rich products of the country. It is from this that Rome supplied itself with the oil needed for the gymnasiums and the public baths. The vine is in a fair way toward recovering in Algeria and Tunis the ground it has lost; it will soon make the fortune of these countries. But the chief products of cultivation were the cereals; all the world extolled the abundance of the African harvests; they had become proverbial." In order to indicate that a man possessed an incalculable fortune, it was said that "he had in his granaries all the corn that was raised in Africa." † The corn from Africa

* C. I. L., 11,824.
† Horace, *Carm.*, i., 1, 10: "quidquid de libycis verritur areis."

was reputed to yield much more than any other; the story is told of a procurator of Augustus, to whom one day corn was sent which yielded four hundredfold.* Yet these harvests were obtained by the most simple means; " I have seen there," Pliny tells us, " after the rains, the earth turned over by a plough, to which were harnessed on one side a poor little ass, on the other a woman." † It is a sight that may still be seen, and Tissot, who has often been a witness to it, tells us that the native of to-day feels no more scruples than the Libyan of former years in harnessing his wife to the yoke with his ass, especially if the former is old. ‡ Let us add that the plough of the Roman epoch, like that which is used to-day, was thoroughly primitive in its simplicity. The ploughshare scarcely grazed the soil; but what matter? The land was so naturally fertile that there was no need of much tillage in order to make it productive. Let there come a favourable rain in the beginning of the spring, in a few weeks the plain would be yellow with corn. When the harvest was finished and the pits full, the farmer piled the crops upon his ass or into a wretched waggon and took them to market.

The Africans of that epoch frequented the markets a great deal, as their descendants still do; it is a custom which, like so many others, has been preserved. There was no lack in the cities of comfort-

* Pliny, *H. N.*, xviii., 21.
† *Ib.*, xvii., 3, 6.
‡ *Geogr.*, i., 306.

able, luxurious, and well-equipped markets, the ruins of which still exist. There were some also in the midst of the fields, near the large estates, in places where the peasants from the environs could gather together. The wealthy landlords, who found it to their interest to settle near them, asked permission of the Senate to do so, if the province was senatorial, or of the representative of the prince, if it was imperial. There was in the time of the Romans, at the foot of the mountains that separated the proconsular provinces from Numidia, and which to-day is the boundary of the regency of Tunis, on the height of Tebessa, a very important estate, called *Saltus Beguensis* (to-day, El-Begar); there have been found there in the middle of a field the still visible remains of a great portico which surrounds some less important débris, in which have been recognised ruined shops. This, then, was a market, and he who built it, L. Africanus, who wished to make known to all the world that it was authorised, took care to thrice reproduce the *Senatus consultum* which decreed the building of it. We have two copies of it with the signatures of the witnesses who affirmed its authenticity. It says in it:

"that L. Africanus, in the province of Africa, on the territory of Begua, occupied by the Mussulmans, in the place called *Ad Casas*, has the right to hold a market twice each month, the fourth day before the nones, and the twelfth before the calends (the second and the twenty-first of every month); that people from the vicinity and strangers shall be allowed to gather there, but only for the purpose of buying and selling (political reunions were always feared), and on condition that they commit no illegal act and harm no one." *

It was to the interest of the proprietor to draw to his mart the petty farmers of the neighbourhood and to make his estate the centre of an important commerce. This kind of traffic always benefited the richest; as his wealth allowed him to wait and as he could store his harvest in his granaries, it was lawful for him to profit by circumstances, to buy grain at a low price in times of plenty and to sell it again at a very high price in hard times.

A part of the grain which was harvested in Africa was reserved for the supply of Rome. There had been a long period during which Rome was unable to support itself; at first it had had recourse to the nearest provinces, to Sicily and Sardinia, in order to supply what it lacked; but they did not suffice for long. It was necessary then to apply to Egypt and Africa, which, after the time of Augustus, became its chief resource. Good citizens were sadly grieved at this necessity: " They groaned," Tacitus tell us, " at seeing that the subsistence of the Roman people was the plaything of the winds and the tempests." †
But what was to be done about it? They could not think of restoring the farmers of Italy to the fields that they had left in order to live in the cities.

---

* C. I. L., 270 and 11,451. The sign-board of another of these markets has been found in Numidia. C. I. L., 6357.

† *Ann.*, xii., 43; see also iii., 54.

What was better, since they were forced to apply to the neighbouring countries, was to avoid all disappointments and to take precautions against all surprises by regulating in a fixed manner the portion that each country must furnish, and by taking measures so that it might reach its destination without hindrance or delay; this is what was done. It was decided that Egypt and Africa should each send a third of what was consumed at Rome, almost 1,800,000 hectolitres; the remainder was to come from Sicily and Italy. The Africans were thus paying a part of their taxes in products of the soil.[14] The grain that they owed the State was gathered under the surveillance of the procurators of the Emperor, and by them brought to the ports, whence it was shipped. It is known that at *Rusicade* (Philippeville [15]) immense granaries were built in which it was stored until the day of sailing.* In order to bring the corn from there to Italy, Commodus organised a special fleet, after the example of that of Egypt, which, at a regular time, was to convey it to Puzzuoli (*Puteoli*) and Ostia.† We know that the arrival of these fleets filled the Italian ports with great animation; people, in order to see them come in, rushed to the jetties and along the shores; they followed with their eyes the small ships, which were recognised by their light sails, and which preceded and announced the approach of the large galleys loaded with corn; they saluted from afar those vessels, im-

* C. I. L., 7975.
† Lampride, 17.

The Surrounding Country

patiently waited for, which brought food to Rome.* It is well known that the service of supplies, or, as it was called, the *Annone*, was of very great importance; therefore they deified it. The *Annona Sancta* was a divinity represented with her shoulder and arm bare, a crescent moon on her head, in her hand swords, and before her horns of plenty. She was greatly fêted at the seaports where the corn was received and shipped to Rome, and which thus owed her part of their life. Porters, measurers, and workmen of every kind, whose living the *Annona* helped them to earn, showed their gratitude by erecting altars to her. The Romans also must have felt a great veneration for her, for they well knew that they would be liable to die of hunger if she should ever distribute her gifts less freely among them. Africa was, therefore, according to the saying of a writer of the times, the soul of the Republic; and Juvenal was right in demanding that they treat with respect those valiant harvesters who supplied Rome with food, and allowed her to give herself up without fear to the pleasures of the circus and the theatre:

"Qui saturant urbem circo scenæque vacantem." †

III

Having studied the condition of the small estates of Roman Africa, let us occupy ourselves for a while with the larger.

---

* See the picture that Seneca draws of the arrival at Puzzuoli of the fleet from Alexandria. (*Epist.*, 77.)

† Juvenal, viii., 118.

In the celebrated passage in which Pliny the Elder attributes the ruin of Italy to the growth of the large estates, he adds that the evil had reached the provinces, and that six landowners possessed the half of Africa.* It is easy to understand how these enormous estates were organised. After their defeats, the natives had been more than once either transported in a body to distant countries, or cantoned among the mountains. The lands which they left free belonged by right to the conquerors. The State no doubt retained a large part of them; but it must also have sold or have given some to a few persons of importance; and this was not an evil, for capital was necessary in order to undertake works of public utility and to make productive a fertile soil which had been but little cultivated. From the close of the Republic, great speculations in real estate were carried on in Africa. There the father of Cælius, a Roman knight of Puzzuoli, acquired the fortune that his son knew so well how to spend.† Cornelius Nepos states that a certain Julius Calidus was put on the list of proscriptions in order that the immense lands he possessed in Africa might be seized.‡ The movement continued under the Empire; men of importance, whom the prince sent to command the troops or to govern the province, attracted by the richness of the country, did not fail later on to buy lands there and to invest a part of their fortune

---

* *H. N.*, xviii., 35.
† Cicero, *Pro Cælio*, 30.
‡ *Vita Attic.*, 12.

The Surrounding Country 167

in them. Julius Martialianus, who was legate of Numidia in the time of Alexander Severus, possessed considerable estates at Mascula in the environs of Lambèse; it is possible that his sojourn in Africa, where he commanded the third legion, gave him the idea of acquiring them. Thus, in time, illustrious families of Rome settled in this country; the *Lollii* at Tidsis, and the *Arrii Antonini* at Milève, as well as many others. These great nobles built for themselves sumptuous residences, with granaries for their commodities, stables for their animals, and lodgings for their servants. Naturally there must have remained more traces of those vast structures than of the humble homes of the poor farmers of whom I have just spoken.

Chance has preserved some remains of one of these great dwelling-houses, and by visiting them we can picture to ourselves the way in which the African aristocracy lived on their estates.* On the road from Constantine to Setif (*Sitifis*)[16] near the little village of Oued-Atmenia, in a great undulating plain which to-day is still fertile and well watered,

* The excavations of which I am about to speak were made by the Archæological Society of Constantine, one of those which in Algeria have best served the cause of science. Monsieur Poulle, who was at that time the president, has given an account of them in a carefully prepared Memoir of which I will merely give a *résumé* (*Mém. de la Soc. Arch. de Const.*, 1878, p. 434 *et seq.*). The Society has published also a plan of the building and a reproduction of the mosaics in some very beautiful plates of which Tissot has made use in his *Géographie de l'Afrique*, and Monsieur Durny in his *Histoire romaine*. Unfortunately it has since been discovered that the plates were not always perfectly accurate. In order to be informed as to the liber-

an Arab, who was ploughing a field, struck an obstacle which broke his ploughshare; the ground was dug up in order to find the cause of the resistance, and there was discovered, first, a wall, and then the beginning of a tesselated pavement which seemed very well preserved.

The work of excavation was continued with care, and at length there were brought to light the remains of a building which measured more than eight hundred square metres. It was easy to see that these were the baths, and that nothing was lacking in them that was found in establishments of this kind at Rome and elsewhere. At one end was the hypocaust, which, in order that the service might be facilitated, was surrounded by corridors in which were stone benches where the slaves rested whose duty it was to light and keep up the fires. Then came the chambers in which one passed through the various degrees of heat, the *calidarium*, the *sudatorium*, and the *tepidarium;* the floor was raised on brick pillars, so that the heat might come from below; the marble plinths covering the walls were separated from the thick masonry by a space of three centimetres in order that the steam might be

---

ties which the designer took with the original, I applied to Monsieur Mercier, the present president of the Society of Constantine, with whose kindness I was acquainted, and who is known by some excellent works on the history of Algeria. Monsieur Mercier kindly pointed out to me the slight mistakes in detail which have been corrected in the copy, and had a new reproduction made for me, this time perfectly exact, of a part of the mosaic which covered the floor of the *atrium*. He adds that to-day everything is irretrievably lost.

diffused everywhere, while sandstone pipes distributed it through the passages and prevented the bather from passing too suddenly from one temperature to another. There were other apartments, both large and small, round and square, with apses at their extremities which must have been used for amusements, for conversation, for meals, and for all of those occupations which made the bath one of the greatest and most complicated pleasures of ancient life. But the most sumptuous and the best ornamented part was a court (*atrium*) almost ten metres long, divided into three compartments by marble pillars ornamented with Corinthian capitals. The *atrium*, which must have been a charming meeting-place and promenade, opened upon a great swimming-tank, surrounded by a semicircular gallery. The whole consisted of twenty-one chambers, and must have formed a structure of rare convenience and perfect elegance. All the rooms were paved with mosaics which were found in a marvellous state of preservation; the débris of the marble and stucco ornaments which probably covered the walls lay strewn on the ground.

In the presence of so vast and so rich a monument, the inclination was to believe that such an outlay was not made for one person alone, but that the public baths had been discovered. It is difficult, however, to hold to this opinion. If these baths were public, for whom could they have been used? It is not known that there was a single Roman city in the vicinity nearer than twenty or thirty kilometres. No important ruin has been found within a radius of several miles; it is therefore probable that one estate occupied the whole plain. The owner, who must have been very rich, and who no doubt lived there with his family, must have combined in it every convenience of life; he had this beautiful edifice built for himself and his family, and we have no reason to be surprised that it is so vast and so sumptuous, when we consider that, throughout the whole extent of the Empire, especially in Africa, the baths had become a necessity for everyone, and that the wealthy displayed an extravagant luxury in them." Seneca relates that having gone to visit the villa of the elder Scipio, at Liternum, he was amazed to find how plain, narrow, bare, and dark were the baths there.

"Who would be satisfied with them to-day?" says he. "Who would not consider himself a beggar if he bathed in a chamber, the walls of which did not sparkle with the light of precious stones? If the Egyptian marble was not inlaid with Numidian marble [18] and encircled by mosaics? If the ceiling was not panelled in crystal? If the *piscina* was not cut from Parian marble? If the water did not flow from silver faucets? And I speak as yet only of the baths of the common people; what will it be when we come to those of the freedmen? What statues and pillars, supporting nothing and which are purely ornamental! What masses of water falling with the crash of a cascade! We have reached such a refinement of delicacy that our feet can no longer tread on anything but precious stones." *

* Seneca, *Epist.*, 86, 1, 6.

These were the follies that the wealthy Romans allowed themselves in the first century of the Empire. The example of Rome was imitated throughout the whole world, and we understand that a great landlord of Africa, who wished to be in fashion, strove to reproduce something of this extravagance.

If he had such magnificent baths built for himself, we may be sure that his dwelling-house was larger still and more beautiful; but no trace of it remains, or at least none has been discovered at the present time. Fortunately there is no need of our making excavations in order to know what it was like; without leaving the baths we can form a picture of the house. I have just spoken of the mosaics which cover the ground; their character is such as to make them especially valuable. The owner, like many others, might have been satisfied with having an ordinary subject copied on them, the triumph of Amphitrite or of Bacchus, the labours of Hercules, etc.; but he wanted something which should be for himself and which would belong only to him; he requested the artist to reproduce his dwelling-house, his park, and his gardens, with their attractions, as our kings sometimes have had their palaces decorated with pictures or tapestries representing their principal residences. The artist of mosaics no doubt took great licence with the reality; he could not have attempted to give to a purely decorative work the perfection and the accuracy that belong to finished works of art; it is a rough sketch which must be judged of as a whole, but, nevertheless, it gives us an idea of a great Roman estate in the time of the Empire. Since it is before our eyes, let us not resist the temptation to look it over for a moment.

In the first place, let us thank the artist of mosaics for the valuable information he has given; as he feared that his pictures might not always be understood, he resorted to the expedient of placing by the side of each legends which help us to understand the places and the people. Above the house stands out in large letters the name of the owner: it was Pompeianus. His dwelling-house, which occupies the upper part of one of the mosaics, does not present the widely developed façade and the beautiful appearance of regularity which have been so much in vogue with us, especially since the Renaissance. The Romans seem to have cared but little for them. Their villas, made for use, were composed, as a rule, of a collection of various structures, situated near one another rather than connected, and built as they had felt the need of them. It was in this way that the villa of Emperor Hadrian at *Tibur* (modern Tivoli) was built, which was looked upon as a marvel. When seen from afar, with its structures of every size and its roofs of every shape, it must have resembled a small city. Pliny the Younger uses this very expression in describing the appearance of the pleasure-houses along the bank of the Ostia: *Præstant multarum urbium faciem*. In that of Pompeianus, although it was planned on a very large scale, the symmetry is somewhat preserved. The wings consist of two great, square pavilions, surmounted by a kind of dome; in the centre, by the side of a monumental portal, rises a tower three stories high, such as was found in every Roman villa, from which the owner could enjoy the view and the fresh air; then comes a number of buildings with great arched windows, which seem to light an interior gallery. On both sides of the villa, two small houses, exactly alike, complete the dwelling of the master and the slaves. They open upon gardens, and in order to indicate this, the artist has placed in the background tall trees, the tops of which rise above the roofs; at both ends, hedges of boxwood, such as are found in the park at Versailles, surrounded the groves and enclosed the paths; this fashion was preserved from the time of the Romans to that of Louis XIV.

Beneath his dwelling-house, Pompeianus had his stables, thus showing his tastes and preferences. They were those of almost everyone in that country. The natives, then as now, loved their horses above all else; they cared for them and were proud of them. Those that Pompeianus shows us, the best, no doubt, that he had at home, have their names written above their stalls; they were called *Delicatus, Pullentianus, Titas,* and *Scholasticus* *; but Pompeianus

* It is in the painting of these horses that the artist seems to have committed his greatest errors. "He made a mistake," Monsieur Mercier writes me, "in putting between them a kind of manger which was never there. Moreover, the picture gives the idea that they are covered with a flowery hood like the *djellal* of our natives, when, in reality, they are without covering, the artist intending merely to show the play of light on their shining coats."

is not always satisfied with merely naming them; he occasionally adds some words of flattery and affection which show how greatly he admires and loves them. Addressing himself to the one called *Altus* (the High), he says: " Thou art without parallel, thou makest bounds like the mountains" (*unus es, ut mons exultas*). Above another are these words: " Whether or not thou art winner, we love thee, Polidoxus" (*vincas, non vincas, te amamus, Polidoxe*). This one, evidently, is a race-horse, trained to carry off prizes.

Racing was the fashionable amusement throughout the Empire, but, apparently, it was enjoyed nowhere so much as in Africa. A very curious relic remains of this passion. At that time it was believed that when complaint was made against anyone, there was no surer way of making the injury efficacious than to entrust the vengeance to the dead; therefore the name of the one who was to be injured was written on a leaden blade which was inserted into a tomb; it was supposed that the dead would undertake to carry the request to the infernal gods. Quite a large number of these blades have been found in Africa and probably still more will be brought to light. Some acquaint us with unimportant and unknown Romans; these are sometimes lovers who complain at having been deceived, and who demand the punishment of the guilty. "O Thou that rulest the Lower World," says one of them, " I recommend to thee Julia Faustilla; come and seize her as quickly as possible and place her among the number of thy subjects." In most cases these blades were inserted by charioteers who wished to rid themselves of their rivals. They invoke the deities of every country; one after the other they name all the horses which are about to contend with them for the prize; they implore the gods to render them powerless:

"Stop them, chain them down, remove all their strength, that they may be unable to leave the stable, to pass the gate of the hippodrome, to advance a step on the track, and as to those who drive them, paralyse their hands that it may be impossible for them to see or to hold the reins or to stand up; hurl them from the chariots, throw them down and let them be trampled under their horses' feet. Without delay, without delay; immediately, immediately!"*

These wild supplications show the ardour that was put into contests of this kind. Victory gave not only reputation to the horses and to the drivers who had obtained it; it brought them wealth also. An inscription found some years ago at Rome tells us that the driver Crescens, of Moorish origin (the drivers were at that time African, as to-day they are English), in ten years won 1,500,000 sesterces (a little more than 300,000 francs).†

Pompeianus entered horses for the races, and this

* C. I. L., 12,504 *et seq.* They were so thoroughly convinced of the efficacy of this witchcraft, that a law of Valentinian condemned to death those who resorted to it.

† This inscription was published, with a learned commentary, by Countess Hercilia Lovatelli.

explains the importance he attached to his stables. He greatly loved hunting also, and was careful not to omit this diversion from his mosaics. It is the subject of two pictures: one shows simply the park in which he kept the gazelles, *sæptum venationis;* the other, which is much more complicated, contains ten or more characters, and represents what to-day would be called the attendants of a hunting-party of Pompeianus. There are seen in it dogs, *Fidelis* and *Castus*, in pursuit of an animal, with horsemen and outriders, whose names, as usual, we are carefully told. They are dressed like certain mountaineers of to-day, in trousers which are tight at the knee; they wear a flat head-dress, a sort of close coat, and a cloak thrown back over the shoulder, after the fashion of Spaniards. The horsemen have their lances couched; those on foot hold a sword in their hand; the master of the house, on a rearing horse, leads the hunt; he is dressed like the others, but is without weapons.

Assuredly the artist was not able to picture every detail of the life as it was lived on these great estates; he has reproduced only a part of the buildings which surrounded the dwelling-house of the owner. But he indicates, at least, the most important of them: here, it is the residence of the shepherd of the flock (*pecuarii locus*); there, that of the forester (*saltuarii janus*), an enormous structure, with its roof of red tiles, pavilions of four stories, and its less important outhouses.*

---

* The very interesting mosaics which Monsieur de la Blanchère has

But here is a picture which is even more curious and interesting; the artist has represented an orchard, with trees of various kinds, about which climbs a vine. At the foot of a palm-tree laden with ripe fruit, a lady, like a dignified matron, is seated on a chair with a back to lean against. She is elegantly gowned and carries a fan in her hand; before her, a young man, wearing a short tunic, leads a little dog by a string, and with the other hand shades the lady with a parasol. In the upper part of the picture are the words: *filosofi locus.* We are therefore clearly informed; we have before us the grove occupied by the philosopher. But the philosopher himself, where is he ? Must we find him in the young man who holds the dog and the parasol ? I am at first rather tempted to think so, when I recall the malicious accounts of Lucian, who shows us the wise men of his time very assiduous in their attentions to great ladies and amusing them by pretty speeches, while they are making their toilet. He even cites one, the stoic Thesmopolis, who, like our young man, assumes charge of the little dog Myrrhine, and even carries complaisance to the point of receiving her puppies in his cloak.

collected in the *Alaoui* at Tunis contain some reproductions of farmhouses which bring before us, in a very vivid manner, the rural labour of the Roman epoch. The most curious are those that have been found in the Godmet farm at Tabarca. One of them shows the picture of a house of several stories, perfectly preserved, with ducks and hens in the lower court. In another, the horse is tied to the door of the stable, while a woman seated on a bench spins as she watches the sheep. These are scenes from the country life of the Romans taken on the spot.

I think, however, that in this case the word philosopher must not be taken literally. Toward the close of the Empire the title was given to every man of letters, and even to all clever men of whatever art or science. " The place of the philosopher " is the place of agreeable and intellectual conversation in which one touches in a discreet manner on literature or the sciences, and, upon occasion, the place of elegant conversation, in which were read those little verses which were fashionable in Africa, a few of which have been preserved in the *Anthology*. There is, therefore, some place in this magnificent dwelling-house for the refinements of life; but while it is Pompeianus who directs the hunters and pursues the antelope, it is his wife who, in a charming flower-garden, gives audience to wits and presides over polite conversation.

IV

Among the great landowners who occupied the best part of Africa, we must place the Emperor first. The princes who were masters of Rome during the first two centuries, the *Julii*, the *Flavii*, and the *Antonini*, belonged to very wealthy families who possessed estates almost everywhere.* Their private

---

* To cite one instance only: as the name of *Matidia* has been found in two places in the tables of Peutinger, as well as on an inscription, the conclusion has been reached that this niece of Trajan, who was very wealthy, possessed estates in Africa, and that they must have been part of her inheritance. There is a discussion concerning this inheritance in the letters of Fronto, and it may be seen by it that

fortune, which was considerable, accrued from the public wealth. Out of the estates taken from the conquered, the State everywhere reserved for itself an important part, which formed what was called *ager publicus populi Romani*. Under the Empire, the *ager publicus* very soon became confounded with the private patrimony of the prince; this, as would be said to-day, was his civil list, which allowed him to provide for all his needs. The Emperor constantly increased it by the confiscation of the property of the condemned, and it often happened that people were condemned merely in order that their goods might be seized. In the passage from Pliny which I have quoted, and in which he says that the half of Africa belonged to six landowners, he adds that Nero ordered them killed and seized their estates. It was thus by a single blow that the half of Africa was added to the part which he must already have possessed.

The large estates, especially in Africa, sometimes bore the name of *saltus;* they were so called because they were originally composed of wood- and pasture-lands. Afterwards great clearings were made; grain-fields took the place of unproductive pasture-lands, and the vine and the olive were substituted for the brushwood; but although their nature was greatly

---

Marcus Aurelius, perhaps through some feeling of delicacy, was unwilling to accept it. This fact displeased his wife, who was much less particular than he. It is probable that in this case, as always, Faustina succeeded in getting the better of him, and that the estates of *Matidia* were added to the African imperial domain.

changed, their ancient name was preserved. These *saltus* were usually enormous cultivated tracts which Frontinus tells us " equalled and even surpassed the area of a city." *

This reminds us of the Enfida, that contains more than 150,000 hectares. " In the centre," adds Frontinus, " rises the *villa* of the owner, surrounded by a line of villages like a belt "; in another place he speaks of " a race of cultivators " which fills the fields. The most important of these *saltus* belonged to the Emperors.

In one of them, called *Saltus Burunitanus*, which was situated in the valley of the Bagradas, an inscription was discovered, a few years ago, which without doubt is one of the most interesting that Africa has preserved.† It is a petition from the cultivators of the *saltus*, addressed to Emperor Commodus, with the reply of the prince; it is interesting in that it shows how those vast territories were administered. In the first place, there was a *procurator* of the Emperor who had charge of the whole estate, and who himself was under the orders of the *procurator* of Carthage; below him were *conductores* and *coloni*, who were not the same in rank. The *conductores*, as their name indicates, leased a part of

* *Gromatici*, ed. Lachm., p. 53.
† C. I. L., 10,570. This inscription has often been studied. Among the most important works that have been written on it, I will mention that of Mommsen (*Hermes*, xv., p. 385), those of Messieurs Cagnat and Fernique (*Revue archéol.*, 1880), and of Monsieur Fustel de Coulanges (*Recherches sur quelques problèmes d'histoire*, p. 53 *et seq.*).

the *saltus*, cultivated it at their own risk and expense, and paid the landowner a rent stipulated by contract. Their lease, as in the time of the Republic, was renewed every five years. At the end of this period the farmer either retired or made a new lease, which might be like the first or might contain different clauses. The condition of the *coloni* was wholly different. In the first place, they were poor, while the *conductores* seem to have been rather wealthy; probably they tilled the less arable portions of land which the *conductores* did not care to lease. It does not appear that they paid the landlord a fixed rent; it is more probable that they shared the profits with him. In fact, it is nowhere stated that there was between them and the landlord a lease which it was the custom to renew at a fixed time, like that of the *conductores*. Their privileges, like their duties, were determined by what was called the *lex Hadriana* or *forma perpetua*, a law which was made once for all, and which remained the same for almost a century. The *coloni* were not under the orders of the *conductores*; they owed them merely a certain number of *prestations*.[19] At a time when work was pressing, or labour scarce, it was understood that the *coloni* should aid the workmen employed by the *conductor*. This was a cause of perpetual conflict; wherever the *conductores* and the *coloni* lived near one another we see these wretched prestations engendering quarrels which never ended. However, Emperor Hadrian, who so thoroughly understood how to preserve order everywhere, took the trouble to indicate in the clearest manner the duties of the *coloni;* they owed to the *conductores* two days' labour, two days' weeding, and two days' harvesting; that was all, but the *conductores* exacted much more, and they found the means of obtaining what they demanded. As they were rich, they purchased by gifts the good-will of the *procurator*, who allowed them to do as they pleased. This is precisely what the inscription found in the *Saltus Burunitanus* says in detail. As a result of one of these acts of injustice, the wretched *coloni*, finding that they had nothing to hope for from their natural chiefs, conceived the idea of complaining directly to the Emperor. Evil betided them; the *procurator* of Carthage, bribed by the *conductores*, and doubtless furious at seeing his administration denounced to the prince, sent soldiers to the estate. The malcontents were seized and punished; some of them were thrown into prison, others were beaten with rods, although they were Roman citizens. But he was dealing with energetic people, who did not allow themselves to be easily frightened. They sent a new petition to the Emperor, which, this time, reached him, and the Emperor answered it with a letter signed by his own hand, in which he ordered that the precepts of Hadrian be respected, and that there be exacted from the *coloni* only their due. And yet this Emperor was Commodus, a very bad man; but under the most wicked princes affairs went on in their usual way, and the provinces had less to suffer from than might be supposed. The joy, as may well be believed, was great in this little world which had finally obtained justice. As they were associated together (we should say to-day formed into syndicates) in order the better to protect themselves, the president (*magister*) of the association was charged to have printed several copies of the petition of the *coloni* and of the Emperor's reply*; and on the Ides of March in the year 181 or 182, when the inscription was dedicated, there must have been a festival among the *coloni* of the *saltus*.

They were, however, a very wretched people, and not at all assuming. "We are," they say, "only poor peasants, who gain our livelihood by the work of our hands"; and, farther on, addressing themselves to the Emperor: "Have pity on us; let not thy peasants, the children of the soil, who have been born and brought up on it, be troubled by the farmers of thy estate." These expressions have made an impression on historians and jurists, who have questioned whether the people calling themselves *vernulæ, alumni saltuum imperatoris* were not already colonists attached to the soil, such as are found in the beginning of the Eastern Empire, and whether the institution of the *colonat*, which usually is made to date from Constantine, is not much more ancient. What is certain in any case, is the fact that if it did not exist under its legal and permanent

---

* Monsieur Cagnat found in Tunis, thirty kilometres from Souk-al-Khmis, a fragment of an inscription which contains another copy of the petition of the *coloni* of the *Saltus Burunitanus*.

form in the time of Commodus, it was about to appear. There is not a text which tells us that the peasants who were born on the estates of the Emperor had no right to leave them; the law which must forever attach them to the estate was not yet promulgated; and yet they lived on them, they had lived on them for several generations, and probably would always live on them, not from compulsion, but because they had acquired the habit of living there, and because they had not the means to live elsewhere. They were therefore, in reality, forced to remain there, although they were not forbidden to leave, and the law which, a century later, would attach them permanently to the soil would change nothing of their true condition. Thus the *colonat* was not wholly created by the legislator of the Eastern Empire; it was in embryo in the statute of Hadrian, which itself was probably only an application of a custom dating back to the origin of Rome.*

In this Roman world, which is the triumph of logic and of the spirit of order, nothing is done all at once, nothing happens by chance, and it is a great pleasure for the historian to see the institutions slowly forming and emerging from one another by a sort of natural generation.

The imperial estate was composed not only of the immense *saltus* which resembled provinces; the

---

* A new inscription, relating to the administration of the *saltus*, was recently found near *Aïn-Ouassel* in Tunis by Dr. Carton, an army surgeon, to whom African archæology is indebted for so many important discoveries. He published it in the *Revue archéologique*

mines also, or rather what were called by the general name of *metalla*, were a part of it; by this were understood not only the mines of gold, silver, copper, and lead, but the quarries of marble, of stone, and even of salt. Almost all the *metalla* throughout the whole world were acquired or confiscated by the Emperor, and administered by his intendants. Although but little is said about those of Africa, nevertheless there were some there, and they were not without importance. To be compelled to work in the mines was one of the greatest punishments inflicted on the Christians during the persecutions. We have the brave letters that the sufferers wrote to their priest Cyprian, begging him for his prayers, and the beautiful response of the priest. They show what a wretched life was led by the workers in the mines; they were scantily clothed and poorly nourished; they slept on the ground; they shivered in winter; in summer they were parched with the sun; and these sufferings, hard for everyone, seemed intolerable to old men, women, and children, to those accustomed to the comforts of cities, and who were unacquainted with misery. But they were sustained by faith, happy to suffer for truth's sake. And when a letter from the priest reached them all misery was forgotten:

"The condemned bless you," said they to him, "for

(1892, p. 214). Many versions have been given as to the meaning of this inscription. I adopt here the conclusions of a work which Monsieur Mispoulet brought out in the *Collections du Musée Alaoui*, published under the direction of Monsieur de la Blanchère.

having revived their courage. Their limbs no longer feel the sting of the whip; it seems to them that their feet are no longer bound; light shines among the shadows of their prison. These horrible mountains become smiling plains, and the frightful odour of the lamps in the sombre creep-holes is changed into the perfume of flowers."*

The mines of Sigus,[20] in the heart of Numidia, whence the martyrs addressed these beautiful words to St. Cyprian, have not been found, but the quarries of *Simittu* (Schemtu), which furnished the famous Numidian marble, are known and worked. This marble was in great vogue during the Empire. Hadrian had his villa at Tibur ornamented with it; and Constantine had some of the columns that supported the vaulting of St. Sophia made from it. There are still some blocks at Schemtu which were taken from the quarry more than fifteen centuries ago, and which, for some unknown reason, were not used; they bear, besides the number indicating their order, the name of the place from which they were taken. At *Simittu* there was a certain number of stone-yards; the royal " Stone-yards " which perhaps dated back to the time of the Numidian kings, the " New Stone-yards," and those of the " Genius of the Mountain." In the time of the *Antonini* the work seems to have been the most active; it was sufficient to lead to the founding of a city, the importance of which is indicated by its ruins.

* Cyprian, *Epist.*, 77.

Possessions so extensive, so numerous, and of so different a character demanded a whole army of officials, some distributed here and there, others collected together, either in the chief town of the various districts (*tractus*), or in the capital of the province. The most important of them are known to us, but we might have been unaware of the more humble ones had not a happy chance rescued some of them from oblivion. Father Delattre in making excavations at Carthage, near Malga, discovered two cemeteries in which rested the bodies of some slaves and freedmen who had been attached to the administration of the imperial estates. Their tombs are very simple and correspond to their humble condition; they usually consist of a stone cippus, in the interior of which are set two or three urns of various shapes. The characteristic feature of the urns is the brick tube which surmounts them and which opens either at the top or at the sides of the cippus. By means of this tube libations were sent to the ashes of the dead. It was the same tube into which were inserted the small leaden blades of which I have spoken and which contained imprecations against certain persons. On the front of the cippus one or more marble tablets bear the epitaphs of those whose remains are buried beneath them.*
They are of interest from the fact that they acquaint us with the inferior degrees of the imperial domestic service which had been transplanted into

---

* The inscriptions are collected in the C. I. L., 12,590 *et seq.*, with a *résumé* of the Memoir by Father Delattre.

Africa. They were people attached to the service of officials of high rank (*pedisequi, medici*); agents of every kind who worked in the bureaux of impost and of the estates (*notarii, librarii, tabularii*); land-surveyors (*agrimensores*), runners who bore despatches everywhere, and who formed an association (*collegium cursorum et Numidarum*); all, with the exception of the latter, who were peasants, seemed to come from Rome, and appeared to regret the land of their birth. One of them, who lost a young wife twenty-six years of age, complained bitterly that Fortune did not allow him to return with her to Italy.* These were already the troubles of the officers who looked upon themselves as exiles in the countries which they governed.

I have been able to give, in the preceding, only a very general and a very incomplete sketch of the state of the African suburbs under the domination of Rome; it is not possible, at present, to do otherwise. The information in detail follows; in studying each section of country and almost each estate separately, an effort is made to learn, when possible, what the Romans derived from it, in what way they exploited it, and how they rendered it so fertile. This study, I doubt not, will be of great advantage; it is good to profit by the experience of others. But besides these great works of public utility with which time and observation will acquaint us, it is a more general cause which singularly aided the prosperity of Africa; it is the security that Rome gave to those

* C. I. L., 12,792.

who lived under her domination. In order that agriculture might prosper, it was first necessary for the peasants to be sure of harvesting the grain that they sowed; for the crop, when gathered, to run no risk of being stolen either by the tax-gatherer or by chance plunderers; in a word, for the government to protect them from others and from itself; it was necessary, moreover, that outside of their country business be easy, and that they should be able to trust the routes by land and by sea for exporting the surplus of their crops. This is what the *Roman peace* assured to them *; and for which they were so grateful. We have given it to them, and already the benefits are beginning to make themselves felt; the rest will come later.

TRANSLATOR'S NOTES TO CHAPTER IV

1. "*Capsa* stood on an oasis surrounded by an arid desert; it was the treasury of Jugurtha, and was destroyed by Marius, but was afterwards rebuilt and made a colony."—Wm. Smith, *Ancient Geog.*

2. "*Takape*, at the innermost point of the Lesser Syrtis, was noted for its hot sulphur-baths."—Wm. Smith, *Ancient Geog.*

3. The capital of *Byzacium* was *Byzacina*, which corresponds to modern Beghin.

4. "*Thysdrus*, between Thenæ and Thapsus, a Roman colony, is known as the place where the Emperor Gordianus set up the standard of rebellion against Maximin. Extensive ruins, especially a fine theatre, exist at *Jemme*."—Wm. Smith, *Ancient Geog.*

---

* At least in a general way, for it was seen at the close of the preceding chapter, that this peace was often disturbed by the incursions of the natives.

5. "*Thelepte* lay north-west of Capsa, and had a treasury and arsenal in the Roman period."—Wm. Smith, *Ancient Geog.*

6. "*Hippo Zarytus* was called *Zarytus* on account of the frequent inundations to which it was exposed. It is more correctly written thus than in the Greek form *Hippo Diarrhytus*, which seems to be merely an imitative translation of the native name."—Chas. Anthon, *Ancient Geography.*

The French Government has, during the past few years, created a fortified port here.

"The town was fortified by Agathocles and was made a free city and colony by the Romans."—Wm. Smith, *Ancient Geog.*

7. *Maisons d'exploitation* are companies or associations founded for the purpose of developing the resources, mines, etc., of a colony or country.

8. "The *Bagradas* rises in Mount Mampsarus and flows in a north-east course into the bay of Carthage."—Wm. Smith, *Ancient Geog.*

The character of this river is well described in the following:

"Primaque castra locat cano procul æquore, qua se
Bagrada *lentus* agit, siccæ sulcator arenæ."—Luc., iv., 587.

9. See Smith's *Carthage and the Carthaginians* for cisterns, pp. 377-378-379; also Beulé, *Fouilles*, p. 61; also Alfred J. Church, *Story of Carthage*, p. 143, for cross-section of cistern wall (from Daux).

10. "*Tupusuctu* (Tubusuptus) stood about 18 miles south-east of Saldæ, and was a Roman colony under Augustus."—Wm. Smith, *Ancient Geog.*

11. For cut of reservoirs of Carthage, see Morris, *Hannibal*, p. 43; also Church, *Story of Carthage*, p. 142.

12. *Mapalia* or *Magalia*. Virgil, *Georgics*, iii., 340 : *Raris habitata mapalia tectis*, and *Æn.*, i., 421: *Miratur molem Æneas, magalia quondam.* They were made of branches of trees daubed with clay.

13. For description of African harvests, see E. H. Bunberry, *Ancient Geog.*, vol. ii.

14. In this connection, see, for taxes paid by cognate Phœnician cities to Carthage, Polybius, i., 72; also Livy, xxxiv., 62.

15. *Rusicade*, on the *Sinus Olcachites*, or *Gulf of Stora*, was regarded as the port of *Cirta.*

16. "*Sitifis*, an important city, was enlarged by the Romans and made a colony. It was the capital of *Mauretania Sitifensis*."—Chas. Anthon, *Ancient Geog.*

17. For special baths see Valerius Maximus, ix., 5.

18. "The Numidian marble, on the possession of which even the Romans prided themselves."—R. B. Smith, *Carthage and the Carthaginians*, p. 29; also Horace, *Odes*, ii., 18, 4; Juvenal, *Sat.*, 212.

19. *Prestations*, the labour imposed on each member of a community for repairing public roads, etc.

20. Sigus (Siga?). "The latter was a commercial town at the mouth of a river of the same name. Neither the river nor town has been identified. It was destroyed in Strabo's time, but was afterwards restored."—Wm. Smith, *Ancient Geog.*

CHAPTER V

THE CITIES—TIMEGAD

THERE were certainly cities in Africa before the arrival of the Romans, but there could not have been any great number of them. The Romans had no difficulty in comprehending that if they wished to become permanent masters of the country, and to destroy its spirit of independence and rebellion, it was to their interest to increase the number of towns. In the surrounding country, the native, even when attached to the soil, and after he had become a cultivator and farmer, still came into frequent contact with barbarism, and could easily return to it; in the cities he escaped it to a greater extent. As he lived in the midst of civilisation, he became the more quickly imbued with it.

It was, therefore, natural that the Romans should do much for the cities of Africa. We know, in the first place, that under their domination the ancient towns became more important. *Thysdrus* (El-Jemm) was only a straggling village in the time of Cæsar*; at a later date, it must necessarily have increased greatly in size and population, as an amphi-

---

* *De Bello, Afric.*, 97.

theatre was built there which was almost as large as the Coliseum. But the Romans were especially active in founding a great number of new towns; large cities arose where, formerly, there had been only villages, and even in places which had been entirely uninhabited. But it was not all done in a day. It is necessary to note this in order to reply to impatient friends who complain that our progress is not sufficiently rapid, and who find that after half a century of occupation there still remains much to be done. We can say to them that the Roman progress was slower than ours. Carthage, restored by the Greeks, emerged very slowly from its ruins; Pomponius Mela said, in the time of Claudius, that " it is more celebrated for the remembrance of its past misfortunes than on account of its present good fortune,"* and it was many more years before it became the " wonder of the universe," as Aurelius Victor calls it.† Pliny the Elder gives us to understand that in his time there were, in Africa, with very few exceptions, only *castella*, or fortified stations. ‡ It was under the *Antonini* especially, during the wonderful prosperity of the Empire, that the cities became more numerous and more flourishing. There are countries in which a happy chance permits us, in a way, to follow step by step the progress of each town; we see it coming into existence and growing almost beneath our eyes. § West of the

---

* i., 34: *Priorum excidio rerum quam ope præsentium clarior.*
† *Cæs.*, 19: *Carthaginem, terrarum decus.*
‡ *Hist. Nat.*, v., 1 *et seq.* § See C. I. L., p. 173.

proconsular province, in a fertile plain not far from the Mejerda, there have been found the remains of several wealthy cities which apparently were crowded together; some beautiful ruins attest their ancient glory. Among these cities were *Thibursicum Bure* (Tebursuk), *Thignica* (Ain Tunga), and *Thugga* (Dugga); the last especially seems to have been the largest and the most beautiful of all. The inscriptions which, happily, are not lacking, show us by what steps they attained this prosperity. They were, at first, small towns (*vici*) formed by the meeting together of a few peasants; each town had its individual magistrates, and even after they had drawn together and united, they preserved their separate governments for some time. Then the governments united; the small, straggling villages constituted a city (*civitas*), and the city, in turn, became a municipality or colony. At each change, the Emperors, in order to favour it, accorded new privileges, and the city, proud of the patronage, hastened to add their names to its own; in order to show its gratitude, it was glad to style itself *Aurelia*, *Antoniniana*, or *Alexandriana*. This prosperity reached its height during the dynasty of the *Severi*, who, being African by descent, delighted in conferring all sorts of favours upon their compatriots.

I have no intention of discussing every Roman city in Africa of which ruins have been found. It is better to study one carefully, as this will help us to know the others. If I choose Timegad, it is certainly not because of its importance or reputation;

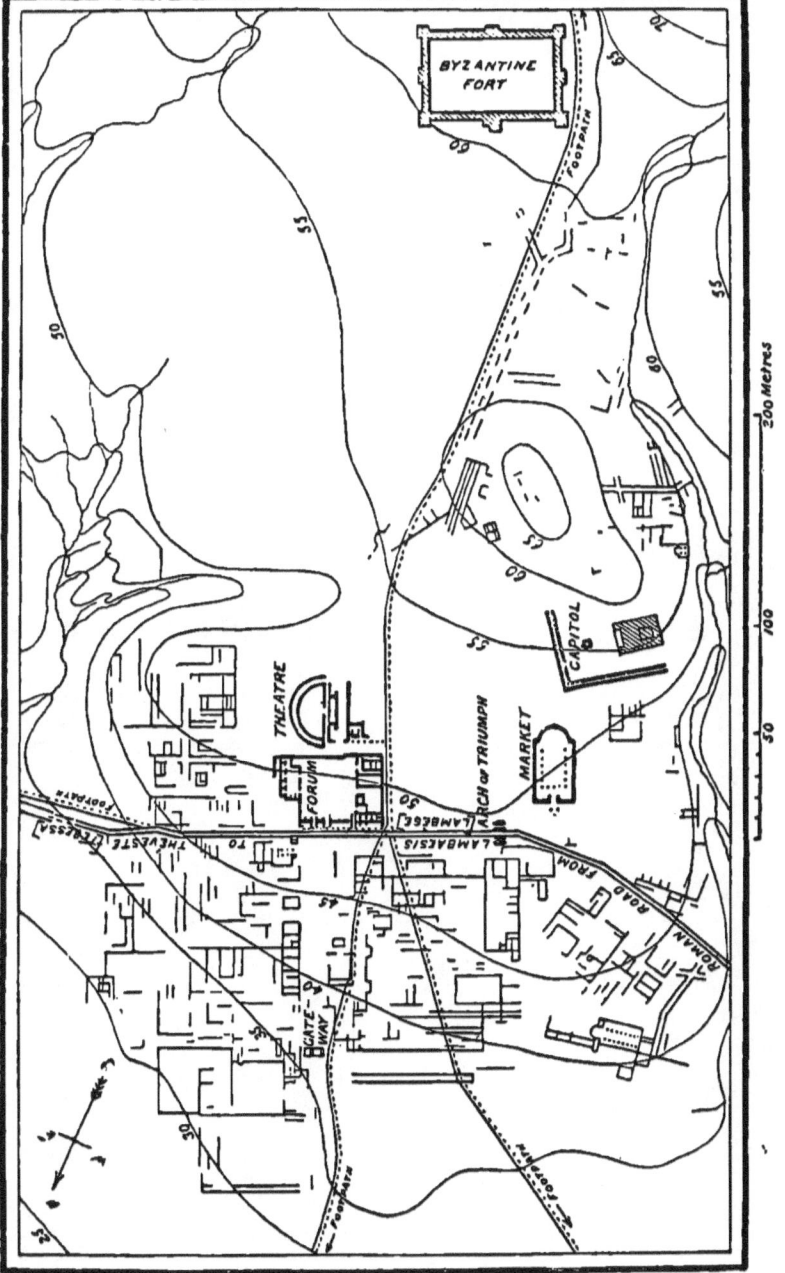

it seems to have taken no part in politics, and historians, with the exception of one or two who mention it incidentally, make no reference to it. It is not likely that it was largely inhabited, and it is certain that it was only of medium size; yet it is the one of which we have the most, and, on the whole, the best preserved ruins. This fact is due, no doubt, to the manner in which it perished. Procopius states that upon the approach of the Byzantines, the mountaineers of the Aurès, who did not wish to see strangers settling in their neighbourhood, destroyed Timegad in order to prevent them from establishing themselves there.* The Byzantines came, however, and they even dwelt there long enough to build a very strong fortress and a church. But it is probable that the city was not rebuilt; the owners of the overthrown houses did not return to occupy them anew, and when, in its turn, the Byzantine garrison departed, the only inhabitants left in the land were the natives, hidden in their mountains. The country being thus deserted, the stones of the ancient houses remained undisturbed, and are found to-day by simply removing the earth which covers them. The Commission of Historical Monuments was, therefore, happily inspired in devoting all its resources for several years to the excavation of Timegad. The work has

* *De Bello Vand.*, ii., 1. It is probable that fire was resorted to in order to hasten the destruction. Bruce, who visited the ruins of Timegad in the middle of the last century, found great blocks of calcined marble in the Temple of Jupiter.

been skilfully conducted,* and it is sufficiently advanced for us to be able, from now on, to study its results to advantage. Not only are the majority of the principal monuments restored, but very many curious inscriptions have been found among the ruins, which inform us as to those who built and frequented them. A visit to Timegad will show the life of a city of Roman Africa in the time of the *Antonini* or the *Severi*.

I

The city of *Thamugade*,† to-day called Timegad, is situated in the ancient province of Numidia, on the last spurs of the Aurès. It occupies the centre of a plateau, which, on the northern side, slopes gradually to the plain. In order to reach it, it is necessary to follow, first, the road that leads from Batna to Tebessa. After going thirty kilometres

---

* The excavations were begun by a very distinguished architect, Monsieur Duthoit, aided by Messieurs Milvoy and Sarrazin; to-day they are entrusted to Monsieur Roger Ballu. Messieurs Bœswilwald and Cagnat have undertaken to publish the sketches and the drawings of those who have worked there, with a detailed description of the city and its monuments. This publication will form a magnificent work, three volumes of which have already appeared (*Timgad, une cité Africaine sous l'empire romain*, Paris, Leroux). I shall make very great use of this excellent work. I have borrowed two maps from it, that of the city and of the Forum, which will aid the reader in understanding the following descriptions.

† It has been proved that this is really the name of the ancient city and that it was not called *Thamugas*, as was supposed, but *Thamugade*. Terminations of this kind are not uncommon in the names of Berber cities.

The Cities—Timegad

or so, the traveller leaves the highway and enters a path, or, as it is called, an Arabian trail, which runs bravely across fields, and in which one stumbles at every step against stones and roots. After crossing a dry *oued*, and painfully re-ascending the steep bank of the river, the ancient city appears. It is a picturesque mass of walls and columns, the first sight of which, in the midst of the surrounding desolation, causes great surprise. Then, following a well preserved Roman road, as the journey continues the ruins on both sides increase. The traveller finally arrives in front of a triumphal arch surrounded by the remains of ancient structures, and finds himself in the heart of the city.

This triumphal arch is one of the most elegant existing in Africa, where there are such large numbers of them. Although it was made somewhat heavy in order to be solid, it produces a very fine effect. Like that of Septimius Severus at Rome, it has three portals, the centre one for chariots and horsemen, the other two for pedestrians. The façade is ornamented with four marble columns having Corinthian capitals; in the panel, two niches, framed in smaller columns, held statues, doubtless images of princes of the imperial family; they are found everywhere at Timegad. An original and rare feature in monuments of this kind is the circular domes which surmount each of the two wings above the niches, and stand out from the straight line of the centre. No arrangement could be more graceful.

At the foot of the triumphal arch, an inscription has been found which has fallen from the top; it was meant to tell in a few words, in the language which was so simple and yet so dignified, and which the Romans spoke better than any other people, the way in which the city came into existence. It reads as follows: " Emperor Trajan Augustus the Germanic, son of the divine Nerva, high Pontiff, Father of the country, when consul for the third time, and clothed, for the fourth time, with tribunitial power, with the help of the third Augustan legion, founded the colony of Thamugade; L. Munatius Gallus being imperial legate and *pro-prætor*." *

Therefore it was in the year 100 of our era that Trajan, who had been Emperor for only two years, decided to found a city between Lambèse and Mascula. It is very likely that on the site on which he chose to build it there had already been some little fort, a *burgus*, such as could shelter a small garrison. All the passes of the Aurès were carefully guarded, and as not far from Timegad there opens a passage about three kilometres long through which flows one of the small *oueds* which conduct the mountain streams into the Great Sahara where they disappear,† this defile must, also, have been guarded like the others. But Trajan no doubt thought that the lessons they had given to the plunderers of the desert were sufficient, that they

---

* C. I. L., 2355.

† I take this detail from the little pamphlet by Monsieur Moliner-Violle, on *Timgad, ses fouilles et ses découvertes*.

need fear no further invasion from that side, and that they could, without danger, replace the embattled *burgus* by an open city. This city he had built by the faithful legion which, for a century, had maintained order in Africa, and which was to defend it up to the time of Diocletian. The Roman soldier was fitted for everything; he threw bridges across streams, cut roads through the mountain, and handled the pickaxe as easily as he did the *pilum*. In the camp at Lambèse, in which we know that there were engineers, land surveyors, and workmen of every kind, there must have been architects also. The work was carried forward very rapidly. We have proof that in the year 117, upon the death of Trajan, the chief buildings of the Forum were completed; yet in spite of this haste, it is evident that they were not poorly constructed, since after eighteen centuries there still remain such beautiful ruins.

When the triumphal arch has been passed, the traveller walks straight ahead, following the principal street of the city, which has been cleared for several hundred metres. This street, which is very beautiful, is wider and more even than those of Pompeii. This is because it was a new city, built at one time, in an open space, unobstructed by ancient edifices.

The street on which we are walking at present was the principal highway between Lambèse and Theveste, and as it ran through important cities and fertile and populous suburbs, it must have been much used; this fact is evident from the deep ruts that the chariot wheels have left on the pavement. On both sides a wide path was reserved for pedestrians who wished to enjoy seeing the passing travellers and chariots, always one of the sources of amusement in small towns; and in order that they might be more comfortable, a portico, the columns of which have been discovered and restored, sheltered them from the sun. Along the street, two fountains of very elegant shape have remained in place. The passers-by were in the habit of watering their horses there, and the women of Thamugade used to come there to fill their jars. The fountains must have been used a great deal, for their curb is much worn.* In this connexion, I will remark that water is what Timegad most lacks to-day. The few natives who live in tents beside the ruins of the ancient city are obliged to go far for it. Travellers have great trouble in procuring any with which to dilute the *clairet*, or light wine, furnished by the neighbouring tribes. At one time water flowed in abundance; it was brought from the mountain, and

* A square and rather large room is found there also, the use of which it is very easy to perceive. It was the public *latrina;* a wide fountain for the necessary ablutions occupies one of the sides of the room. The other three were provided with twenty-five seats, one of which was found in its place. Each seat was separated from the next by a sculptured dolphin on which the arm could lean. Water flowed in gutters; this preserved cleanliness and conveyed everything to the sewer. Monsieur Milvoy claims that "the management of this chamber was such that in point of comfort, it has not been surpassed in our day."

canals, which still exist, conducted it through the streets. One of these conduits, which descended from the Forum along a flight of steps, having burst, at a time when the municipality was not rich enough to repair it, the inhabitants contented themselves with making, by the side of it, a channel in which the water could run without overflowing the rest of the steps. It continued to follow this temporary bed for so long that it finally deposited a considerable sediment in it, as is the case at the *Pont du Gard*, in the conduits of the Fountain of Eure.

In the middle of the street are the remains of a monumental gate, the posts of which were formed by two beautiful columns ornamented with Corinthian capitals. This was the principal entrance to the Forum. After passing beneath the gate, and ascending a wide flight of ten steps, the square is reached. Before studying the Forum in detail, let us take our position in the centre, in order the better to judge of the whole.

The Forum, at first, seems very small. This is the impression received when standing in the centre and gazing about. But it must not be forgotten that the ancients had not the same liking as we have for those great vistas, in which the eye loses itself; and that, for instance, the Place de la Concorde, which is our admiration, would have seemed ridiculous to them. Moreover, Timegad was a small city, and Vitruvius expressly states that the Forum should everywhere be proportioned to the number of inhabitants. " Too limited, it could not suffice for the use to which it is put; too large, the people would seem lost in it." *

What makes the Forum of Timegad seem still smaller to us is the fact that it was not empty; it was filled with statues of every shape and size, scattered about here and there. It was very much the same in every Roman city, and we know, for instance, that at Cirta there were so many statues, and they were so poorly arranged, that it was found necessary to put them in line in order to facilitate traffic. Those at Timegad have been destroyed,† but we still have some of the bases on which they stood, and some of the inscriptions they bore. As is rightly supposed, it was for the Emperors that this honour was at first reserved; and naturally, too, the most ancient, Antoninus, Marcus Aurelius, and Caracalla, finding the space empty, took the best places. The others were put wherever there was room. Maxentius was on the staircase, Cæsar Galerius beneath a portico, and Julian on a small hexagonal base, directly in front of one of his predecessors, whose face he must have hidden. On the other side, toward the entrance, and apparently in somewhat crowded groups, were the benefactors and patrons of the city, people of less importance, to whom were raised more modest statues, the number of which was constantly increasing. In the long run this must have become somewhat troublesome.

* *De Archit.*, v., 1.
† Or at least there remain only a few rather insignificant fragments of them.

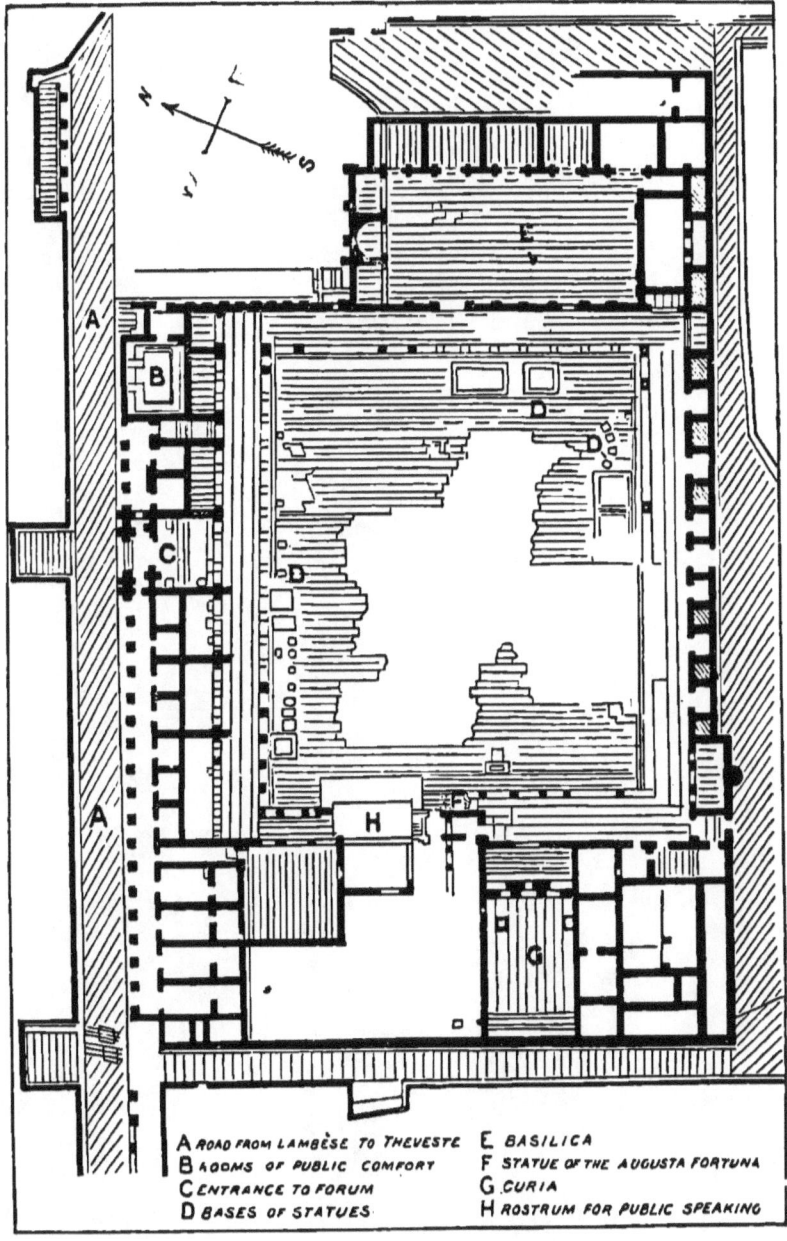

FORUM OF TIMEGAD.

The Forum was encircled by a broad walk which was raised two steps above the ground, and was shaded by a portico, most of the columns of which have been found, some almost intact. Thus the place, in spite of the variety of the buildings which surrounded it, had the appearance of regularity. These structures of different shapes and sizes rose on all sides behind the portico. As there no longer exists anything but the foundations and some portions of the walls, it is not always easy to know for what they could have been intended. I wish to mention here only those the use of which is positively assured. The east side is occupied almost entirely by a large building about which it is not possible to be deceived: it is a basilica. It does not resemble, in every detail, structures of the same kind, such as, for instance, the basilica of Tebessa, and it is not one of those which were so easily turned into Christian churches. There are no rows of columns, as is often the case, which divide it into several aisles and support the ceiling. The wall at the extremity is straight and does not terminate in an apsis, as is usual, but there is a stone platform which was called the *tribunal*, and on which the judges sat. By a peculiar arrangement, the apsis is in front, on the wall opposite the tribunal. It is a great circular niche, which must have held some statue. Was it not that of Trajan, the founder of the city? He well deserved to occupy the place of honour. This fact is certain, however, that images of the princes of his house were placed all around the walls, as though to form a *cortège* for him.

On the west side, opposite the basilica, are found the most interesting and the best preserved monuments of the Forum. In the first place, there is, in the centre, a large base, three metres long by one and a half high, terminating in two simple but elegant pilasters. Thanks to the inscription which is engraved between the two pilasters, and which has been preserved, we know what this base supported when intact. It informs us that two women, in order to carry out the wish of their father, raised to the Augusta Fortuna a statue worth twenty-two thousand sesterces (four thousand four hundred francs), and that they added to it, from their own income, a little shrine which cost them four thousand five hundred sesterces (nine hundred francs).* From its position, which attracts the eye from every side, this statue, on its stone base and in its small chapel, seems to be the centre of the Forum of Thamugade. At the time of its dedication under Hadrian, the Empire had reached the height of its glory and splendour. The new city, in placing itself under the protection of the Augusta Fortuna, thought indeed that it was assuring to itself a long-lived prosperity.

The two edifices at the sides of the small monument of the Augusta Fortuna are of great interest. On the left is an immense room, entered from a vestibule, to which one ascends by four steps; two

* C. I. L., 17,831.

beautiful fluted columns rise at the entrance. The interior must have been very rich; delicate mouldings decorated the basement; the walls were covered with marble of various shades; there was so much of this that a whole cartload might be carried away, and there would still be some left. The use of the monument has been revealed by an inscription discovered near the centre of the chamber, in the place of honour. It informs us that a statue had been raised to the Concord of the order of decurions (*Concordiæ ordinis*).* Such a statue would scarcely be appropriate except on the spot where the decurions, that is to say, the municipal council, were in the habit of meeting in order to deliberate; no place was better suited for preaching concord. It was, therefore, the curia, or, as we say, the town hall, of Thamugade; and what proves this conclusively is the fact that, among other inscriptions, there have been found those that contain the list of the decurions of Timegad in the fourth century.

The monument which was built on the north side to form a counterpart to the curia is in a very bad condition; it seems to have suffered from earthquake more than the others. However, it was evidently a temple, although we do not know to what god it was consecrated. An ancient centurion of the legion of Lambèse, having received his dismissal, raised two statues on the façade in honour of the victory of Trajan over the Parthians (*Victoriæ Parthicæ Augustæ sacrum*).† The façade has a remarkably

---

*C. I. L., 2354.   †*Ibid.*, 2341.

peculiar feature: it has no broad flight of steps in front of it, like the others, leading up to the temple; the steps are relegated to the sides, while in front of the temple there extends a platform which must have been surrounded by a balustrade. The same arrangement occurs at Pompeii, in front of the Temple of Jupiter, which occupies the centre of the Forum. At Timegad, as at Pompeii, this platform, which projects onto the public square, must have been the place from which the magistrates addressed the people. The African towns had their tribunal as did the metropolis, and we know that they did not hesitate to give it the glorious name of *rostrum*. There were, therefore, *rostra* at Timegad, and it has been noticed that the colonnade which surrounds the whole place ends abruptly in front of them. It was necessary, in short, for the speaker on the platform to have a free space before him, and for him to be seen and heard from every point; this shows that, even in this little town at the end of the civilised world, a few leagues from the Great Sahara, a value was set on the art of speaking, and that the *rostrum* had its own importance.

II

Let us not leave this deserted Forum without trying to catch a glimpse of what it must have been, and what must have been done there, when the city was alive and peopled. A few words will suffice to tell what can be learned about it.

In the first place, it was a meeting-place and promenade for a large part of the inhabitants. Idlers were in the habit of lingering beneath the porticos to seek shelter on rainy days and a little shade during the days of summer, and no doubt they discussed the gossip of small towns. There the open-air meetings called *circuli* were held, in which the news was repeated and, when need be, invented, and where even the pleasure was indulged in of occasionally slandering the authorities. The most idle seated themselves on the steps and passed their time in gambling. There has been found, cut in one of the great slabs of the pavement, one of their card-tables (*tabulæ lusoriæ*), which probably answered to our draught-boards; it bears these words, which give a very clear idea of the sentiments of those who traced them: " To hunt, to bathe, to gamble, to laugh,—this is living." *

But the Forum was used for more serious purposes as well; it was the centre of public life for the little town. It is easy to imagine what usually took place when it was necessary to elect or install magis-

* Venari   Lavari
Ludere   Ridere
Occ est   Vivere.

Occ will be noticed for *Hoc;* African Latin is not always correct. It is probable that, in that *tabula lusoria*, each letter formed a sort of square in which the players successively placed pebbles, which took the place of dice, moving them according to rules which we do not know. On other slabs of the Forum are found series of little holes which seem meant to receive marbles. Everything, therefore, seems to prove that they played a great deal in the Forum of Timegad.

trates, elect others in their places, or discuss the affairs of the town; we have only to recall what was done elsewhere. He who knows one Roman city knows all, at least as far as the essential points go, for the municipal institutions differed but slightly. It is not one of our least surprises, when studying the Roman Empire, to see to what an extent, from one end of the world to the other, they resembled one another. How could peoples of such different customs and origins submit so completely to the same laws and customs, and bring themselves even to live for the most part in the same way? There would be less surprise if it were proved that Rome used violence to compel them to give up their own customs, and to accommodate themselves to new laws. Victorious as it was, it would not have met with resistance if it had given formal orders. But it was not the ordinary policy of Rome to impose on conquered nations a prescribed method of government; it willingly left them their ancient form when there was no danger in doing so. It is therefore probable that in Africa, as elsewhere, it desired nothing more than to respect the customs of its new subjects. The African cities, under the domination of the Carthaginians, were governed by Suffetes. Rome left these to them, and some of the cities retained them until after the time of the *Antonini* *; they renounced them in order to receive the title of towns or colonies, and from the way in which they thank the princes who gave them the title,

* See in the "Index" of the C. I. L., the term *suffetes*.

it is very evident that they gave up their ancient magistrates without regret. They all seemed very glad to enjoy Roman administration. Timegad proudly assumed the name of *Respublica Thamugadensium,* and those who spoke of the council of the decurions did not hesitate to call it *splendidissimus ordo,* as though it were a question of the Roman Senate.

Among the customs in vogue in Roman towns was one which was practised everywhere, but which the inscriptions of Africa perhaps make better known than those of other countries. Although it has often been spoken of, it is necessary to refer to it here, for it aids us in comprehending why we find, at Timegad and elsewhere, the ruins of so many beautiful monuments.

In those days the cities not only did not recompense their magistrates, but the magistrates had to pay those who were under their administration. At each election, in order to acknowledge the honour which was bestowed upon them, it was necessary to give a sum of money, which was called *honoraria summa.* Hence there was this difference between the ancient cities and those of our time, namely, that what ruins us enriched them; as we are interested in lessening the number of officials, so it was to their interest to increase it; evidently they did not fail to do this. The list of the decurions, of which some fragments were discovered in the curia of Timegad, must have been very long; one of these fragments alone contains seventy names; it is probable that there were at least as many on the others *; it is rather the parliament of a kingdom than a council of a small city. The towns, apparently, were on the watch for every opportunity to increase their resources in this way. As soon as a citizen became rich, they hastened to open to him the ranks of the curia; he was one more taxpayer, and they hoped that, if he attained the highest honours, he would pay dearer for them than others, because he would be more flattered by them. Sometimes they went as far as the neighbouring city, to seek for some wealthy citizen, who was very proud of being appreciated away from home; thus he became magistrate of two countries at the same time.† Of this twofold office there were some duties to which he could not attend; but he had paid and was released from the rest. It happened also that they would apply themselves to some freedman who had made a comfortable fortune in commerce; he could not be elected an out-and-out decurion, as the law accorded this honour only to those who were free-born; but they overcame the difficulty; instead of vesting him with the honour itself, they conferred on him its ornaments (*ornamenta decurionis*); he became, so to speak, honorary decurion, and gave money as though he had been a regular decurion.‡ We cannot but admire the ingenuity

---

* See these lists, C. I. L., 2403 and 17,903.

† C. I. L., 2407. The same personage was *flamen perpetuus* at Thamugade and at Lambèse.

‡ *Ibid.*, 2330.

with which all these cities knew how to make, from the vanity of their citizens, a revenue which, for centuries, greatly helped their finances.

The stipulated sum, for the various honours, was not the same everywhere; it was natural that it should vary with the importance of the town; and furthermore, it is supposed that it changed also according to the wealth of the candidate. We are told, in some inscriptions, that under certain circumstances the tax was increased (*ampliata taxatione*).*
At Timegad, the highest honour of the city, the duumvirate, paid four thousand sesterces (eight hundred francs)† ; but in reality the expense was much greater. In the first place, it did not seem suitable to be satisfied with the amount demanded by law; the merit of giving only what was impossible to refuse! Therefore the candidate promised more, and for fear that once elected he would forget his promise, care was taken to have it inscribed in the *acta publica*.‡ It even happened, as a rule, that he gave more than he had promised. He strove to satisfy his compatriots, to show his gratitude, and to merit their admiration. It was like an emulation of liberality among the various magistrates, no one wishing to be less generous than his predecessors or his colleagues. The inscriptions show how the most unpretending were finally piqued into prodigality.

* C. I. L., 12,018.
† *Ibid.*, 2341. The honorary sum of the ædileship at Thamugade was three thousand sesterces (six hundred francs). See *ibid.*, 17,838.
‡ *Ibid.*, 15,576.

In a small city of Byzacium, the very name of which we do not know, and which has left no relic beyond a few ruins, the " honorary sum " for becoming decurion was sixteen hundred sesterces (three hundred and twenty francs). A well disposed candidate promised to give double, then he assumed the debt of his brother, decurion like him, who perhaps was unable to free himself, and doubled it like his own. This money was used to repair a temple; but the expense was greater than was anticipated, and the granddaughter of the decurion, who completed the work begun by her grandfather, had to add to it five thousand six hundred sesterces of her own money. Thus it cost our man twelve thousand sesterces (two thousand four hundred francs) to be a municipal councillor of a hamlet.* Imagine, then, what must have been expended in the large cities, when it was not a question of repairing a chapel, but of building great edifices; without counting the fact that on the day of dedication it was considered in good taste to give scenic plays, to have gladiatorial shows, or at least to distribute money among the magistrates and to give a banquet to the people.

In time, this extravagance must have had serious consequences. In the case of the wealthy, it became a cause of bankruptcy, and made public offices a sort of bugbear and punishment; but at first it brought about very happy results. We owe to it most of the magnificent monuments, the ruins

*C. I. L., 12,058.

of which are astonishing. At *Calama* (Guelma), a great lady, who was appointed priestess of the Emperors, gave a theatre to her fellow-citizens, which fact excited such gratitude among them that they at once raised five statues to her.* At *Theveste* (Tebessa), an officer of the legion, of high rank, over and above a considerable sum which he bequeathed to the city to be used for giving plays and for ornamenting temples, erected a tetrastyle arch of triumph in honour of Caracalla and the African dynasty of the *Severi*.† This is still standing at the entrance of Tebessa, and is the admiration of travellers. It cost fifty thousand francs.

The desire of all these generous citizens was to beautify their native place, *exornare patriam*, as the great lady of Calama said. They possessed, in those days, a love of the magnificent; each citizen wished his city to present a fine appearance, and to be more sumptuous than the neighbouring cities. Hence the great number of monuments, the ruins of which surprise us. But our wonder increases when we think that they were built without exhausting the municipal funds or resorting to the help of the State, and that almost all of them are due to the generosity of individuals.

In traversing the Forum of Timegad it is impossible not to be impressed by the fact that almost all the monuments have been erected in honour of princes, and consecrated to them. We had already noticed this at Lambèse; but Lambèse was a mili-

* C. I. L., 5366. † *Ibid.*, 1858.

tary city, and it seems natural that the Emperor should have been especially honoured there. He was the commander-in-chief, the *imperator* of the army, which bore his image on its standards; he took the auspices for it; he was reputed present when it engaged in combat; he triumphed when it was victorious. It is surprising, however, to see that outside of the army the Emperor received the same homage as in the camp, and that what occurred at Lambèse was repeated everywhere. Throughout the whole Empire, in the most distant and the least known countries, there are no cities or villages in which these proofs of love and devotion are not found. It is difficult to admit that these unanimous protestations are only a combination of servility and flattery, and that the whole world, for four centuries, agreed to lie. We must not forget that the marks of homage were addressed not to one man only, but that Rome shared them with him. Sometimes this is expressly stated (*Romæ et Augusto*); in the provinces in which the whole formula is not used, as in Africa, it must be understood. In praising the Emperor, it is Rome that is thanked for the peace that it gave to the world, and as wicked princes maintained peace almost as vigorously as good ones, and as, in the words of Tacitus, their tyranny weighed especially on those who lived in their neighbourhood,* when one had the good fortune to be far away, one rendered to them almost the same honours as to the others, and scarcely

* *Hist.*, iv., 74.

any distinction was made between Caracalla and Trajan.

In Africa, as elsewhere, these honours were summed up in the imperial worship. To-day, since its signification and consequences are better understood, there is less temptation to be indignant or to smile at it. The cause of its long period of good fortune lies in the fact that it was the expression of two sentiments which seemed irreconcilable, but which were united in it. In the first place, it was a burst of gratitude for the sovereign authority which governed the world, and under the laws of which men protested that they were happy to live. Furthermore, as the worship of the Emperor was celebrated in the chief city of the province, by his delegates and at his expense, the province was recognised, and found itself in these celebrations; it regained the consciousness of self which had been lost since its conquest by the Romans; under the suzerainty of the Emperors it began to revive. It was then at once a fête for the entire realm and for the individual province, and in these ceremonials in which was commemorated the unity of the Empire, there came into expression a revival of a national feeling for the province itself.

The details of the imperial worship varied according to the country. Sometimes it was addressed especially to the dead Emperors who had been deified (*Divi*); sometimes to the living Emperor (*Augusto*); the authority of the priests charged with the celebration, and the name given them, were not the same in every case. These differences suffice to convince us that it was not instituted all at one time and by a decree from Rome. The first move must have come from the provinces and the cities, each one in its own way imitating the neighbouring city, and seeking at times to surpass it. But these differences are only superficial; at heart, the spirit of the institution is everywhere the same; so much so that at one time some Emperors conceived the idea of making this worship the centre of resistance to Christianity, because it was the most wide-spread of all, and the one on which all the peoples of the Empire were in the greatest accord. Almost everywhere it was celebrated at the same time, in the capital of the province, in the name of the whole province, and in every city. It was therefore both provincial and municipal.

Timegad, for instance, to mention it alone, took part every year in the great festivals of Numidia; the provincial priests were sometimes chosen from among its citizens, and the city was very proud of this.* But Timegad had its special worship as well, to which it clung tenaciously. In order to celebrate it, the city appointed flamens, who, when their term of office expired, were permitted to retain

---

* At Simittu the inhabitants raised a statue to one of their citizens, a priest of the province of Africa, *qui primus ex colonia sua hunc honorem gessit*, C. I. L., 14,611. At Timegad, mention is made, in the *album* of the decurions, of two ancient priests (*sacerdotales*). As they are placed immediately after the patrons of the city, and before the other magistrates, it must be that they were ancient priests of the province, whom they wished to honour by thus giving them this prominent position.

the title, in order that the glory of the office they had once filled might brighten their whole life. In this way, at least, is usually explained the presence of the names of thirty-five *flamines perpetui* on the lists of the decurions of Timegad; they were placed immediately after the duumvirs, the highest magistrates of the city, and before the pontiffs and the augurs. This fact shows the importance that was attached to this honour, and that it was ranked above the other sacerdotal offices. The city, having been founded by an emperor, had special reasons for being devoted to the Empire; it was proud of its origin, grateful for the favours it had received, and very ready to show its devotion to the prince. Therefore the imperial festivals at Timegad may be considered the most beautiful of all. It is easy to picture the concourse of citizens crowding under the porticos, against the statues, and on the steps of the buildings; the city magistrates advancing slowly, with their fasces and their lictors, as though they were senators of Rome; the priests crowned with flowers, and clothed in robes bordered with purple; while before them chosen youths bore on pikes gilded bronze busts of the deified Emperors; all surging, amidst the shouts of the throng, toward the temple of the *Divi*, in which the sacrifices were to take place. On such a day as that the Forum of Thamugade should have been seen.

III

The Forum is the most curious monument of Timegad, but it is not the only one. Other buildings have been excavated, which, although not of equal importance, are none the less interesting.

Let us once more take the street by which we came, and again pass under the triumphal arch. On our left we see a rectangular building terminating in an *exedra*, which no doubt was the base of an apsis. As basilicas are usually of this shape, we at first suppose that this is one; but we must yield to evidence; an inscription informs us of its real use, which perhaps we should not have guessed. It is a market, and, like most of the other monuments of Timegad, it is the result of the munificence of a wealthy citizen. Plotius Faustus, after having commanded cohorts and wings of the auxiliary troops, and won the title of Roman chevalier, returned to end his days with his wife, Cornelia Valentina, in his native city, which hastened to honour him with priestly dignities; and it was in order to acknowledge this honour that Faustus and his wife had the market built.* In it were placed their statues, of which some fragments have been found. The centre of the rectangular court was ornamented with a graceful fountain; porticos surrounded it, the columns of which strew the ground. I thought I saw that the capitals bore drooping leaves, less elaborate than the acanthus leaf and more like the

* C. I. L., 2398.

palm. The porticos doubtless sheltered merchants and buyers during the heat of the day; and those who could not find room circulated about in the uncovered part around the fountain. The apsis at the farther end must have been reserved for more important business.

Seven shops, separated from one another by a wall, and in a very good state of preservation, can also be seen. In one of them a granite slab is still fastened to the wall at both ends. The slab, which served as a table on which the merchandise was displayed, was placed in front of the shop; as there is no door at the sides, the merchant, when he wished to enter, must have stooped down and passed underneath. I have seen this done more than once in the *souks* of Tunis. These countries are conservative by nature; their customs never change. Vases of various shapes, which are perfectly intact, have been found in the shops of Timegad. They must have contained the fruits or liquids sold by the merchant.

On a hill behind the market is a mass of enormous ruins, the most considerable of all which cover the plain. It was evidently an important building, which has suffered still more than the others from time and man. We should find it difficult to imagine what it could have been were we not very clearly informed by an inscription which formerly ornamented the fronton. This tells us that in the reign of Valentinian I., the porticos of the Capitol, which were crumbling from old age, were rebuilt by the municipal magistrates, and that the work was dedicated by the consular Ceionius Cæcina Albinus, an important figure of the Empire, and one of the last of the pagans.* We have therefore before us all that remains of the Capitol of Timegad. Every city which wished to assume a Roman air took care to build a capitol in which Jupiter was worshipped between Juno and Minerva. There were many capitols in Africa. That at Constantine was filled with very rich relics and ornaments, a list of which has been preserved.† We do not know what the interior of the Capitol of Timegad contained, or whether there was in it " a silver statue of Jupiter with a crown of oak on his head, the leaves of which were modelled in silver, and bearing in his hand a silver globe with a Victory holding a silver spear "; but the exterior must certainly have been sumptuous. The square, in the centre of which it was built, was enclosed by a portico, like that of St. Peter's at Rome. The columns supporting the fronton of the temple measured, at the base, one metre fifty centimetres in diameter; the walls were decorated with a profusion of precious marbles. " Nowhere else in Algeria," says Monsieur Milvoy, " have I discovered them in such great numbers and variety." Of all this magnificence very little remains to-day. The ceilings, in falling, have broken the slabs of the pavements, and exposed the subterranean vaults under the temple, in which, according to Varro, were placed the objects of worship not in use. It is probable, however, that these ruins will soon

* C. I. L., 2388. † *Ibid.*, 6981.

assume another aspect. The Commission of Historical Monuments, to which we owe the restoration of the Forum, is at work excavating them. They are unearthing capitals, friezes, cornices, and balustrades, and are raising on their bases the beautiful columns which have fallen at full length, like those at Selimonte; and when all this is restored to its place, we shall have some idea of the Capitol of Timegad as it was in the fourth century, when dedicated by Ceionius Albinus.

If we walk straight before us, in an easterly direction, from the steps of the Capitol, we soon reach the theatre, which is separated from the Forum by a wide street. According to a very common custom, the theatre of Timegad was built against a hill, which did away with a great deal of masonry, and assured the solidity of the edifice; the steps were cut out of the rock. The building has been wholly freed from the rubbish, but with great difficulty, as it formed a sort of funnel in which the ruins were piled up almost to the height of seven metres. Of the façade, which reminds one of that in the theatre of Ostia, there remains the base, with numerous fragments of columns, which upheld a portico, where, no doubt, the spectators took refuge in case of a sudden storm. The stage has wholly disappeared. The site can be perceived, however, which again proves how narrow were the stages of the ancient theatres. As may readily be supposed, the wooden floor composing the *pulpitum*, or *proscenium*, no longer exists; but the three rows of stone pillars which supported the boards are still visible. The *pulpitum* terminated in a small wall which must have been richly ornamented. All around the orchestra, which is the best preserved portion of the building, where the tiers of benches begin, there are three steps, so wide that presumably the benches of the city magistrates were placed thereon. In this way they could see the play without inconveniencing one another; the centre was no doubt reserved for other people of note, or remained empty for certain mime dances. Beyond the three steps was the orchestra, enclosed within a small wall, or *podium*, composed of smooth slabs, which are still standing in place. There remain almost seven rows of benches, more or less intact, which formed the first precinction.[1] What seemed new to me was that between this precinction and the next there are traces of another *podium*, which would make a new division. Must we infer that at Timegad, as at Rome, above the orchestra where the magistrates of the city sat, a certain number of rows were set apart for the chief citizens ? These seven tiers of benches would thus be equivalent to the fourteen rows that the law of Roscius Otho reserved in the theatres for knights. Above this *podium*, nothing can be distinguished.

When we consider that Timegad is on the confines of barbarism, the sight of a theatre of such elegant proportions and so exactly like those which are admired in the most civilised countries, cannot fail to excite surprise. Doubtless all the nations, even the most barbarous, that were conquered by Rome, very soon learned to enjoy the public games; it is evident, however, that all games would not please them equally well. To refer to Africa alone: the crowd of Roman immigrants, who were not always the flower of their country, and the natives, who were still more unpolished, would naturally care for gladiatorial combats; we find that this was the case. Such spectacles were delighted in, and much gratitude was evinced toward the magistrates who went to the expense of arranging them in order to amuse their fellow-citizens.* Horse-races were enjoyed no less than the athletic contests, and the gymnastic exercises, which were sometimes given in the public *thermæ*. Diversions of this kind do not require a very cultivated mind nor a very sensitive soul; but the plays which were presented at a theatre were of another character, and it seems that they did not please everyone. I asked myself as I wandered through the theatre of Timegad what could have been given there. The ancient theatres, being larger and less shut in than our own, were suited to the presentation of entertainments of various kinds. "It is there," said Apuleius, "that the mime actor utters

* In the environs of Hippo an inscription has been found which says that all the curiæ (corresponding to the districts of the city) erected statues to a wealthy citizen "because of the magnificence of the gladiatorial combat, which lasted three days and surpassed all those which could be remembered, and also because of his integrity" (C. I. L., 5276). It is easy to see that the gladiatorial combat made a deeper impression upon the people of Hippo than the virtues of their fellow-citizen.

his foolish speeches, that the comedian rants, that the tragedian shouts, that the actor gesticulates, that the rope-dancer risks breaking his neck, and that the prestidigitator performs his tricks," * not to mention the philosopher, like Apuleius himself, who sometimes gave lectures. But aside from these occasional entertainments, it may be said that the kinds of which the theatre was the true home were the mime and the pantomime, the comedy and the tragedy.† There can be no doubt that the pantomime and the mime were played in the theatre at Timegad; from the beginning of the Empire, it was the spectacle preferred by the populace of Rome, and none was better suited to a provincial public. The Fathers of the African Church describe the lewd gestures of the actors as those who have seen them with their own eyes; they often refer to the insults uttered and the affronts received. But if such plays were usually given in the theatres of Africa, as in other places, must it be supposed that nothing else was seen there? Is it possible that comedy and tragedy were never played? To be sure, comedy and tragedy were no longer fashionable, but there was such need of variety at the theatre, that it was found necessary to make new things out of old material, and this was the reason for reviving from time to time the ancient plays which seemed new because forgotten. Arnobius

---

* Apuleius, *Florida*, i., 5.

† There should be added the vocal or instrumental concerts, which were sometimes fashionable in the Roman theatres.

says that when Jupiter was to be propitiated, the *Amphitruo* of Plautus was performed, but concludes that perhaps it was not a good way of pleasing the god to recall to him his old follies.* In this manner, barbarians at the ends of the world gained some acquaintance with the masterpieces of antiquity; and even supposing that plays of only an inferior quality were acted, such as the mimes and the pantomimes, the representations were not without some benefit in the education of their minds. There were often very keen observations in the mimes, in spite of their usual grossness, and Seneca at times found more wisdom in the farces of Publius Syrus than in the words of professional philosophers.† As for the pantomime, it presented characters and stories from ancient legends; occasionally it borrowed its subjects from the greatest poets. We must remember that they danced in the theatres to the lines of Virgil and Ovid. It seems, in the first place, that such representations were not given in order to interest the vulgar; and yet we have proof that the latter took pleasure in them. The inscriptions of the proconsular province and of Numidia mention the scenic plays at least as often as the gladiatorial combats, and once we are told that they were given at the request of the populace, *populo expostulante.* ‡ It may therefore be stated that, in their way, they aided Roman civilisation in Africa. By their means this civilisation was spread among those who had not passed through the

* *Adv. Gentes*, vii., 33. † *Epist.*, viii., 8. ‡ C. I. L., 958.

schools or who had only made a beginning in education; merely by listening and looking they acquired some idea of it. Therefore I am tempted to look upon this little theatre of Timegad with respect, when I think that the unlettered of the city and its environs, who once occupied these benches, not only passed some agreeable hours here, but also, in the words of Varro, carried some knowledge of literature to their homes.

The theatre visited, there is only one more monument for us to see. On an eminence toward the south, about five hundred metres from the city, rises a Byzantine fortress. It is a large rectangle, one hundred and twenty metres long by eighty wide. It is surrounded by solid walls and flanked at the corners by square towers. Every trace of habitation has disappeared from within; it must have contained only temporary places of refuge which were not intended to last; in one of the towers, however, there is a casemate protected by a double ceiling, which must have been proof against the stone bullets hurled by the ballista. The generals of Justinian, after the defeat of the Vandals, made a great effort to assure for themselves the control of the conquered territory; they surrounded the cities with walls and fortified the heights. But as speed was necessary, they made use of the materials at hand. The ancient monuments had fallen in ruins; they hastened the destruction of them and used the material for their new buildings. At Timegad, the walls of the fortress are composed of stones from tombs, shafts of columns, friezes of temples, and slabs of pavements. The wonder is that this chance accumulation is solid and that it has lasted. The ramparts, constructed in haste from stones picked up almost anywhere, with both good and bad united, have sustained furious assaults. In the insurrection of 1871, the inhabitants of Tebessa and of the neighbouring cities successfully coped with the Arabs of Mokrani behind the walls built by Solomon, fifteen hundred years before.

IV

I advise those who visit Timegad to pause for a time on the central bastion of the Byzantine fortress; this is the best place from which to view the plain, and the beautiful mountains which surround it. Below are the excavated monuments which may be seen in detail; and the unevenness of the ground indicates the position of those still buried. It is therefore easy to distinguish the form and the extent of the city; and if the traveller is fortunate enough to be there at twilight, when the last rays of the sun are lighting the snows of the Chélia, he can scarcely resist the illusion that the ruins over which the shadows are beginning to steal have suddenly been restored, and that the ancient city is again throbbing with life.

As I gaze, there comes to my mind one of the most brilliant passages in the works of St. Cyprian, the *Lettre à Donat*. In order to convince his reader of the futility of worldly life, in imagination he transports him to a height from which he points out all the movements of a great city. Here are the preparations for a gladiatorial show, " men fattened for death, and about to be killed for the amusement of other men "; there is an obscene spectacle of mime dances and pantomime which attracts the crowd to the theatre; in another direction " the Forum resounds with the angry shouts of litigants "; in the streets, the early client goes to salute his patron in order to receive the sportule²; the magistrate, preceded by a retinue of friends and hangers-on, betakes himself to the tribunal, " while within the houses, when the hour for the repast is come, they bring out crystal goblets ornamented with precious stones, and spread golden couches covered with tapestry and feather pillows on which the guests recline."

In drawing this picture, St. Cyprian was thinking of the city in which he had always lived, and of which he was bishop; he wished to describe Carthage. Surely the little town above which we are standing at this moment could not have had the audacity to compare itself with the capital of Africa. But we have already said that Roman life was more or less the same everywhere. It is therefore probable that the town as we might have seen it, eighteen centuries ago, would have resembled St. Cyprian's description; like him, we should have seen litigants disputing in the basilica, candidates canvassing the popular votes in the Forum, devotees ascending the steps of the temples, and the crowd pressing into the theatres. It is the sight that every Roman city must have presented from one end of the world to the other. I suppose, therefore, that it is useless to lay stress upon it, since it repeats itself everywhere and teaches us nothing new. It appears to me more important, in the presence of this ancient city, which seems to live again under our eyes, to come back to our own times, and to ask ourselves if it cannot explain to us in what respect the customs of the Romans, when they settled in a conquered country, differed from ours. These differences are not only interesting to note, but they can be useful as well; it is not impossible to derive an occasional lesson from an example.

We, too, have often been led to found cities in the countries in which we wished firmly to establish our domination. Like the Romans, we have sometimes had them constructed by the army, and, in most cases, on a uniform plan. But there the resemblances end. In order to see how much our manner of building differs from that of our predecessors, it is sufficient, I think, to compare Timegad and Batna. Between these two neighbouring cities, founded on the same plan and almost under the same conditions, comparison is easy as well as profitable. We seem to have been desirous of aiming only at the useful. Wide streets, very regularly laid out, intersecting at right angles, and lined with modest houses, one story high; here and there barracks, shops, and hospitals, distinguishable only by their size and massiveness; in the centre of a square *place*, a church, as simple as possible, when the builder has not had the poor taste to give it the appearance of a mosque—such are usually the cities that genius constructs for us. How different were those built by the Roman army! They were lavishly ornamented. Timegad, when seen from a distance, gives the impression of a forest of pillars rising in a desert; and a nearer view shows that what remains is but the smallest part of what once existed. At every step one stumbles against shafts or capitals, to say nothing of fragments of altars, statues, and bas-reliefs. It is said that the English have a sort of mania for never making a change in their mode of living and that they expect to find in India or Australia their *home* of London or Edinburgh. In the same way it seems as though the Romans were anxious to transport everywhere with them their entire civilisation. At the foot of the Aurès, as on the borders of the Rhine or the Danube, they wished to have before their eyes squares filled with statues, temples surrounded by porticos, *thermæ* and theatres—all that they were accustomed to see in Italy. Must it be supposed that they were influenced merely by a narrow-minded vanity, and that they were slaves to petty habits? I think not; it seems to me that their policy found its reward.

We shall be convinced of this by reflecting on the results brought about, in time, by the numberless constructions, ever being undertaken and renewed. In order to build these edifices, in order to ornament and repair them, it was necessary for schools of artists and artisans to be founded in these barbarous countries. There was, in short, a large number of such schools, and we find that the Emperors were greatly interested in aiding them. "We need many architects," wrote Constantine to the Proconsul of Africa; and he asked him to influence young men of eighteen, who were completing their studies, to enter this profession.* As an inducement, they and their parents were to be exempted from taxation; and a suitable salary was to be given to them while they were occupied in studying. Painters were no less favoured than architects. A law of Valentinian I. provided them gratuitously with shops and workshops in which to carry on their art; it ordered, furthermore, that the magistrates should not demand of them portraits of the imperial family, or ask them to decorate the public monuments free of charge, which no doubt often happened.† As to sculptors, it was clearly necessary that there should be some in cities like Timegad, where there was such a great number of statues. Those of the patrons of the city with which, as we have seen, they were in the habit of filling the Forum, could have been executed only on the spot. It often happened that those whose likenesses were reproduced belonged to the humblest class. At *Auzia* (Aumale³), an ancient decurion had a statue of himself and of his wife placed on his tomb, and bequeathed a yearly income of three *denarii* to the keeper of the monu-

---

* *Codex Theod.*, xiii., 4, 183.   † *Ibid.*, xiii., 4.

ment in order that on certain anniversaries he might clean, perfume, and crown them with flowers, and light two tapers before them.* It is not probable that the decurion had a renowned sculptor brought from afar for this purpose; he must have found one in the city or its vicinity. Moreover, these artists in small towns, ever ready to execute the orders of their compatriots, must have had on hand a certain number of ready-made statues, the market for which was assured, as for instance those of the most honoured gods or of the Emperor and his family,† of Victory, the Augusta Fortuna, or other official deities with which the public squares were filled. An *ædile* of Constantine who, the fifth day before the Ides of January, promised his fellow-citizens to raise a statue to Concord, dedicated it less than two months later, which fact clearly proves that he bought it ready made.‡ Works of this kind, which were copied from one another, and which were found in the shops in large numbers, must often have been sold at reduced rates. At *Calama* (Guelma), where the worship of the god of the seas was very popular, a beautiful Neptune, worthy of figuring in the Forum, could be obtained for fifteen hundred, and even for eleven hundred francs.§ It is evident that at this price it

* C. I. L., 9052.

† It is true that, as the Emperors changed rather frequently, sculptors were likely to have on hand statues of the dead or dethroned Emperor, but in those days they had an expedient; they were in the habit of replacing the head of the former prince by that of the new. This is a method to which they often resorted.

‡ C. I. L., 6942. § *Ibid.*, 5298, 5299.

was not possible to expect a masterpiece; but they did not demand perfection; these good people of the provinces were more easily satisfied. Thus the art which seemed to be best suited to them is the mosaic. It was perfectly adapted to the climate; it accommodated itself strictly to a certain mediocrity of execution; it could be very pleasing even when limited to reproducing simple ornaments which required of the artist less talent and care than the human figure. The mosaic, therefore, could be made for any price, which fact permitted its being used in the decorating of private houses, even the humblest. Thus the mosaic penetrated everywhere throughout Africa.* Very fine works were executed in it, but even the most mediocre have their interest, when it is remembered that they show how the poor people, in proportion to their means, procured the enjoyments of the rich and the cultured. Thus there was a sort of education which existed all by itself in the large cities, and from the influence of which no one escaped. By means of having before their eyes the monuments with which the cities were filled, and from being constantly with

*For the mosaics of Africa, the works of Monsieur Héron de Villefosse and of Monsieur Gsell may be consulted. Monsieur de la Blanchère has collected in the museum of the Bardo, at Tunis, a very large number of them which give a very good idea of African art. As a rule, the artists who executed them did not put their names to them, and are to-day unknown. However, we know one of them called Amor, a native of Carthage; he studied in the studio of Sennus Félix, at Puzzuoli, and signed, in conjunction with his master, a composition which has been found at Lillebonne in Gaul. (District of Caux.—Tr.).

artists who had erected or decorated them, the people became familiar with the arts and succeeded in acquiring a taste for and a knowledge of them.

But it was not enough that the result made itself felt among the inhabitants of the cities. There was no need, after all, to take so much trouble for them. From the moment that they consented to shut themselves up in a Roman city, they were half won over, and would soon become wholly Roman. But there were others to be thought of—those who held themselves apart, and who persisted in living on their steppes or in their mountains. How act so that Roman civilisation should reach them? Happily they had a habit of which I have already spoken, and which could be turned to account: they loved to leave their solitude occasionally in order to buy or sell in the vicinity. Reference has been made previously to the markets established in the country near the large estates; but there were some in the towns which were also greatly frequented; we can even imagine that certain cities, which seem to have been founded under special conditions, and in which, as has been noticed, the monuments are of far greater importance than the cities themselves, must have been above all else meeting-places for the peoples of the neighbourhood, and that besides the permanent residents there were many others who were frequently in the habit of coming thither for pleasure and business. I wonder whether Thamugade was not of this number. Up to the present time but few private houses have been discovered there, and although it is very possible that, being built of lighter materials, they may have withstood less than the rest, it is probable that they were not very numerous. The wall, a trace of which, now and then, is easily discerned, does not seem to have been very extensive, and public monuments occupied the greater part of the town. Perhaps the city was only a great mart whither the peasants of the Aurès were in the habit of coming on certain days, to bring their commodities, and to provide themselves with what they needed. They must have led a very wretched existence at home; those who did not live in their solitary *mapalia* dwelt on the side of steep rocks in the vulture-nests that Sallust has described, and of which the Kabyle villages can give an idea. Their surprise may be imagined when, for the first time, they entered a Roman city! They passed beneath one of the triumphal gates which the conquerors had erected at the entrance of even the smallest towns in order to commemorate their victories; they visited the squares, filled with statues, and surrounded by temples; they glanced at the *thermæ* [1] which contained every comfort and convenience of life; they paused to take the air beneath the porticos; they followed the crowd into the theatres, the circuses, and the amphitheatre. Their surprise soon changed to admiration. They caught sight of a new world, of the existence of which they had never dreamed. The thought of comfort, the idea of elegance and luxury, awoke confusedly in their minds. They became, gradually, more sensitive to those pleasures as they began to be better acquainted with them, and, now and then, they even strove to introduce in some measure into their villages and homes what had charmed them elsewhere. It may readily be supposed that attempts of this kind did not succeed without some opposition. The innovations could not please everyone; many, no doubt, mistrusted them, and wished to remain true to ancient traditions. So there arose among them and the followers of progress, struggles, the remembrance of which is not wholly lost. Some leagues from Setif, an interesting mosaic has been discovered representing the head of the god Oceanus, with nereids mounted on marine monsters. Below are two distichs, of which the following is a translation:

"At this divine spectacle, may envy burst from spite, and may insolent tongues cease to murmur. In the love of the arts we surpass our fathers. It is a joy to see this marvellous work shining in our homes."*

The encomium is certainly greatly exaggerated; there is nothing "marvellous" or "divine" in the mosaic of Setif, but this burst of naïve enthusiasm shows us the pleasure that their initiation into civilised life caused those awakening souls. It cannot be doubted that it was in visiting the Roman cities that the desire " to surpass their fathers in the love

*C. I. L., 8509.
"Invida sidereo rumpantur pectora visu,
　Cedat et in nostris lingua proterva locis.
　Hoc studio superamus avos gratumque renidet
　Ædibus in nostris summus apex operis."

of the arts" came to them, and that is why the Romans took so much trouble and spent so much money in building the cities. As these cities were unwalled, they could not serve as a defence; they were rather a bait held out to barbarism, and in order that it might be caught, it is evident that they were made as sumptuous as possible.

Such were the thoughts that came to my mind as, from the Byzantine citadel, I watched the sun sink behind the ruins of Timegad. On my return, as I passed the Forum, and strolled by the theatre and the Capitol, I said to myself that a critic who was difficult to please, fastidious, and accustomed to the perfection of Greek art, would doubtless find much here to censure, and that all this official architecture might seem to him monotonous and cold. But whatever criticism may be made on the monuments when compared with those from which they were modelled, it is only just not to treat them with too much severity, and, in judging them, we should not forget the part they played in the civilisation of Africa.

TRANSLATOR'S NOTES TO CHAPTER V

1. "Precinction. In the ancient theatre, a horizontal passage of communication, subdividing the carca or auditorium. In the Roman theatre it was bounded at the back by an elevated podium."—Funk & Wagnalls' *Standard Dict.*

2. *Sportule*, distribution of food or money to clients.

3. "*Auzia* (Aumale or Hamzale) was near the Gariphi Mountains, and was a considerable town under the Romans."—Wm. Smith, *Ancient Geog.*

4. For interesting description of thermæ at Pompeii and Rome see Bulwer-Lytton, *Last Days of Pompeii*, bk. i., chap. vii.

CHAPTER VI

AFRICAN LITERATURE

I

THERE is no reason for astonishment at the fact that among the ruins of African cities we have not come across schools. Since, as a rule, they were held under the porticos, or in the upper stories of private houses, naturally nothing is left of them; but we may be sure that there were schools almost everywhere, and that they were largely attended. St. Augustine relates that he received his early instruction at Thagaste, a very small town, where he was born. When the master at Thagaste could teach him nothing further, he was sent to Madaura, a town near his home, where the schools were more flourishing; then, as he won great success there, his family, although very poor, sent him to complete his studies at Carthage.

There were many Africans, however, who, not content with the instruction given at Carthage, went all the way to Rome to obtain their education. A law of Valentinian shows that the African students there were very numerous, and often very dissipated; the Emperor issued an order that if they were seen too frequently at the theatre, if they attended festivities that were prolonged into the night, " if, in a word, they did not conduct themselves as the dignity of a liberal education demanded," they were to be put on board ship, and sent home as quickly as possible.*

This zeal for learning and the value attached to knowledge have left their traces in the inscriptions of Africa as well as in the works of contemporaries. When a father had the misfortune to lose his young son, he did not fail to tell us, in an epitaph, that " he was being bred as a scholar, that he died while studying at Carthage, and that he had already become proficient in the art of speaking." † At Calama, a poor man sadly bewailed the fact that his two sons, whom he had made to study, *in studiisque misit*, had both died young, " and that after so much expense, he could not enjoy either of them." ‡ At Mactaris, it is a young man who speaks: he tells us that he was beloved by his masters; that from childhood he had given himself up zealously to study; that at the age of fourteen he read stenographic characters in Greek (probably his parents intended him to be *notarius*, a very important profession at that time); and he adds, not without some pride, that " he knew how to speak well, write well, and paint well." § Apropos of others, who died at the same age, we are told that " they had a wonderful knowledge of the two known languages (Latin and

---

* *Codex Theod.*, xiv., 9, 1.
† C. I. L., 8500, 9182, 12,152.
‡ *Ibid.*, 5370.
§ *Ibid.*, 724.

Greek); that they excelled in composing dialogues, letters, and idyls; that they could improvise on a given subject, and that, in spite of their youth, they drew a crowd when they declaimed." *

It is evident that Rome encouraged this taste which attracted African subjects toward literary pursuits. Everything that attached them to Latin civilisation was of profit to Roman domination; more enlightened, more lettered, and less barbarous, they became more submissive, and were in consequence easier to rule. Tacitus relates that his father-in-law, Agricola, who was a very intelligent man and a clever politician, after having vanquished the Britons, succeeded in overcoming their resistance by gathering into schools the children of the chiefs. In order to encourage them to study, he praised their diligence, and professed surprise at their progress; as he knew that in everything they were very jealous of their compatriots, the Celts of the continent, he affected to prefer " the natural intelligence of the Britons to the acquired talents of the Gauls." " In fact," adds Tacitus, " he succeeded so well that those who at first scorned the Latin language soon became enamoured of rhetorical exercises." † The Romans must everywhere have pursued this policy which was so advantageous to them, and everywhere it must have brought them the same results. We do not see, however, that they took official measures, as we do in our day, to open schools and to organise courses of instruction

* C. I. L., 5530. † *Agricola*, 21.

in the conquered countries. The emperors favoured the professors of elocution or of rhetoric by granting them privileges and exemption from taxation; they founded some chairs of rhetoric or philosophy at Rome or at Athens; but, as a rule, they let the cities take the initiative in these matters. For the rest, they had no need to trouble themselves; Roman civilisation exercised an invincible charm upon the peoples of the Occident. It was not necessary to resort to compulsion in order to induce them to speak the language of the conqueror or to read the masterpieces of his literature, as well as to imitate his way of living. They were impelled to it of their own accord. When one realises the zeal with which they set themselves to learn, it is impossible to pretend that they became Roman in spite of themselves.

It was rhetoric more than anything else that conquered them. To-day, this study does not enjoy a great reputation, and it is difficult for us to believe that it was ever of great importance. It is none the less true that it was the soul of the education which spread throughout the whole world and which civilised the most barbarous nations. There was a time when, from the Atlas to the Rhine, and from the Euphrates to the Atlantic Ocean, no more refined pleasure was known than that of listening to good speaking; when a special effort was made to learn the rules which governed it, and when a knowledge of it was looked upon as the feature which most distinguished the civilised man from the savage. The Greek or the Latin rhetorician followed the legions, settled in the countries through which they had passed, and completed their conquest. It is remarkable that the art which he taught became acclimated so quickly that pupils of overnight were masters on the morrow. Spain, which resisted Roman arms for so long, produced as early as the first century such orators as Porcius Latro and the Senecas, who were examples to those at Rome. Gaul was so delighted with the art it had just learned that it spread it among the neighbouring nations; it was Gaul, Juvenal tells us, that made the orators of Britain:

"Gallia causidicos docuit facunda Britannos."*

Britain, in turn, acquired such a liking for oratory, that Thule,¹ the island at the end of the world, spoke of providing itself with a professor of rhetoric:

"De conducendo loquitur jam rhetore Thule." †

Africa also gave such a kindly welcome to rhetoric, studied it with such zeal, and thronged the chairs where it was taught, that at the end of a few years the country of Jugurtha and the Numidians deserved to be called by the same Juvenal a nursery of advocates, *nutricula causidicorum.* ‡

II

These advocates were not only the great provincial men whose reputation was confined to the city in which they practised their profession. Some

---

* *Juvenal*, xv., 111.   † *Ibid.*, xv., 112.   ‡ *Ibid.*, vii., 148.

crossed the sea and made a great name even at Rome. The most ancient advocate of whom mention is made lived toward the middle of the first century, in the time of Vespasian and his sons. This was Septimius Severus, the grandfather of the Septimius Severus who became Emperor and founded a dynasty. He was born at *Leptis* (Lamta),[2] which was not considered a very literary city; but this fact did not prevent his winning one of the foremost places among the orators of Rome. Statius,[3] whose friend he was, expressed the general opinion when he said to him: " Who would ever believe that Leptis, hidden in the midst of the Syrtes (Tripolis),[4] was thy native country ? Is it possible that such a brilliant mind passed its early years far from the hills of Romulus ?" And he added these words, which afterwards there was occasion to apply to many others who came from the same country as Severus:

> " Non sermo pœnus, non habitus tibi,
> Externa non mens : Italus, Italus." *

The number of lettered Africans who made themselves known at Rome soon increased. A few years later, in the early part of the century of the *Antonini*, the foremost orators of the age were counted among them: Cornelius Fronto,[5] born at Cirta, the master and friend of Marcus Aurelius; and Sulpicius Apollinaris, a native of Carthage and a celebrated rhetorician. Aulus Gellius, a friend and great admirer of

* *Silv.*, iv., 5, 45.

both, pictures them to us on the Palatine discoursing together on literary subjects while waiting for the Emperor to arise. They could meet there with several of their compatriots, Servilius Silanus of Hippo, Eutyches Proculus of Sicca, Postumius Festus, Annæus Florus, and many others also who had become men of note.

If I were to choose from the number the one who seems to me the best representative of African literature, I should not take Fronto, notwithstanding his reputation, and despite the fact that in his time he was regarded as the head of a school. Fronto did not forget the land of his birth; we read that he consented to be patron of Calama and of Cirta, and he was delegated to thank the Emperor, in a pompous address, in the name of the Carthaginians, for some favour they had received from him. However, it is probable that, his fortune once made, he remained at Rome, held there by his high position and his friendship with men of note. He soon ceased to be a provincial in order to become one of the great personages belonging to the entire Empire. But there was at that time another writer almost as celebrated as he, who remained more truly African: this was Apuleius. No doubt Apuleius led a very wandering life; yet a sort of charm always drew him back to his native land, and it is he who has best preserved the character of its literature.

Apuleius was born in an old Numidian town on the borders of the Gætuli, that is to say, a few steps from barbarism.[6] Madaura, his native place, the ruins of which may be seen as one goes by rail to Tebessa, is situated on a vast plain, watered by numerous streams and surrounded by wooded hills. Above the hills the picturesque mountains of the circle of Soukara are seen along the horizon, and, farther on, the jagged crests of the chains of Tunis. The ruins of the great monuments which to-day still cover the ground indicate that the city must have been rich, important, and well populated. Monsieur Gsell, who collected many inscriptions on a recent visit to the ruined city, points out that although it was very ancient, dating back to the time of the Numidian kings, it seemed wholly to have given itself up to the domination of the Romans.* Berber names are much less numerous than in the neighbouring city of *Thubursicum Numidarum* (Khamisa). On the other hand, we find there the *Julii*, the *Claudii*, the *Flavii*, the *Cornelii*, and the *Munatii*, the greatest names of Rome. This, without doubt, was one of the centres of Roman influence in Numidia, where literature and the arts must have been cultivated. From the large number of priests found there it is evident that the town had many temples; we know that even in the time of Theodosius the city was very devout, and that statues of the gods filled the Forum. The family of Apuleius held an important position, and his father filled the highest municipal offices. It would be interesting to know the real origin of this family: whether it was directly descended from the ancient inhabitants

* Gsell, *Recherches archéol. en Algérie*, p. 293 *et seq.*

of the country, or whether it came from another land and settled there with the veterans sent thither by Rome to form a colony. Perhaps it would have been difficult even for Apuleius himself to tell us; after several centuries the two races were so thoroughly intermingled that it was no longer possible to distinguish them. However, he regarded himself as an African, and he happened once to say, when boasting of his fine connections: "I have known many great orators of the Roman race," *multos romani nominis disertos viros cognovi*,* which shows that he looked upon himself as of a different race from them. It is very probable also that Latin was not the first language he spoke, as, when he came to settle in Rome, he was compelled to learn it from the very beginning.

His father left him two million sesterces (400,000 francs), which allowed him to make a tour of the world in order to enrich his mind. He went first to Carthage, where he studied rhetoric, which was taught there with brilliancy, and where he gained a knowledge of philosophy. It was doubtless in order to perfect himself in this science that from Carthage he went to Athens, the schools of which were at that time very celebrated.' At Athens he conceived such an admiration for Plato that from that time on he desired to inscribe himself at the head of his works, " the Platonist of Madaura." But philosophy alone did not occupy him; he studied, besides this, natural history, astronomy, astrology, medi-

* *Apol.*, 95.

cine, music, and geometry. He wished to learn what appertained to everything at one time; he must have cultivated every branch of literature and of science. To speak of literature alone, there is almost no style that he neglected. He wrote discourses and philosophical works as easily as romances, besides dialogues and verses in every metre. It is evident that he was tempted to display all these talents, of which he was very proud, in the capital of the Empire; this was the rendezvous of important and distinguished people from the whole world who hoped to make a reputation for themselves; they came thither from every direction out of curiosity or ambition, in order to enjoy the sights that the city offered, or to bring themselves into notice. If he were not a fool, a man might reasonably hope to better his position or his fortune there. Apuleius, who, like others, had decided to undertake this journey, speaks of it with a sort of awe; he takes care to note, as an important date in his life, that it was the night before the Ides of December that he made his entrance "into the holy city." * He arrived there very poor. Journeys were expensive, and his sojourn in the schools of Carthage and of Athens had greatly diminished his fortune; he tells us that he ruined himself in relieving the needs of his friends and his masters, and even in giving dowries to their daughters. Perhaps, too, he did not always lead a regular life. We know that he wrote love poems, which fact seems

* *Métam.*, xi., 26.

little suited to a philosopher, and which suggests rather dissipated habits. It was therefore necessary for him to earn his living in the great city and to profit by his talents. In the first place, he mastered Latin, which he spoke rather poorly; then he became an advocate. He succeeded in this profession, and was enabled to live at ease, although it did not bring him a fortune, as it did others. A few years later, in the argument that he wrote for his defence, he was obliged to admit that he was poor; but he consoled himself by recalling the fact that poverty had always been the faithful companion of philosophy, and the mother of every virtue, while wealth had the disadvantage of engendering every vice.*

I am tempted to believe that it was during his sojourn in Rome that he composed his *Metamorphoses*.† In the first place he himself implies this when he tells us in the beginning of the story that "a short time ago he left Athens" ‡; furthermore this period

---

* *Apol.*, 48.

† This is not the opinion of everyone I know. As there is no mention of the *Metamorphoses* in the *Apology*, it is often supposed that it was not composed until later, that is to say, that it belongs to the second part of the life of Apuleius. It is indeed difficult to comprehend why his enemies, in order to prove that he was a magician, did not make use of his romance, if they were acquainted with it. Whatever the weight of this objection, I cannot bring myself to see in the *Metamorphoses* anything but a youthful production. May it not be supposed either that he neglected to answer the charges brought by his accusers against his book, not knowing what to say to justify himself, or that the work, although already written, was not as yet widely circulated?

‡ *Métam.*, i., 4.

of his life is the one to which the work seems best suited. When read with care, it is very evident that it marks a sort of crisis in his life. After much wandering he comes to be the object of divine favour; Osiris deigns to appear before him and speak to him; in return he, as he expresses it, enrolls himself in the sacred band, becomes a *pastophore*,[8] and even one of the masters of the college. This is the time when he admits that he renders homage to the gods by recounting the sins he has committed, and the generous pardon he has received. Later, when he became a serious man in earnest, and a sort of priest, it was no longer the time to confess his frivolities and culpable desires. The writing of the *Metamorphoses*,[9] if we place it at this period of his life, separated the latter into two parts: the age of dissipation was past, henceforth he was about to devote himself undividedly to rendering homage to the gods, and to preaching wisdom.

It was in his native land that he wished to put into practice this kind of apostleship that he imposed upon himself. He left Rome and probably settled at Carthage. In like manner his fellow-countryman, St. Augustine, having received baptism at Milan, returned to Africa, there to serve the god to whom he had just consecrated himself. But it is not likely that Apuleius remained quietly in the city which he had chosen for his home; being of a wandering disposition, he must often have visited the neighbouring countries. On one of these journeys he met with an adventure that caused a great sensation and that brought about the writing of one of his best works.[10]

He had started for Alexandria, but on the way, in the city of Œa (Tripoli, in Arabic, *Tarábulus*),[11] he met one of his old comrades from Athens who detained him on his journey, and afforded him an opportunity to make himself heard and applauded. Apuleius, charmed with the reception he received, remained several days, then several months, and finally ended by marrying the mother of his friend, a wealthy widow, who had fallen in love with the young student. Unfortunately, discord soon arose in the family; the sons of the widow, who at first seemed delighted at having Apuleius for a stepfather, became frightened at the ascendancy which he was gaining over his wife, and, fearing for their fortune, accused him of having used witchcraft in order to make himself loved. In vain did Apuleius reply that the infatuation was explained in the most natural way in the world; that a woman who was no longer young, and who had never been beautiful,* could easily fall in love with a brilliant young man, whom his enemies accused of being too fine a fellow for a philosopher, without any other witchcraft than that of his face and of his mind; nevertheless he was dragged before the courts. It was a serious affair; Roman law treated magicians without mercy. Happily the charges that were advanced by the enemies of Apuleius in order to convict him were absurd, and he had no trouble in refuting

* *Mediocri forma, at non ætate mediocri, Apol.*, 92.

them. He probably won his cause before the judges,[12] but I imagine that the public was not wholly convinced of his innocence. A man who had a knowledge of so many things, who dissected fishes, magnetised children, and cured epileptic women, was looked upon with suspicion. In spite of his brilliant defence, some doubt still remained, and who knows? perhaps Apuleius himself was willing that it should do so; it could not have been displeasing to his vanity to be regarded as one who possessed secret powers, and who, in case of need, could perform miracles.

The chief occupation of Apuleius, during the second half of his life, seems to have been to give addresses, full of eloquence and philosophy, before the literary men of Africa. It is a pity that none of these discourses has been preserved intact; but there remains a little book which gives an idea of them. It is a sort of anthology (*Florida*[13]), and, as it were, a bouquet, composed of the most beautiful flowers of his rhetoric. He who made this collection was not a man of taste or of sound judgment; his work often shows glaring faults; he admired assonance and antithesis more than reason; but we must forgive him for much, since, after all, he has given us a knowledge of what might be called the teaching of Apuleius.

He did not have scholars in the real sense of the word, and he did not give consecutive and regular lessons. We should say to-day that he gave lectures. Lectures at that time were very fashionable. We have just seen that throughout the Roman world people were very fond of hearing good speaking. About this same time Lucian was travelling through Gaul and Italy, charming the literary men of the large cities by his brilliant declamations, and winning much fame as well as a goodly sum of money. The subjects of the lectures of Apuleius must have been borrowed from philosophy; we have seen that he professed to be a disciple of Plato, but this fact did not prevent him, in speaking, from giving at least as much attention to the style as to the ideas. The mission of his philosophy—as he himself tells us—was to teach the art of correct speaking as well as of right living: *Disciplina regalis tam ad bene dicendum quam ad bene vivendum reperta** ; and he seems to have devoted himself particularly to the art of speaking. He knew that this was the one feature which was especially demanded by those who came to hear him; it is probable that they would have been rather indifferent to some error of doctrine, but we may be sure that they would not have suffered a fault in language. " Which of you," said he to them, " would forgive me for committing a solecism ? Who would not be annoyed if I mispronounced a single syllable ? " † We are here enlightened as to the tastes of the auditors of Apuleius; philosophy served as a pretext, but it was really an exercise of rhetoric at which they assisted.

Lectures were given almost anywhere; in private houses, temples, or basilicas, even in the theatre at

* *Florida*, i., 7. † *Ibid.*, i., 9,

Carthage. One may at first be shocked because a theatre was used for a lesson in philosophy, but Apuleius reassures us. The place in itself, he tells us, is indifferent; it is not necessary to ask where one is, but what one comes to see and hear; intention purifies everything. " If it is a mime actor, he will make you laugh; if it is a rope-dancer, he will make you tremble; the comedian will amuse you, but by the philosopher you are instructed."* No matter! behold the philosopher in strange company. The truth is, that there was no other place large enough to hold those who wished to hear Apuleius, and even the theatre itself scarcely sufficed. This great audience made him very proud. He does not fail to tell us that no philosopher before him had drawn such a crowd, and he gives amusing pictures of those who pushed and elbowed one another, without always succeeding in getting a place.

For the rest, the success of Apuleius is very easy to comprehend. He possessed a fund of wit, he spoke well, he pleased the people both by his good and by his bad qualities. No one knew better than he how to turn a phrase and make a period in such a way as to charm the ear. It was a concert that he gave the people of Carthage each time he was heard. Let us add that the man was as attractive as the orator. It is indeed his own portrait that he wished to paint when he speaks in his *Metamorphoses* of the young man " who is tall without being long, slender without being thin, ruddy without being

* *Florida*, i., 5.

red, with blond hair which has no need of art in order to be well arranged; with piercing eyes, full of life; with a face on which is painted the flower of youth, with a carriage at once noble and natural." * This fine fellow prided himself on his elegant manners. He speaks rather lightly of mendicant philosophers, who ran about the world with wallet and staff, becoming poor in order the better to preach to the poor. † He cared to know only people of position; he was the friend of the most influential men of the city, and associated with the proconsul; it was indeed necessary for him always to be dressed with care, in order that he might not be out of place in that company. He was even criticised for being a little too fastidious in his toilet, which seemed but little suited to the dignity of a philosopher. He was accused one day, as of a crime, for having written stanzas in honour of tooth-powder ‡; whereupon he gravely replied that since people washed their feet, it could not be criminal to cleanse their teeth. A final charm which the philosophy of Apuleius possessed for the people of that age was the fact that it was strongly tinged with mysticism. This

---

* *Métam.*, ii., 2.
† *Florida*, i., 7.
‡ *Apol.*, 6 ; here are some of these curious lines :
"   Misi, ut petisti, mundicinas dentium . . .
      Tenuem, candificum, nobilem pulvisculum
      Complanatorem tumidulæ gingivulæ,
      Converritorem pridianæ reliquiæ,
      Ne qua visatur tetra labes sordium,
      Restrictis forte si labellis riseris."

rhetorician was also a priest; he always spoke with unction of the gods, and referred to them as often as possible; as he had in his audience scarcely any but pious and literary people,—everyone was such at that time,—his auditors were delighted to hear him mingling prayers with rhetorical feats of skill. One day when he wished to extol Æsculapius, the great deity of the Carthaginians, whose temple, built on the summit of the Byrsa, dominated the city, he recited a dialogue in which the speakers expressed themselves alternately in Greek and Latin, and concluded with a hymn in both languages. Rhetoric and religion! Latin and Greek! Prose and Poetry! The applause which must have resounded throughout the theatre of Carthage on that day may be imagined! *

They were not satisfied with applauding Apuleius; we know that several statues were erected to him at Carthage and elsewhere. He was chosen priest of the province, which position, he says, was the greatest honour that could be obtained. †

I do not know why St. Augustine was surprised that Apuleius, with his birth, his talent, and his power, did not fill some judicial office in his own town.‡ I suppose that he did not care for it. In fact, it is difficult to see what a man who was looked upon as the greatest orator of his time and of whom his country was proud, would have gained by becoming *decurion* or *duumvir* of Madaura.

---

* *Florida*, iv., 18.   † *Ibid.*, iii., 16.   ‡ *Epist.*, 138.

III

To return to the romance of Apuleius, to which I have barely referred; it is the most important of his works; therefore it is fitting to pause before it.

Its subject is taken from a simple Greek legend, of which there were several versions. It is the story of a young virtuoso, who, chancing to see a sorceress change herself into a bird by rubbing herself with a certain unguent, tries to imitate her; but, having made a mistake in the flagon, he finds himself changed into an ass. Fortunately, he knows that he will be able to return to human form by chewing roses. His evil fate ordains that he shall have great trouble in finding them, and thus retards his deliverance. The adventures in which he takes part, up to the day when he again assumes his own form, are the basis of the romance. On this rather slender woof the author has embroidered all sorts of strange episodes collected from all quarters. The accessory becomes the principal, and, to speak of only one of the episodes, the most charming of all, the story of "Cupid and Psyche," " alone comprises a third of the work. The various elements are not always well blended, and sometimes they differ greatly in character; for instance, there are some episodes which are more than frivolous, with conclusions of lofty devotion. The whole is, notwithstanding, very piquant and pleasing. "The Golden Ass" (" L' Âne d'Or "), to give it its proper title, must have been a popular book in the second century. It is probable that people read it eagerly, but in secret, without daring to admit the fact, and Septimius Severus criticised his rival Clodius Albinus, an African like himself and Apuleius, for having made it his favorite reading.*

The tale possesses the disadvantage of perplexing us from the very outset. The hero himself relates the story of his adventures; but who is this hero? He tells us in the beginning that he is called Lucius, and that he was born at Patræ, in Thessaly. This is, in fact, the name given him in the original Greek, whence the legend is taken. But immediately, as though to throw us off the track, this Thessalian adds that he is descended from Plutarch,[15] who, as we know, was a Bœotian, born at Chæronea. Then he tells us that he went to Rome, where he learned Latin with difficulty, and he begs that he may be forgiven if he does not always speak in an irreproachable manner; of these facts the Greek legend says not a word. The thought, therefore, arises that the author must have blended his own history with that of his fabulous Lucius; in fact, the assimilation is complete at the end. The Thessalian has disappeared, and we are told positively that it is the man of Madaura (*Madaurensis*), that is, Apuleius himself, whom Isis, having delivered, receives into her sacred band.† But then, if it is to him that the goddess has given back the human form, it is he also who lost it; it is he who was the lover of Photis, he who surprised the secrets from the old magician, and who by his imprudence was exposed to so many

---

* Capitol, *Vita Albini*, 12. † *Métam.*, xi., 27.

perils. It was not, therefore, entirely a mistake to confound Apuleius with Lucius and to attribute the adventures to him. Evidently it pleased him to let hover over this entire legend an ambiguity from which it seemed to him that his reputation would profit. I said just now that if he deemed it necessary to defend himself before the judges from the charge of being a magician, in order to escape the punishment of the law, he was not sorry, however, that some suspicion remained of his having been such. The *Metamorphoses* succeeds in proving this. He doubtless thought that, in the future, this renown would give to him a special halo of glory, and this is what really happened.

In this amusing display of vanity, and in this desire for extraordinary fame, Apuleius differs wholly from Petronius,[16] with whom one is apt to compare him. Roman literature has had but two novelists, Petronius and Apuleius, and they conceived the novel in almost the same manner; with both of them the plot is of little importance, and the whole interest consists in the episodes which they introduce. These episodes are borrowed by both from Greek story-tellers, and especially from Milesian fables. But if their methods are almost identical, their work is very different; never did two writers resemble each other less. Apuleius brings himself into notice as often as possible, and voluntarily assumes fine airs; he wishes people to share the good opinion he has of himself, to know that he is a great orator, and to suspect him perhaps of being a magician. He presents himself as a protégé of the gods, and relates the favours they have heaped upon him. Petronius is entirely the opposite; he never speaks of himself, and takes as much pains to hide himself as the other does to bring himself into notice. Nevertheless, his true sentiments may at times be suspected. For instance, it is very evident that he detests rhetoricians, pedants, and scholars, that is to say, those whom Apuleius particularly admires. His attacks upon them are full of spirit and animation. A light and pleasing irony runs through his whole book; he spares no one, not even himself. It has been remarked that his ideas on the decadence of the arts, on epic poetry, and on the dangers of oratory, on all of which he lays much stress, are put into the mouth of a ridiculous poet, who in giving expression to these ideas discredits them. He wished, no doubt, to avoid the appearance of esteeming himself too highly, of being too confident and too set in his opinions. It is a curious fact, however, that, of the two, the one who does not pride himself on philosophy, who does not have on his books the title of Platonist, is by far the more acute observer and the more profound moralist. What a picture he has given of the extravagant luxury of the freedman, and how he has avenged the great nobles for the foolish self-conceit of the *parvenus!* What an amusing image of the chase after heritages which, at Rome, was the profession of so many! And when he descends still further to the lower classes, of which he gives but a glimpse, how quickly does he apprehend and depict their characteristics! What truth in the manner in which he makes the petty workmen and the important men of the village speak! How he reproduces their language and their ideas! It is certain that there is nothing as vivid or as profound in Apuleius. The latter's observation always remains on the surface, and however amusing his work may be as a whole, his characters never become types like *Trimalchio*.

But the greatest difference between them is their manner of writing. There is no style that is at the same time more pleasing and graceful than that of Petronius. With him there is nothing forced, nothing artificial, nothing affected; he resorts to no emphasis or rhetoric; wit flows spontaneously; even his somewhat stilted love-passages seem natural, so accurately do they reproduce the language of the society of the Empire. Cicero says of certain men and women of his time, that they speak well almost without wishing to do so, and, in any case, without an effort, solely because they have always heard good speaking. It is the same with Petronius; he was a good writer by birth and habit. Apuleius, on the other hand, was a provincial; Latin was not his native language; he had to learn it, and did not speak it easily, as is readily perceived.

It cost him effort and labour to give expression to his thoughts, and though the result was often happy, the effort was always apparent. This offers a marked contrast to the pleasing facility of Petronius. While the one speaks the Latin of the whole world, and speaks it better than anyone else, the other makes use of turns and expressions which constantly disconcert us, and which do not seem to belong to the common language.

This is a source of surprise to those who are familiar with Latin writers, and causes the work of Apuleius to appear strange as a whole. Mingled with what is assuredly Roman we find elements of a foreign origin, and we wonder, at first, how he could have come by them. It is not easy to determine this, and yet it would be interesting to know. We shall see the various ways in which this question has been answered.

IV

At first one is tempted to believe that, because Apuleius was African by birth, he borrowed from Africa what he did not obtain from Rome. This, in fact, is the general opinion, and Monsieur Monceaux, one of the last writers to make a study of Apuleius, thinks that " he clearly reproduces the image of his native country," and that " he would appear like a Bedouin in a congress of classics."

Is this really true ? I think not. This " Bedouin " has taken the trouble to tell us as plainly as possible from what source he has drawn for the foundation of his work. He states, in beginning his romance, that he is about to relate a Greek story: *fabulam græcanicam incipimus*. We know, in fact, that the adventures of Lucius of Patræ had a certain popularity in Greece, nor is there any doubt that the loves of Psyche have the same origin; moreover, among the other legends, which are shorter and less important, is there a single one that can be suspected of being of African origin? He might, indeed, have borrowed them from the peasantry; the Numidians must have been as eager for this sort of story as their descendants are, and in our day collections of Kabyle tales have been made, several of which date very far back. But those of Apuleius come from elsewhere; he did not hear them during the night-watches in the *mapalia*. In order that we may know where he found them, he himself calls them " Milesian stories."[17] These charming legends made the round of the world throughout antiquity, and it may be said that their journey still continues; if some of them, thanks to Boccaccio and La Fontaine, have entered into modern literature, others are circulating about more obscurely in the faithful memory of the people; they pass from one country to another by roads with which we are unacquainted, changing, renewing, and constantly repeating themselves. Petronius had already drawn from this inexhaustible source. He owed to it the *Matron of Ephesus*, a masterpiece of light literature. Apuleius, who has less grace and delicacy than Petronius, also borrowed some very interesting material from the same source; the *Tub*, afterwards imitated by La Fontaine, and the *Slippers of Philetærus* are very amusing fables, the origin of which is recognised at first glance. It is the same with the characters whose story he tells: the deceived husbands, the frivolous women, the adventurers, the highway robbers,—all come straight from Greece. This was not a reason for their seeming to be foreign to Africa. The Africans, since the time of the Numidian kings, had given a kindly welcome to Greek literature, and had become familiar with it; they spoke Greek fluently throughout the Proconsular Province*; on the side bordering on the frontiers of Egypt, toward Byzacium, it was the language preferred by the genteel class; perhaps it was used more familiarly than Latin at Madaura, and in the family of Apuleius. Therefore it is not surprising that he should have early become familiar with this charming literature, that it should have made a deep impression upon him, and that, when he began to write, his mind being thoroughly imbued with it, he should have imitated it in almost all that he composed.

So much for the groundwork of his stories; it is Greek, and I do not believe that, with the best intent in the world, anything African can be found in it. As to his style, that is a more complicated question."[18] Here, again, he imitates the Greek to a great extent; but does he not imitate something else? We must remember that around him Punic and Libyan were spoken; these languages were

---

* Tertullian, who lived later than Apuleius, in the time of Septimius Severus, wrote in Greek and in Latin, which fact proves that in his age both languages were heard almost equally at Carthage, at least in literary circles. From that time on Latin completely supplanted the Greek in Africa.

probably the first that fell on his ear, and he never wholly ceased hearing them. Is it not probable that they had some influence on his style of speaking and writing? It is so natural to believe this, that even at that time the scholars of antiquity were seeking for traces of Punic in the language of the Africans. Those of our day, with more patience and with better methods, have taken up the same study; but neither the one set nor the other has had much success in these researches; what is claimed as coming from the Semitic patois is wholly insignificant, or is not of the origin to which it is attributed. In short, the turns and expressions which are used most frequently by Apuleius, and which characterise his style, when studied closely, are easily explained by the Latin and the Greek, without need of resorting to other languages.* The conclusion may

* This is not the place in which to discuss a question of philology. I wish, however, to say a word regarding one of the figures most common with Apuleius that seems characteristic of him. It is a sort of relation between adjectives and verbs, which correspond two by two and three by three with a regularly recurring assonance. This makes his writings seem like rhyming prose. Let us take, for instance, the first sentence of the *Florida*. To begin with, we find a succession of rhymes in *e*: "Ut moris est votum postulare, pomum adponere, paulisper adsidere"; then rhymes in *a*: "Aut ara floribus redimita, aut quercus cornibus onerata, aut fagus pellibus coronata"; then rhymes in *e* and *us*: "Vel colliculus sepimine consecratus, vel truncus dolamine effigiatus, vel cœspes libamine fumigatus, vel apis unguine delibutus," etc. This figure, which recurs everywhere in Apuleius, is especially used in his oratorical works. There it repeats itself with a wearying insistence and like a sort of mania. But if Apuleius uses it more than others, he is not the first to have employed it. The abuse of it belongs to him; the use was much older than

therefore be drawn that the Libyan and the Punic which he heard spoken in his childhood, and which perhaps he himself spoke, have introduced none or almost none of their idioms into the sometimes unusual Latin of which he made use.

In order not to be too greatly surprised at this, we must remember the importance of the schools in Africa. The school is almost everywhere the mortal enemy of patois; the master, proud of his knowledge, and always somewhat pedantic and solemn, does not suffer the beautiful language that he teaches to be injured by popular expressions; he mounts guard about it, and makes a special effort to preserve it from its nearest enemies, who are the most dangerous. In this struggle, which begins anew every day, he has allies and accomplices. The family of the young man labours also to hunt down the ill-sounding expressions which may escape him. How could it permit them, since the use of them gives the impression that he is a poorly educated

he. It dates as far back as Isocrates, who suggests placing at the end of phrases or parts of phrases, syllables with like terminations ($\delta\mu οιοτέλευτα$). Cicero and his successors did not disdain to do this in moderation; but I firmly believe that it was Apuleius who made the trick popular. It won a fortune after him. We find it very often in the delightful work by Minutius Felix (see *Latin Literature*, by J. W. Mackail.—Tr.) and still more in the *Manteau* of Tertullian, a sort of oratorical revelry, in which every resource of rhetoric is squandered. As these two authors are compatriots of Apuleius, some might be tempted to believe that a method employed by so many Africans was a peculiar feature of African literature; but we have just seen that it did not originate in Africa, and that here again Apuleius has drawn very freely and sometimes without reason from a Greek source.

man, unaccustomed to the world, and that he has spent much time in the village or the lobby, which is something that good society does not forgive ? It is really necessary to have lived in the countries in which the various patois struggle for good or evil against the disdain of good society, in order to know how unweariedly they are attacked, and to understand how it happens that men of the world succeed in guarding against them. It is probable that the prejudices which govern us already existed in the literary Africa of the second century, and that the schoolmasters and the fathers of families were of one mind in combating the influence of the ancient native tongues. Apuleius seems wholly to have shared the scorn that was felt for them. He says somewhere, in order to bring disgrace upon a poorly educated young man who ran away from school and spent his time with gladiators: " He never speaks anything but Punic, and can scarcely even remember the Greek that he learned from his mother. As to Latin, he neither knows nor wishes to know it."* He evidently thought that a man of the world should not speak Punic, and very naturally, therefore, put forth every effort that no trace of it might be found in his Latin.

Assuredly this Latin was not of the best; in order to perceive this, it is sufficient merely to glance at a few pages of his books. But what is original and even at times bizarre in his style is

---

* *Apol.*, 68 : " Loquitur numquam nisi punice, et si quid adhuc a matre græcissat ; enim latine neque vult, neque potest."

easily explained when one remembers the manner in which he acquired his education. He tells us, as we have already said, that, when already a grown man, he gained his knowledge of Latin at Rome, and he adds a very important fact, namely, that he learned it without a master.* This study, carried on boldly and somewhat at random by a very independent spirit, must have developed some capricious and extravagant results. He did not voluntarily follow ordinary rules; his style of writing is wholly individual, and is that of a man who is self-trained. Much of his seeming originality, however, may be credited to his erudition rather than to his creative faculty, his memory often coming into play when he seems to be inventing.

For instance, in regard to words, I believe that no writer has taken greater pleasure in making use of those that are strange, surprising, unknown, or but little known. His vocabulary is marvellously rich. Evidently this Roman of late date was anxious to show that he had at his command a language which was richer and more varied than that of the old Romans. But the words which seem new are, for the most part, only ancient terms revived.† This was a popular practice at that time. As to the words that he coined outright, and which he used much less frequently

---

* *Métam.*, i., 1: "nullo magistro præeunte."

† Monsieur Kretschmann shows this very clearly in his memoir, entitled *De latinitate L. Apuleii Madaurensis*. I refer especially to p. 33, in which he discusses what is called the *Africitas* of Apuleius.

than might be supposed, he formed them regularly and according to the usual methods. Often he joined two words together, making a compound which expressed his meaning in the quickest and most vivid manner. It is in such a way that he refers to the interested caresses of the courtesans as kisses that cost money, *oscula poscinummia*. It has been noticed also that he was very fond of diminutives. In a certain passage of the *Metamorphoses*, eight have been found in two lines, which is a little too much, and this does not include the diminutives of diminutives, such as *tantillulum* or *pullulus*, which were not displeasing to him. He often obtained very agreeable effects from them, as, for instance, when, apropos of a woman in love with a fine fellow, he tells us that she nibbles (*mordille*) him with her eyes, or when he gives us to understand in a single word that a matron is all attention to him, *me matrona curitabat*. In the long run, however, this use of little caressing words makes his style somewhat affected and weak; but the method of writing was at that time very common, and Apuleius only exaggerated what was done by authors of renown.

He cannot, therefore, be characterised entirely as a barbarian, and as a solitary exception among contemporary writers. In reality, he followed, in his own way, the fashions of the day. It is impossible to believe that a man as proud as he was of his Græco-Roman education, in order to be different from others, ever conceived the idea of seeking in the uncouth idioms of the peasants expressions with which to ornament his works. He took them from the classic languages, the Greek and the Latin, or, if he felt the need of coining new ones, he followed the usual methods by which the Latin was little by little revived and enriched. But, as he was impetuous and extravagant, as he had learned the language without an instructor, and as, moreover, he did not live in the midst of the old Romans, who were filled with the genius of their language and who could impose some restraint upon a rash innovator, he employed these methods without discretion; as a result, his style was often bizarre, but whatever may be said of it, it does not possess any foreign element.*

With Apuleius begins what is called African literature. This term is just and deserved if we wish to say merely that, for four centuries without interruption, Africa produced a succession of talented authors who wrote in Latin. But it is unquestionably a mistake if we mean to imply that these writers resemble one another, that they bear the same stamp and form a compact group. Strictly speaking, I clearly discern some common traits in them which give them a likeness. For instance, I see that Apuleius, St. Cyprian, Arnobius, Lactantius, and St. Augustine, the greatest of them, were rhetori-

* Among the words used by Apuleius are *cambiare*, to change, and *minare*, to lead, evidently taken by him from the language of the people. This proves that the popular Latin of Africa was often the same as that spoken by the humble classes of Gaul.

cians by profession, and that rhetoric left its mark upon them all; but it is the same in other countries; everywhere, writers who have received only the education of the world are becoming rare, and literature is being recruited more and more from the schools. I notice also that the African rhetoricians were at the same time devotees; Apuleius frequented all the temples, was initiated into every mystery, and enrolled himself in the band of Isis; the other writers were fervent Christians, priests, bishops, and defenders of their faith. But there again they differed but little from the writers of other countries; there were no longer any but believers, and the time was approaching when priests and monks would be almost the only ones to know how to write. Thus the points in which they resemble one another are those which they possessed in common with the writers of other nations. For the rest, it often happened that they differed greatly from one another; it is therefore somewhat difficult to define African literature by any general characterisation of its writers. Shall we say, as has sometimes been said, that the writers born under that flaming sky are to be recognised by their violence, that they were ardent spirits, intemperate, and incapable of self-government and self-restraint? These are, indeed, the characteristics of Tertullian; but, on the other hand, St. Cyprian was wise, moderate, politic, thoroughly master of himself, and a man always inclined toward reasonable solutions. If Apuleius appeared to be a romanticist in quest of brilliant images and unusual expressions, who cared little for rules of grammar and usage, Lactantius wished to pose as a pure classicist; he affected to imitate the phrases and to reproduce the expressions of Cicero. As for St. Augustine, he does not exactly resemble anyone, and sometimes not even himself, so great a difference is there between some of his writings; for instance, between the *Philosophical Dialogues* and the *Confessions*, the *Soliloquies* and the *City of God*.[19] Perhaps it is fitting to conclude that these very differences are what best characterise African literature. It has been remarked that the writers of Gaul, to speak of them alone, have more points in common. They strove to write well, that is, to write like those who wrote well; and as they worked from the same models, they grew to resemble one another in style. They were men of good sense, who refrained from extravagances, and who, as far as possible, strove to be simple, clear, exact, and correct. The African writers did not appear to have the same scruples. Each one wrote in his own way and according to his liking. They were, as a rule, less careful of elegance and appearance, less hampered by rules and more personal, and they gave themselves up more fully to their individual genius. In this, I believe, lies their true originality.

V

Mommsen remarks that Africa, which is so rich in great orators, has had no true poets. This is not because poetry was scorned there; on the contrary, the Africans early conceived a very lively admiration for it. From the time of Augustus they began to acquaint themselves with the latest poetical works, and strove to understand them. Horace tells us that when the first rage for them was over at Rome, they were piled into a ship and sent to Ilerda or Utica *; the booksellers were sure that in Africa or Spain they would always find a sale. And not only were the Africans very fond of poetry, but they practised it commonly. Perhaps more metrical inscriptions have been found in Africa than anywhere else. I have already said that at Scillium in Byzacium, the son of an old soldier, T. Flavius Secundus, who had become a person of note in his town, and priest of the province, conceived the idea of erecting a beautiful tomb for his family. It was a very lofty pyramid, with several rows of superposed steps, bas-reliefs, and columns which seemed suspended in the air. On the top of the building a rooster flapped his wings; on the side, the stone, which was pierced by small holes, housed swarms of bees. This monument, which must have been the admiration of the peasantry, and of which Secundus was very proud, did not seem to him complete without some lines of beautiful poetry inscribed upon it. Among his friends was a certain literary man, from whom, no doubt, he begged the lines which were composed and engraved on the stone. They consisted of ninety hexameters, followed by some dis-

* *Epist.*, i., 20, 13.

tichs.* This was a great deal, but it is clear that in evincing this immoderate taste for poetry, there was an evident desire to pose as an educated man who had attended school, and who knew how to live. This kind of vanity was very common in Africa, where, as we have seen, a high value was set on education. It was easily carried as far as pedantry. Those who wished to appear more skilful were not satisfied with ordinary metres; they wrote iambics of different measure, and even minor ionics; they attempted what, until then, had been an impossibility, and made a great effort to write the acrostic. Moreover, not only persons of importance, but also very insignificant ones, a peasant, for instance, or a jeweller, indulged in the luxury of metrical epitaphs. A poor man of Carthage, a messenger who carried official despatches, tells us that he built himself a tomb, and that it was a pleasure for him, when crossing the plain, to read the verses that he had had engraved upon it.†

Unfortunately, the verses of the African poets are almost all frightfully halting; as a rule, they possess neither quantity nor metre. This is so often the case that one wonders if the mistakes were entirely involuntary, or if such marked and such frequent errors were not the result of a sort of system or affectation. It has been thought that the writers may have belonged to a particular school, which made a habit of disregarding ordinary rules because it had a special method of versifying, and that, for

*C. I. L., 211, 212. †*Ibid.*, 1027.

instance, accent was substituted for quantity. This is giving too much credit to the poor poets; as a matter of fact, they respected accent no more than metre, and composed false verses because they did not know how to write others. St. Augustine admits that the Africans were absolutely ignorant of the quantity of Latin words, and that they did not distinguish long syllables from short.* Therefore they were not very exacting; it sufficed if the line which they composed, and which seemed to them a verse, terminated in something which resembled a dactyl or a spondee; they asked no more. Their ear, which was not hard to please, caught in it an echo, as it were, of the beautiful hexameters of Virgil which they had been forced to admire at school, and they were proud to imitate them to the best of their ability; they hoped that the one whom they wished to honour by an inscription would be grateful to them, as far as Tartarus, for what they had tried to do:

" Credo tibi gratum, si haec quoque Tartara norunt." †

Procilius, the silversmith of Cirta, who passed his long life so gayly " in laughing and amusing himself with his dear friends," congratulates himself heartily upon having taken the precaution to compose his own epitaph:

" Titulos quos legis vivus meæ morti paravi." ‡

* *De Doctr. Christ.*, iv., 24 : " Afræ aures de correptione vocalium vel productione non judicant."
† C. I. L., 2803. ‡ *Ibid.*, 7156.

It is certain, however, that if he had left this task to his friends, they would have had great difficulty in writing worse verses than his. But these good Africans did not seem to suspect that their prosody was so bad; on the contrary, they seemed very proud of their poetry; they drew the attention of the passer-by to it, and when he went on his way, they thanked him for having paused a moment to read it:

" Valeas, viator, lector mei carminis." *

There must, however, have been exceptions to this; in a country where poetry was studied with so much zeal, it was inevitable that some writers should be found who succeeded in getting into their heads the quantity of syllables, and who versified almost correctly. As this talent was not natural but acquired, and most laboriously acquired, their poetry, as a rule, lacks ease and grace; it seems stiff, affected, and artificial; it somewhat resembles that of our own scholars, when with the aid of the dictionary they painfully grind out Latin verses. However, these witticisms, as well as their authors, were much esteemed. At the close of the Empire, during the invasion of the barbarians, there was at Carthage, in spite of the unfortunate times, a flourishing school of poets, a part of whose works has been preserved in the *Latin Anthology*. The sudden arrival of the Vandals disconcerted this little group that had become thoroughly accustomed to Roman civilisation. They must have felt a violent hatred

*C. I. L., 5370.

for the intruders who disturbed their quiet life and their literary enjoyments; but as it had become the habit of the Africans to make friends with the powerful, and to seek favours from them, the poets at length composed verses in honour of the Vandal kings, as they had done previously to extol the Roman proconsuls. This justice must be rendered them, that they particularly praised what was worthy of praise ; they encouraged the efforts to repair the evils of invasion and to continue the work of those whose places they had taken; for it came to pass in Africa, as in Spain and in Gaul, that contact with the vanquished gradually modified the uncouthness of the barbarians of the North; they became sensible of the pleasures of a more civilised life, and began to appreciate in some slight degree the charm of literature and of the arts. They themselves restored the monuments which were in ruins, and built new ones. Carthage seemed to have become alive again, and the poets were glad to sing of its resurrection:

> " Victrix Carthago triumphat,
> Carthago studiis, Carthago ornata magistris ! " *

VI

Among the fine minds that were admired in the schools, and that were considered even greater than the ancients,† because they composed laboured and

---

* *Anthologie* (Riese), 317.

† *Anthologie* (Riese), 87 : " Certum est, Luxori, priscos te vincere vates."

trivial verses "to a magpie that chattered like a woman," or "to a cat that was strangled while swallowing a mouse," there is one that deserves to be remembered. Not that he was free from the faults of the others, but he had distinguishing qualities which gave him a place apart. Is it not the irony of fate that the best Roman poet Africa produced should have lived at the court of the Vandal kings, at a time when it was wholly lost to Rome, and when Latin was beginning to be forgotten there!

He was called Dracontius, a name that causes little stir in the world.[20] His family had held an honourable position in the government of the country, and he seemed destined to fill the same offices as his ancestors, and with the same glory. He was an excellent student and a precocious poet. A few years ago some of his youthful works were discovered in the library at Naples, and were published. They are dedicated to his master, the rhetorician Felicianus, on whom he bestows this encomium: "He brought back to Carthage fugitive Literature, and gathered about his chair Romans and barbarians." *

The works found are merely the verses of a student, but they are of value in that they show how, to the last, ancient education remained faithful to

---

* *Dracontii Carmina minora* (ed. Duhn), i., 13:
 "Sancte pater, o magister, taliter canendus es,
 Qui fugatas Africanæ reddis urbi litteras,
 Barbaris qui Romulidas jungis auditorio."

its customary methods. In the midst of Christianity, poets continued to write only on pagan subjects. Young Dracontius sings of the abduction of Helen, the crimes of Medea, the adventure of Hylas, and the groans of Hercules, "when he sees the heads of the Hydra grow again as fast as he cuts them off." He composed metrical dialogues on the same subjects that had been treated of in prose from the time of Seneca and Quintilian, three or four centuries previous. One of these dialogues had the honour of being declaimed publicly in the thermæ of Gargilius, in the presence of the magistrates of the province.* It is, however, very mediocre, and if Dracontius had never written in any other style, it would not be worth while to rescue it from oblivion; but a violent crisis that changed his life caused the production of a more important work. Misfortune developed a vein of talent hitherto unsuspected.

It is natural that the yoke of the Vandals should have pressed heavily upon all those who cultivated literature, causing them to regret the Roman domination. We have just seen that many among them, although enemies of Germanic barbarity, had, nevertheless, resigned themselves to flattering their new masters. Literature being the only profession of these unhappy authors, this was their only means of avoiding starvation. But there were others to whom this servitude seemed intolerable, and who avenged themselves for submitting to it by writ-

* *Carmina min.*, v.

ing malicious verses, which were freely circulated. Such authors, when discovered, must have been severely punished.* The fault of Dracontius was more serious still: " I was wrong," he says, in his confession, " to sing of one king whom I did not know, and who was not my master, instead of extolling kings full of moderation." †

This strange prince, about whom Dracontius censures himself for having sung, was certainly the Cæsar who was ruling at Byzantium. From the time that the Empire of the Occident no longer existed, he represented Rome. All who remained faithful to the memory of the Romans had their eyes fixed on him; as Dracontius, in addressing verses to him, set himself in open revolt against the Vandals, it is not surprising that he was very severely punished. He was beaten, imprisoned, stripped of his goods, and removed from office. In vain did he try to move the King by his prayers, promising that in future he would consecrate his muse to his family; the King was inexorable. He had good cause to think that the Emperor of Constantinople had not renounced the hope of reconquering Africa, and it was natural that in flattering

---

* We have preserved one of these insulting pieces in which the author, in order to ridicule the barbarians who are occupying Africa, intersperses Teutonic words among his Latin verses (*Anth.*, 285). Terms are found in it which are still used to-day, as, to drink (*ia drinkan*). It is probable that those who lived in the neighbourhood of the Vandal soldiers had the opportunity of hearing them uttered frequently.

† *Satisfactio ad Regem*, 93.

this ambition the culpable poet seemed to him to have committed an unpardonable crime.

Dracontius, therefore, remained in prison, more wretched than ever. "Chains press upon me," said he; "torture crushes me, poverty consumes me; I am no longer covered with anything but shapeless rags."* He complained the more bitterly because no one tried to soften his punishment. "Friends and strangers all turn from me. Those to whom I have devoted my life forsake me; my relatives no longer recognise me; my many slaves have fled, my clients despise me." In this loneliness and misery nothing was left him but God and poetry. Consolation came to him from them.

The poem, in three cantos, which he wrote in prison, and which is entitled *Carmen de Deo*, too often escapes attention. It is very evident that it belongs to an age in which the art of composing was lost. After the fifth century there were few authors who knew how to conceive of a subject as a whole, and how to dispose of its parts. They wrote at random, without connection, without concentration, and without metre. It was the use and the success of the sermon that spread this fault in literature. The priest and the bishop had always to be ready to address the faithful; they had no time to prepare their discourses, and give due thought to their language. With mediocre orators, always the most numerous class, the sermon became a mass of verbiage, inexhaustible and more or less edifying, in

* *De Deo*, iii., 58 *et seq.*

which the chief idea was submerged by narrations, digressions, episodes, and accessory developments. Unfortunately, the preaching was done not wholly from the pulpit, and the same faults occurred in all that was written. It must be admitted that the poem of Dracontius is a sermon also, the thread of which is constantly being lost; but, at times, in the midst of the insufferable digressions, the poet sounds a note of personal feeling and of true sentiment. From that moment, and as though by magic, all this background of haze becomes bright; the idea is clearly stated; the style grows animated and vivid; the preacher has become a poet.

In his poem, Dracontius wished to extol divine mercy, and as the first and greatest proof of the love of God was the creation of man, the first song is consecrated to the story of the Creation. During the Middle Ages, this song was separated from the rest of the work, and was greatly admired under the title of *Hexameron* (The Work of the Six Days). It bears comparison with the poem of Marius Victorinus of Marseilles, and with that of St. Avitus. If Dracontius is less correct than they, he has at times more brilliancy, and a livelier appreciation of the beauties of nature. He knew better how to describe the life which flowed in the newly born world; the earth that was becoming fertile and covered with herbage; the forests, " clothed with verdure and inhabited by prating nests " *; the animals of the land

---

* *De Deo*, i., 257; and (674) two beautiful verses on the sun:
  " Sol, oculus mundi, famulus super astra tonantis,
   Cujus ab immensis languescunt sidera flammis."

and of the sea pulsing with life; and the birds that disturb the air with their panting flight and that sing, in order to thank the Lord who has just given them life.

> "Exilit inde volans gens plumea læta per auras,
> Aëra concutiens pennis crepitante volatu
> Ac varias fundunt voces modulamine blando,
> Et, puto, collaudant Dominum meruisse creari."*

In order to represent man, who has just been born, and to distinguish him, at the start, by his peculiar attribute, Dracontius employs an ingenious method; not only does he depict him as gazing with admiration on the beautiful spectacle of the world, but as a thinking and reflecting being. While the animals placidly exist, man wishes to know what he is, and why he has been created, and he looks about him for someone who can tell him." When he sees the beasts running away at his approach, he is disturbed, and realises his loneliness; it is then that God gives him a companion. Ecclesiastical writers, as a rule, pass over the creation of woman; Dracontius, who is a layman, feels more at his ease; he describes Eve with complacency as she comes before him who is to be her husband: " She appeared before him without covering, her body as white as the snow, resembling a nymph rising from the water. Her hair, untouched by the iron, floated over her shoulders; colour glowed on her cheek;

---

* *De Deo*, i., 240.

everything about her was beautiful, and it was evident that she came from the hand of the Almighty."

> "Constitit ante oculos nullo velamine tecta
> Corpore nuda simul niveo, quasi nympha profundi." *

Then he is happy following them into the flowery groves and the gardens of roses in which they hide:

> "Ibant per flores et tota rosaria bini,
> Inter odoratas messes lucosque virentes." †

Beautiful lines may still be found in the other two books, although they are more rare. The author, however, always lays stress on the divine compassion; he had to believe in it to justify his hope that it would bring him out of his trouble. God is good. He hears every prayer, He helps the unfortunate. One has but to call upon Him in order to be saved, "Judas himself, the wretched Judas, might have been saved had he trusted in Him." ‡ Nothing disturbed this tranquil optimism; he could not imagine that God would condemn anyone who confessed his sins, and it seemed to him that repentance created a sort of right to pardon. No one ever had less conception than he of the terrible Judge of the Scriptures, who punishes the fathers in their children, and sets snares for humanity.§ His God was gentle, tender, compassionate, and resolved to

---

* *De Deo*, i., 393.   † *Ibid.*, i., 436.

‡ For instance, he rewrote in his own way the story of Isaac (iii., 125). He did not wish to admit that God tempted Abraham by demanding of him the death of his son; "Non est tentator habendus," he says, boldly. He forgot that the Bible says: "Tentavit Deus Abraham."   § *De Deo*, ii., 558.

punish only those who were determined not to reform. Therefore he felt for Him transports of love and gratitude which were shown in beautiful passages, or rather in hymns full of lyric effusion. Although somewhat lengthy, I wish to quote one of the passages, in order to show what powerful inspiration at times animates his poetry:

" The company of heavenly bodies," thus he addresses his God, "the planets and the stars, praise their Creator ; the lightning adores Thee, the thunder and the tempest tremble before Thee. The lakes and the rivers sing to Thee in their language ; the scattered clouds shine with Thy light. Through Thee the earth is fruitful, the grass becomes green, the forests put forth their leaves, the flower breathes, the tree is covered with fruit. It is Thou that the wild beast extols ; the fish, the great herds, the birds of the air, the race of vipers and of venomous reptiles that hiss in moving their tongues with triple sting, all these monsters which bring death delight in praising the Maker of life."

> " Agmina te astrorum, te signa et sidera laudant,
> Auctorem confessa suum; te fulmen adorat,
> Te tonitrus hiemesque tremunt ; te stagna, paludes,
> Voce sua laudant, te nubila crassa coruscant.
> Per te fetat humus, per te, Deus, herba virescit,
> Frondescunt silvæ, spirat flos, germinat arbor.
> Te fera, te pisces, pecudes, armenta, volucres,
> Turba cerastarum laudant, genus omne veneni
> Sibilat ore fero lingua vibrante trisulca :
> Auctorem vitæ gaudet stridore minaci
> Materies laudare necis." *

* *De Deo*, ii., 205 ; very beautiful verses on God and Nature are also found in i., 717.

There is no doubt that one capable of carrying on without weakening a period so broad, so full, and of such lofty inspiration,—and I have greatly abridged it,—one who wrote the beautiful lines that I have quoted above; who knew how to bring out at intervals the strength or the grace of the ancient Latin hexameter, was indeed a poet. It is sometimes a matter of regret that he was not born at a time when taste was more decided and language more correct. The language as then spoken, which he was compelled to use, was in its decadence, yet the study of it is not without interest. From among the ashes of corruption a few sparks of life are perceived; beneath this language which is dying out, another about to be born is discovered, and from a few indications it is predicted that it will resemble those which are forming on the other side of the sea.*

Thus there existed in Africa, as long as the Empire lasted, a literary class, that was highly educated and cultured, whose common language was Latin. This Latin had its rise and its fall, according to the times; but it never became one of the provincial dialects which were ridiculed elsewhere. A rhetorician of those days states that even at that time it was preferable to that which was used in Italy.

The Africans did not employ the language of the conqueror merely from necessity, in order to com-

---

* Is not the following verse almost a French phrase:

"Est tibi cura, Deus, de quidquid ubique creasti."
"Thou takest care of (*de*) all Thou hast created."

municate with him, and to discuss their common interests; they had become so imbued with it, they had grown so familiar with it, that they made it the natural outlet for their sentiments and thoughts. A literature developed among them which, for centuries, was the admiration of the world. This proves that Roman culture was not merely superficial, but that it took deep root, at least in the cities and among enlightened people.

But it is not enough for civilisation to conquer the upper classes of a nation; as long as it is not supported by the mass of the inhabitants it remains in the air, ready to fall at the least shock. We must try to find out whether Roman civilisation, which, as we have seen, flourished among the higher classes of African society, descended lower, and, if so, to what depths it penetrated.

TRANSLATOR'S NOTES TO CHAPTER VI

1. " Thule, where there is said to be perpetual daylight, was discovered by Pytheas, who places it at six days' sail from the Orcades, and thus leads us to identify it with Iceland. Ptolemy places it more to the S., in the latitude of the Shetlands, so that we may identify it with Mainland. It was always regarded as the farthest point of the known world ; and this is supposed to be expressed in the name itself, the Gothic *tiel* or *tiule* denoting the remotest land (*tibi serviat ultima* Thule.—Virg., *Georg.*, i., 30)."—William Smith, *Ancient Geog.*

2. " Leptis Magna was favourably situated on a part of the coast where the central table-land descends to the sea in a succession of terraces, as at Cyrene. It possessed a roadstead, well sheltered by the promontory of Hermæum. The old Phœnician city was situated

similarly to Carthage, upon an elevated tongue of land at the point where a small river discharges itself into the sea ; the remains of seawalls, quays, fortifications on the land side, and moles are to be seen on its site, which is still called Lebda. At a later period a new city, named Neapolis, grew up on the west side of the old town, which henceforth served as the citadel alone. Its ruins are deeply buried in the sand, and a small village, Legatah, occupies its site."—William Smith, *Ancient Geog.*

" Proxima Leptis erat, cujus statione quieta
Exegere hiemem, muibis flaminisque carentem."
Luc., ix., 948.

3. Statius Cæcilius, the successor of Plautus, is said to have especially distinguished himself by the more artistic treatment of the subject.—Mommsen, vol. iii., bk. iii.

For Statius, see *Silv.*, II., 11., 6 ; III., v., 28 ; iv., 11., 65; Quint., III., vii., 7 ; *Ibid.*, III., v., 31 ; *Silv.*, IV., 11., 65 ; also Nisard, *Poètes de la Décadence*, vol. i., p. 303 ; also *History of Roman Literature*, edited by Charles T. Cruttwell.

4. "Syrtes Major and Minor answer to the Gulfs of Sidra and Khabs. These are the innermost angles of an extensive sea which penetrates between the highlands of Cyrene on the east, and the Atlas range on the west."—William Smith, *Ancient Geog.*

5. For Fronto and Aulus Gellius, see *Roman Literature*, edited by Rev. Henry Thompson, M.A.; *History of Roman Literature*, by Charles T. Cruttwell, M.A. ; also a Dissertation prefixed to the *Criticæ Lucubrationes* of Lambecius.

6. According to Charpentier, Apuleius was born 114 A.D. Teuffel (L. L., ¶ 362, 2) inclines to a later date—125 A.D. Apuleius calls himself *Seminumida et Semigætula* (*Apol.*, 23). The most complete edition of Apuleius is Oudendorp's (*Lugd'. Bat.*, 1786-1823); the best modern edition is Hildebrand's (Leipsic, 1842).

7. In the following metaphorical sentence, Apuleius gives an account of his studies :

" Hactenùs a plerisque potatur ; ego et alias crateras Athenis bibi, Poeticæ commentam, Geometriæ limpidam, Musicæ dulcem, Dialecticæ austerulam, enimverò universæ Philosophiæ inexplebilem scilicet nectaream."—*Florida.*

" Thus much most people drink. I quaffed other cups at Athens ; the cup of poetry adulterated, that of geometry clear, that of music sweet, of dialectics somewhat sour, but that of universal philosophy nectar inexhaustible."—*History of Roman Literature*, edited by Rev. Henry Thompson, M.A.

8. Pontificate of Æsculapius.

9. See Bayle, Fleuri ; *History of Fiction*, vol. i., by Dunlop ; *Lectures and Essays on Latin Literature and Scholarship*, by Henry Nettleship, M.A. ; *History of Roman Literature*, by Cruttwell ; and *History of Roman Literature*, edited by Rev. Henry Thompson, M.A., from which I quote the following : " Two of the stories introduced are found in Boccaccio. The adventure of the wine-skins, in *Don Quixote*, and that of the robber's cavern, in *Gil Blas*, may be traced to the same source." See also, Bishop Warburton's *Divine Legation of Moses*, bk. ii., sec. 4.

10. The *Apologia*, or *Apology*, sometimes called *De Magia*.

11. "Œa, in the interior of the island of Ægina (Eghina), became a Roman colony about A.D. 50, and flourished for three hundred years, when it was ruined by the Rusuriani. On its site stands the modern capital Tripoli. A very perfect marble arch, dedicated to Marcus Aurelius Antoninus and Lucius Aurelius Verus, is the principal relic of the old town."—William Smith, *Ancient Geog.*

12. His case was tried before Claudius Maximus, Proconsul of Africa.

13. See Joann. Woweri, *Præfatio;* also *History of Roman Literature*, edited by Charles T. Cruttwell.

14. It will be found *Métam.*, iv., 28 ; vi., 24. On *Story of Cupid and Psyche*, see Bryant. This fable has been imitated in an old French romance, *Partenopex de Blois*, and is well known to the English reader by Mrs. Tighe's exquisite adaptation of it, and Mr. Rose's elegant versification of the tale of *Partenopex.* It has afforded the subject of a drama to Thomas Heywood and of a narrative poem to Shakerley Marmion. There are good English versions by Sir G. Head, and in Bohn's Classical Library.

15. The mother of Apuleius came of Plutarch's blood.

16. "Petronius Arbiter." See *History of Roman Literature*, edited by Charles T. Cruttwell; also Tacitus, *Ann.*, xvi., 18.

17. Apuleius himself (I., 1) calls the *Metamorphoses* a Milesian tale (see Appendix to chapter iii.). These are very generally condemned by the classical writers, but they were largely read *sub rosa*. When Crassus was defeated in Parthia, the King Surenas is reported to have been greatly struck with the licentious novels which the Roman officers read during the campaign.

18. For excellent description of style of Apuleius, see *Latin Literature*, by J. W. Mackail. See also Kretzschmann, *De Latinitate L. Apulei Madaurensis* (Regimonte, 1865).

19. For St. Augustine and Lactantius, see *History of Roman Literature*, by Cruttwell.

20. For Dracontius see *History of Roman Literature*, edited by Rev. Henry Thompson, M.A.

21. *Nescia mens illis, fieri quæ causa fuisset.* Compare Milton's line:
  "But who I was, or where, *or for what cause*, knew not."

CHAPTER VII

THE CONQUEST OF THE NATIVES

IF we compare the work that we have done in Africa with that of the Romans, it seems to me that we have good reason for being proud of ourselves. In the first place, we have accomplished the conquest of the country in fifty years, that is, in a much shorter time than it took them, and our victory has been not only more rapid, but also more complete. From the Mediterranean to the Great Sahara, all belongs to us, and there is no steppe however lonely, no mountain however wild, over which our flag does not float. On this immense area we have constructed forts, built cities, rendered salubrious the infected plains, and laid out nearly 13,000 kilometres of roads. We are replanting the vine, we have improved the cultivation of the olive and of the cereals, and are in a fair way toward giving back to the country the richness and the vitality that it had lost. These are great things, of which we may well feel proud.

But we must confess that our success is not complete. A part of our task, and by no means the least, has completely miscarried. After having conquered the ancient inhabitants, we have not found out how to win them over. There has been no fusion, no real union between us; they live apart, faithfully preserving their beliefs, their customs, and, what is more dangerous, their hatreds. They reap the advantages of our domination without being grateful for it. Algeria contains two neighbouring but separate populations; they no longer quarrel, and apparently bear with each other, but at heart they are mortal enemies, and in all probability will never blend. This is a serious situation, which renders our authority precarious and gives to prudent and far-seeing minds much food for reflection.

Was it thus in the time of the Romans? Did they know how to obtain the confidence and affection of the conquered peoples? How deeply did their civilisation affect the natives?* Finally, were those who permitted themselves to be won over more or less numerous than those who resisted? This is the question that in concluding these studies I shall endeavour to answer.

* I should state that I give to the word *indigènes*, natives, a somewhat broader meaning than is usually assigned to it. Properly speaking, it should be applied only to the ancient inhabitants of the country, to those who were called Libyans, Moors, Gætuli, etc. I add to them those of the Punic race who, in time, became mingled with them. The Romans made no distinction between them, although they well knew that they were not of the same race, and they coined a word to designate the fusion. Titus Livius tells us that they were called *Libyphœnices* (xxv., 40). The natives of whom I am about to speak are the Libyphœnicians.

I

This, unfortunately, is a very obscure question. The ancients were not great makers of statistics, as we are to-day. At that time no one seems to have taken the trouble to compute, even approximately, the number of the inhabitants of the country who had settled in the cities, who had acquired the customs of the Romans, and who spoke their language, or to ascertain whether it was greater than that of those who had remained faithful to their early manner of living and to their ancient dialects. But even supposing that the Romans did know, which is very doubtful, they were not in the least concerned about our knowing; so that if we wish to make up for this omission, and find some trace of the statistics which they neglected to leave, the documents are altogether wanting.

The inscriptions are almost our only source of information, but it is true that they exist in large numbers. Léon Renier, the first to think of collecting them, has gathered together almost five thousand. The eighth volume of the *Corpus*, which is the work of Willmans, contains ten thousand, and scarcely was this published before he had to set about preparing a supplement. Tunis had just been occupied, and new inscriptions were continually being found. This supplement, which was complied by Messieurs Schmidt and Cagnat, doubled the number of inscriptions that we already knew, and it is probable that soon also it will need to be supplemented.

It is there that we must seek for what, in our day, we should find in official records and in newspapers. The antique inscriptions take the place of both for us; not that the Romans were wholly ignorant of journalism, but they did not realise its power, and made use of it only incidentally. They entrusted to inscriptions all which they did not wish lost: laws, regulations, official decisions, the testimony of their devotion to the gods, of their respect for the prince, and of their affection for their relatives. Carefully studied and interpreted with wisdom and discretion, they will give us a fund of information concerning which history is silent.

Let us try to discover what they tell concerning the question at issue.

The Index to the eighth volume of the *Corpus* begins by taking up the series of proper names that are found in the volume.* As these names figure in Latin inscriptions, we may be sure that in some way the individuals themselves were connected with Roman life. There are almost ten thousand of them, and out of this number there are scarcely two hundred, of which, at first glance, it can be affirmed with any certainty that they belong to natives. The others have all the signs by which a Roman citizen is usually recognised, and many among them even seem to be connected with the most influential houses of Rome. We shall see farther on that this appearance is often deceptive, and that there were

---

* Mention is made here only of the volume published by Willmans. The Index of the supplement has not yet appeared.

many of these so-called Romans whose origin was very different. It is none the less true that in examining the lists of the *Corpus* for the first time, the student almost always believes that he is in the presence of those who came directly from Italy, and who became the founders of families. Let us note that if this were so, the Roman conquest would strangely resemble ours. In both cases, a race of foreigners would have come to invade and govern the country, and the decurions of the cities, as well as the farmers of the surrounding country, whose names are given in the inscriptions, would all belong to the victorious race, as to-day all of our counsellors-general, mayors, and magistrates are French by birth, or are at least Europeans who have become French.

This conclusion, after all, is not surprising. We are told that the Romans were in the habit of settling in large numbers in the countries they had conquered, *Ubicumque vicit Romanus habitat.** These rugged peasants did not despise commerce as much as they pretended; at first, they had been kept from it only through fear of the chances they had to run. As they were as cautious as they were keen, they feared to risk losing, all at once, what they had gained with so much trouble.† But when their conquests had opened to them a vaster and a surer field, they became more confident and set to work to exploit the world as vigorously as they had conquered it. Traf-

---

* Seneca, *Cons. ad Helv.*, 7.

† See the beginning of the *De re rustica* of Cato.

fickers of every kind followed the armies in order to dispose of their merchandise to advantage.* Great banking companies were also formed, which strove to profit from the resources of the country or to take advantage of its misery by loans at a high rate of interest. These banking houses had, ostensibly, for directors Roman knights, but it is well known that the funds were furnished by personages of high rank, who shared the profits. The Roman banker and the Roman merchant penetrated everywhere. "Gaul," said Cicero, "is full of them; nothing is carried on without them." † There were so many in Asia, and they became so odious, that one fine day, at the instigation of Mithridates, they were all massacred; eighty thousand of them are said to have been killed.

Africa, probably, was not treated differently from the rest of the world. Sallust tells us that from the time of Jugurtha there was at Cirta, the capital of Numidia, a large number of those who wore the toga, *multitudo togatorum*. ‡

The day following the victory of the two Scipios, the toga was a sort of safeguard which hid their questionable transactions. We know also that at Vaga and at Thysdrus many Italians were found

---

* It was sometimes the soldiers themselves who undertook traffic. Titus Livius relates (v., 8) that a city of which the Romans had just taken possession, was recaptured by the Volsci while the garrison was dispersed throughout the environs for the purpose of trading.

† *Pro Fonteio*, 4: "referta Gallia negotiatorum est, plena civium romanorum; nemo Gallorum sine cive romano negotium gerit."

‡ Sallust, *Jug.*, 21.

who were in the grain trade.* If they settled there from the first, when there was some peril in carrying on the business, it is natural that they should have come in great numbers after the conquest was complete. Later still, in the time of the Empire, they were attracted thither either by the colonies which were founded almost everywhere, by the administration of the imperial estates, by the service of the *Annone*, or, finally, by the hope of enriching themselves in a country whose marvellous fertility was boasted of. Thus until the time of the invasion of the barbarians there must have been a continual stream of Roman immigrants pouring into Africa.

Can the number of those immigrants be computed in any way? Monsieur Masqueray has endeavoured to do so, and this is how he reasons:

" Since 1830, in spite of the uncertainty of our first settlement, 195,000 French and 182,000 Italians or Spaniards, in all, 377,000 Europeans, have settled in Algeria,† and we may suppose that if our domination continues to strengthen in fifty years, this number will have doubled. But for seven centuries the Romans possessed not only Algeria, but Morocco, Tunis, and the Tripolitana Provincia. It is therefore surely keeping within actual facts to estimate that during that period, without taking into account three of the centuries (the first two

---

* Cæsar, *De bello Afric.*, 37. See also Sallust, *Jug.*, 26, 47.

† The work of Monsieur Masqueray, from which this paragraph is quoted, appeared in 1886. Since then these figures have increased. The census of 1891 gives the following figures: *267,672 French by origin; 215,793 foreigners. Total, 483,465 Europeans.*

The Conquest of the Natives 297

and the last), four million men settled in Northern Africa."

Who, at first glance, does not see that everything in this calculation is hypothetical? It rests on analogies between the present and the past which are taken for granted without having been proved. Are we sure that the condition of the Roman Republic after the conquest of Africa was enough like our own to enable us to draw such a conclusion? And, further, are we justified in believing that the tide of emigration continued without intermission? Circumstances do not seem always to have been equally favourable to it. From the commencement of the Empire, we are told that Italy was depopulated, that the country was becoming deserted, and that the cities were too large for their inhabitants. Is it likely that at that time there set out yearly for Carthage, from the ports of Puzzuoli or Ostia, as many merchants and agriculturists as when the cities and the country were overflowing with people? Moreover, must not Africa have lost much of its attraction as soon as the best localities had been appropriated?

What seems to me the most reasonable explanation is that the number of Romans who settled in Africa was considerable; as to fixing upon the exact figures, I do not believe it possible. We do not, and in all probability never shall, know them.

II

But if the Romans settled in large numbers in the countries they had conquered, it was not their custom to exterminate or even to expel the ancient inhabitants. We do not find that they acted differently from the Anglo-Saxons in America, who simply superseded the natives, and founded States where there was room for them alone. The Romans felt sure of being able to conquer the world, but knew that they were not numerous enough to occupy it. Therefore they always sought to come to an understanding with the people of the country. We have seen that they did not destroy existing institutions, when they were compatible with their own safety; they preserved ancient municipalities and utilised them in order to complete their conquest; they left the authority in the hands of the influential men of the country who offered them guarantees. In this way the vanquished were in time and by degrees initiated into Roman methods of life. When the proper time seemed to have come, the Romans first conferred on them the so-called law of civil right and then the full right of citizenship. Even when political necessity demanded harsher measures, and a colony was sent into a conquered city, Rome did not wholly dispossess the inhabitants; it took from them only a part of their goods, and as the right of war allowed the conqueror to take all—which other nations were in the habit of doing—those who were but half despoiled, instead of complaining of Rome's rapacity, were clearly obliged to be pleased with her moderation. Therefore they very soon forgot their wrongs; when the wound was closed, the old inhabitants and the new began to grow accustomed to living together, and finally amalgamated. This is what happened in Spain, and in Gaul, where the fusion of the races was speedily effected. After a century or two, everyone there was Roman, and it would have been difficult to distinguish those who in reality had come from Rome from those who were descended from the Iberians or the Celts.

Why was the result which was brought about in those two countries not accomplished also in Africa? Had Rome any reason for not following her usual policy? or must we believe that the enemies there encountered were such that it was absolutely impossible to come into accord with them? Usually, the violent antipathies which prevent nations from coming to terms arise either from a spirit of national obstinacy or from the conflict between incompatible religions. But it is easy to see that nothing of this kind existed between the Africans and Rome.

In the first place, it would be wholly wrong to represent the wars of Africa as the struggle of two hostile nationalities; properly speaking, there was no African nationality. Reunited for a time under Masinissa and the princes of his family, the natives soon returned to their usual isolation. They were so little accustomed to agreeing with one another that ancient writers do not seem to have perceived that they belonged to the same race; Pliny's idea of them was that of a collection of small tribes, with nothing in common except mutual hatred,* and St. Augustine seemed greatly surprised when he perceived that they all used a common language.† The fact is, that merely to have the same origin and to speak the same language is not sufficient to constitute a nation; it is also necessary to have lived the same life for a long time, to have stood shoulder to shoulder in prosperity as well as in adversity, to possess, in common, memories of defeat and of success, and all these conditions are found less often than might be supposed.

It is pointed out that the Romans rarely had to fight against compact and united nations. Almost everywhere they profited by local quarrels; and " fraternal hatreds," which are the most violent of all, rendered conquest easier for them. When Cæsar, in his pursuit of the Helvetians, penetrated into the country lying between the Rhone and the Rhine, he found Gauls there, but no Gaul. The various tribes were in the habit of waging desperate war against one another, and of calling the stranger to their aid. Later, when Rome had imposed peace upon them, and when the sixty Celtic cities had grown accustomed to be united around the altar of Augustus at Lyons, they began to be conscious of their common origin. Mommsen is right, therefore, in stating that Rome did not destroy the Gallic nationality, as is sometimes claimed, but, on the contrary, created it.

* *Hist. Nat.*, v., 17 *et seq.* † *De Civ. Dei*, xvi., 7.

The Conquest of the Natives

In Africa, as in Gaul, Rome met with no united resistance. There also the tribes were conquered one by one, and some with the help of others. Victory was difficult to win and pacification but slowly accomplished, for the people were brave and naturally intractable. But it cannot be said that Rome encountered one of those national hatreds which are the soul of great resistances, and over which it is difficult to triumph. The struggle finished and the first prejudices overcome, there remained no serious antagonism between the conquerors and the conquered.

Could the obstacle have been religion? This is so often the cause of division; and this is what to-day makes the natives our mortal enemies. At the present time, they are no more united as a nation than formerly, but it is their religion which commands them to hate us. This creates a deep gulf between them and us; this forms a bond of union between them, in spite of their natural love of living apart; this makes them suspicious of the kindnesses that we bestow on them, and causes them to give ear to those who strive to incite them against us. The war they have waged against us for fifty years is not a national war; it is a religious war. Nothing like it took place in the time of the Romans. The natives had a religion that we know very little about, and of which only one thing can be said, namely, that from the manner in which it accommodated itself to other religions, it did not differ greatly from them. The ancient religions, with their absence of prescribed dogmas, and their unlimited number of gods, were always undefined in outline and of uncertain limits, which allowed them to overlap one another, and often to intermingle. When chance brought them together, they were tempted to find out in what they resembled one another rather than in what they differed, and this is exactly contrary to what happens to-day. Their first idea was not to anathematise and contend against one another; they sought instead to find some means of mutual support and agreement. Thus, the Berber gods seem to have lived on good terms with those of Carthage. It is probable that they sometimes became identified with one another, and that their worship, which must have been very simple, appropriated to itself some of the practices of the Punic religion.* It was still easier for them to avoid conflict with the Romans on religious grounds. It was the policy of Rome to respect the religion of conquered peoples. This was not a difficult matter, however, as the Romans regarded all religions as local and looked upon the god connected with a particular country as its guardian. Consequently they had no scruples in placing themselves under its protection, when they lived in that country, or even when merely travelling through it. In Africa,

* It was in this way that the natives adopted the use of the votive *steles*, so numerous at Carthage. In the Museum of Algiers may be seen the *stele* which was found at Abizar, in Kabylia. It bears a Berber inscription, and is a very curious specimen of native art. If the rough drawing of the figure belongs properly to the Berbers, the form of the *stele* was borrowed from the Carthaginians.

they invoked the god **Bacax**, in his grotto, and Baldir, Ieru, and Motman, praying to them as earnestly as if they had never known any others. It happened still more frequently that, for fear of omitting any, they invoked all of them at once, under the name of Moorish gods (*Dii Mauri* or *Maurici*); they called them protecting gods, saviour gods, and besought them to watch over the safety of the Emperor or the success of the Roman armies. It is rather amusing to read of a governor of the province, who has subdued a rebellious tribe, and made a rich raid on the country, giving thanks to the Moorish gods, that is, the very gods of the people just conquered.*

In return for this zeal, and in order not to be surpassed in good-will, these gods consented, without much persuasion, to become reconciled to the Greek and the Roman gods, and to be identified with them. Tanit continued to be the great deity of New Carthage, as she had been of the ancient; she merely changed her name, which was too Phœnician, and which would have seemed barbarous. She was called " the celestial goddess," and was identified with Juno, Venus, or Minerva. From the moment that she belonged to the group of Olympian deities, it was natural that she should be honoured like the others. They went further; and, since Rome was the natural meeting-place of all gods, as it was of all men,† the *Dea Cælestis* was transferred thither;

---

* Ephem. Epigraphica, vii., 165. " Dis patriis et Mauris conservatoribus præses provinciæ ob prostratam gentem Bavarum prædasque abductas."   † " Dignus Roma locus quo deus omnis eat."

she was placed in the Capitol, and at the risk of exciting the jealousy of Jupiter, they dared to call her " the most illustrious deity of the Tarpeian Rock," *præstantissimo numini montis Tarpeii.**

As to Baal Hammon, the ancient associate of Tanit, there was thought to be some resemblance between him and Saturn, and he received that name; furthermore, in order to be more thoroughly in harmony with the new times, the imperial title was also added, and he was termed *Saturnus Augustus*. Tertullian tells us that he was the most important deity of Africa. It is very evident that his worship enjoyed immense popularity there. Sometimes temples were built and statues raised to him in order that he might be honoured as were the other gods of Greece or of Rome, among whom he was placed; sometimes the ancient form of his sanctuaries was preserved, like those found among all the Semites, vast enclosures open to the sky, with *steles* set up in the ground, or affixed to the walls. The most interesting of these sanctuaries is the one that Monsieur Toutain has discovered and excavated, on the summit of the mountain with the two horns (Jebel Bu-Korneïn), near Tunis. It was one of the " high places " referred to in the Scriptures, on which the neighbouring peoples of the Israelites rendered homage to their gods. From this height one gazes upon an expanse of almost fifty kilometres.

" That country, which was crossed by the two most

* *Notizie delli scavi*, 1892, p. 407.

important watercourses of Tunis, was, in antiquity, covered with flourishing cities like Carthage, Utica, Maxula, Carpis, and Misua, which were on or near the seashore ; and, in the interior, *Thuburbum* (*minus*) (or Teburba), Giufi, *Uthina* (Udena), and many other more modest settlements, the names of which we learn from epigraphy and itineraries. When the priest of Saturn immolated on the altar the victims preferred by the god, a bull and a ram, he could distinguish from the summit of the mountain all these towns lying in the plain or clinging to the sides of the hills." *

The base of the altar, which occupied an area of twenty square metres, has been discovered, besides the remains of almost six hundred *steles*, all belonging to the second century of the Empire, and bearing inscriptions or symbols. Thus Rome did not make war on the ancient religions of the country. On the contrary, under her domination they were as flourishing as ever; and were even developed and propagated. Thanks to her victories, and to the extent of her conquests, the ancient deities of Carthage penetrated into countries where they had previously been unknown. " Rome," says Monsieur Berger, " extended the Punic religion into Africa, as it contributed to the diffusion of Christianity throughout the whole world." † The ancient

---

* "Le Sanctuaire de Saturnus Balcaranensis," by Monsieur Toutain, in the tenth volume of the *Mélanges d'Archéologie et d'Histoire* in the French School at Rome.

† *Le Sanctuaire de Saturne,* at Aïn-Tounga, by Messieurs Ph. Berger and Cagnat.

inhabitants had, therefore, no cause for complaint in this respect; in the inscriptions which cover the *steles* of Saturn, Roman names abound by the side of Punic and Berber. All, both conquerors and conquered, united in the same worship; they frequented the same temples, and together climbed the crags of Bu-Kourneïn to sacrifice to the same gods. So it came about that religion, which separates us so completely from the natives, was at that time a further bond of union with the Romans. It was a bit of good fortune which we may well envy.

III

Thus there was nothing between the Romans and the natives that would necessarily make irreconcilable enemies of them. But is it true that they became reconciled? We must turn to the inscriptions for information.

In Africa, as elsewhere, the most ancient inscriptions are the most scarce. It is not surprising that we have very few dating back to the early times of Roman occupation. Under the Empire they become numerous, and light begins to dawn. One inscription has been found among the ruins of the town of Masculula, near Kêf, which probably dates back to the time of the death and the apotheosis of Augustus. It says in it that the Romans and the Numidians together raised a monument to the new god.* Thus, in the fourteenth year of our era, so

* C. I. L., 15,775.

near the final struggles, in a city near Carthage, Romans and Numidians joined together to honour the memory of the Emperor. It must, however, be noticed that at that time the union of the two different elements was not yet complete. They acted together for a common purpose, but they were distinct from one another; they were always Romans and Numidians. A few years later this distinction had ceased; apparently, at least, they were all Romans.

Does this mean that the native element had disappeared? How could this be? There were cities in Africa before the invasion of the Romans, and some of them were very important. The surrounding country must have been peopled and cultivated, as it already produced corn in abundance,* and merchants came thither from afar to trade in cereals. At what time could the country and the cities have been depopulated? Is it possible that at any time they all could have been exterminated or sent back to the desert, without some remembrance of such an act having been preserved? † We cannot believe this. They must have remained, and there is no doubt that, in spite of the influx of strangers, they always formed the main part of the population of Africa.

But if they continued to live there, it might be

* Carthage and Numidia furnished Rome with corn in the time of Antiochus. Masinissa, on his own account, gave fifty thousand bushels of wheat and three hundred thousand of barley (Titus Livius, xxxvi., 4).

† After violent wars, some tribes were transported in a mass far from their country, but these were the exceptions.

said, and with truth, that they tried to conceal and disguise their identity. At first glance, the traces of them which remain seem very few. We must remember that in the Index of the eighth volume of the *Corpus*, we observed almost ten thousand Roman names, and, at the most, two hundred names of natives. At first such a difference seems inexplicable. I think, however, that in looking a little closer at the list we shall not have much trouble in accounting for it. A great number of the names denote Romans by birth,—those who came from Italy, or their fathers, in order to settle in Africa. But are we certain that they all had the same origin? Very many, I think, did not come from such a distance, and it is not difficult to prove this. I find, for instance, among the ruins of the city of *Thubursicum Numidarum* * the tomb of a man named Q. Postumius Celsus.† There, apparently, is a true Roman. He is designated by the *tria nomina* (prænomen, nomen, cognomen), which, Juvenal tells us, fill with pride the one who has the right to bear them; and all three are borrowed from the best Latinity. But let us continue: in order

---

* To-day this city is Khamisa, a little village above Souk-Arrhas, between the Mejerda and the Seybouse. Some beautiful ruins are there,—a theatre, a forum, and a basilica. As its name indicates, the city was probably founded and certainly inhabited by Numidians, that is to say, by natives. The numerous inscriptions that have been found are very interesting to study; they show that the Numidians assumed Roman names in place of their Berber names, and bring, so to speak, before our eyes the steps by which a native city became a Roman city.

† C. I. L., 5076.

that we may thoroughly understand the civil state of Postumius, we are told that he is the son of Iudchad (*Iudchadis filius*) that is to say, the son of a native. In this way the information is given; under a Roman name is hidden an African origin. It is the same with a certain Q. Celius Secundus, of the same city,* and with C. Julius, whose tomb has been discovered near Thagaste.† We are not told the names of the fathers, but by the side of the Latin epitaphs are Libyan inscriptions; this was evidently done to show to what race they belonged. These examples, which could be greatly multiplied, prove that we must not believe that all those who bear Roman names came directly from an Italian port. A very great number of them were originally from Africa, Carthaginians or Numidians by birth, and we may be sure that the names of which they boast were not those of their fathers.

Can we learn the reason for their having given up their ancient names? Nothing is easier so far as most of them are concerned. They must have received from Rome the right of citizenship, and, in changing their condition, they changed their name; this was their privilege, and even their duty. But we may be sure that many did so without having any right. They anticipated the favour that Rome must one day or another accord them, and did not wait to become citizens *optimo jure*, before renouncing their ancient names. This is what happened throughout almost the whole of the Empire; and

* C. I. L., 4936. † *Ibid.*, 5209.

the abuse became so frequent that Claudius thought an edict should be issued in order to prevent it.*

In Africa, the appropriation of Roman names must have begun very early. In the year of Rome 742, ten years before our era, a little town, called Gurza, of which some ruins still remain in the environs of Sousse, decided to choose an influential Roman for protector, or patron, as such an official was called. A decree was drawn up in Latin, and signed by the magistrates. But the Latin was very indifferent, and the names of the magistrates were Ammichar, son of Milchaton; Boncar, son of Azrubal; and Muthunbal, son of Sapho †; these were Carthaginians. Seventy-five years later, the city again felt the need of a patron, and drew up a new decree, in order to make the fact known; but this time the Latin was irreproachable, and the names of the delegates charged with carrying the decree to Rome were Herennius Maximus, son of Rusticus, and Sempronius Quartus, son of Iafis. Thus, in less than eighty years, the city had assumed another aspect, and the manifest sign of it was the fact that the important citizens were in haste to renounce their names. ‡

---

* Suetonius, *Claud.*, 25 : " Peregrinæ conditionis homines vetuit usurpare romana nomina, dumtaxat gentilicis."

† C. I. L., 68.

‡ *Ibid.*, 69. As a matter of fact, Mommsen supposes that the inhabitants of Gurza had, in the meantime, become entitled to the right of Latin citizenship, which permitted their magistrates to assume Roman names. But in any case it is not uncommon to see families in which the sons, for some reason unknown to us, resumed the Berber names which their fathers had given up. This proves that the

This change, especially when it was not compulsory, or even when it was forbidden, shows a great eagerness on the part of the Africans to welcome the Roman domination. A man assumed a Roman name, as he wore a toga, from vanity, ambition, or flattery, because he wished to be thought one of the conquerors, or because he hoped to please them. Bold men did this resolutely, all at once; others attained the same result by degrees in order to be careful of public opinion. I ask permission to give another example from the collection of inscriptions; these little details are of singular use in throwing light upon history. In studying the ruins of Scillium, in Byzacium, Monsieur Cagnat came upon a series of funeral *steles* on which are roughly cut figures. As they resemble one another, he judged that they must have belonged to the same family.* These are natives, who, for some time, seem to have resisted the temptation to become Romans, but finally yielded. A certain Masac had two sons; one, named Masul, married one of his fellow-countrywomen and remained faithful to the traditions of his fathers; the other took the name of Saturninus. It was a preliminary step which was not binding. This surname, borrowed from the greatest god of Africa, must have been very common, and was apparently unpretentious. But Saturninus married Flavia Fortunata, who was evidently a Roman, and their son,

---

fathers had resigned them without any right; for if the fathers had been Roman citizens, the sons also would have been.

* C. I. L., 11,308 *et seq.*

who perhaps acquired the right of citizenship, effaced the last trace of foreign extraction by boldly calling himself Flavius Fortunatus.* That is how a family became wholly Roman in three generations. This evolution usually took place when the natives were wealthy, and when, with riches, came the desire to mingle in the best society of their country. It is known that fashionable people scorned those named Miggin and Namphamo, and it was necessary to ape the Romans in order to please. Fashion was so imperious that one dared not act contrary to it even when it might have been of advantage to do so. We read that a great lady, who was very proud of being descended from the ancient kings of the country, and who styled herself " the foremost of Numidian women," nevertheless gave up the name of her ancestors, and called herself Plancina.†

The natives in quest of Roman names, when such were not imposed on them by circumstances, ‡ must occasionally have had some difficulty in choosing them. We remember how embarrassed the Jews were, at the close of the last century, when they re-

---

* Horace says that the children born of mixed marriages were called *hybridæ*, and that they were thought very little of in Roman society. They none the less founded Roman families.

† C. I. L., 16,159.

‡ As, for instance, when the new citizen out of gratitude took the name of the magistrate or the prince to whom he was indebted for his right of citizenship. It has been pointed out that although this right was given especially to the Africans under the Empire, the names of the Emperors, with the exception of that of Julius, are no more numerous than other names in the list of the *Corpus*.

ceived from us the civil state, and, in a few weeks, were obliged to provide themselves with family names. In Africa the difficulty was overcome in various ways. Some called themselves Maurus, Gætulus, Numida, which demanded no great effort of imagination. Others were satisfied with translating by a Latin approximation their Punic or Berber names. The more pretentious created high-sounding names for themselves, or borrowed them from the most illustrious houses of Rome. Nowhere else have there been found in the inscriptions so many *Julii, Cornelii, Æmilii, Claudii*, etc. It is not possible to imagine that they are all descendants or allies of these noble families. Is it probable that this great aristocracy, which was almost extinct in its native country, should have flourished so luxuriantly at such a distance from Rome? Strictly speaking, it may be supposed that some of them were clients or dependents of the illustrious houses, men who had received some favours from them, but how admit this about all? The simplest explanation is that, being obliged to provide themselves with a name, and free to choose what they wished, they decided upon the most celebrated. Apparently, they selected by preference those which had some connection with the history of their country. The Scipios, who had twice conquered Carthage, were well remembered in Africa, as was Julius Cæsar and the overwhelming victory of Thapsus; perhaps there is no other reason for our finding so many *Cornelii* and *Julii*. This is evidently the reason why the *Sittii* are so numerous in the environs of Constantine. Sittius was a bold partisan, to whom Cæsar, whom he had served well, gave up the government of Cirta and of some neighbouring cities. The reign of this adventurer soon came to an end, but his memory was more lasting, judging from the great number of *Sittii* whose tombs have been discovered. They cannot all have descended from a man who lived but a few years; it is more reasonable to suppose that his memory was cherished in the country he had governed, and that people were proud to call themselves after him. It may be thought that it was rather presumptious thus to assume such illustrious names; but the Africans, in this sort of thing, did not pride themselves on their modesty. An inscription tells us that two women of the country, mother and daughter, whose station in life was probably very humble,* wishing to honour their son and grandson, called him, without ceremony, Julius Cicero.

IV

What proves still better the extent to which Roman civilisation penetrated into Africa, is the fact that Latin was spoken almost everywhere. How could this have happened?[1]

* C. I. L., 9114. They were called Sissoi and Sabbattrai, two very barbaric names. It is possible that the young man may have been adopted by one bearing the two illustrious names given him. In this case it is on the father that the criticism of presumption should fall.

The beautiful sentence is often quoted in which St. Augustine gives us to understand that Rome, "the mistress city," took measures to impose on the world its language as well as its government.* This phrase, if taken literally, is not just. The Romans, who, as far as possible, permitted the vanquished to retain their laws, never forced them to renounce their national language. They demanded this only when they gave them the right of citizenship; and then it was necessary. It is said that the Emperor Claudius, a great observer of ancient maxims, crossed out from the number of citizens a judge who knew only Greek.

As a matter of fact, the people of the provinces did not always wait to be forced into speaking Latin before doing so; they often made use of the language of the Roman citizens long before becoming citizens themselves. It was in Latin, as has been seen above, that the inhabitants of Gurza, while still only a Punic city, asked Domitius Ahenobarbus to consent to be their patron. The Suffetes of Avitta, Thibica, Calama, and Curulis expressed themselves in the same language. At Leptis, a Semitic inscription has been found bearing a dedication to Augustus in beautiful Roman characters.

It is true, however, that, as yet, it is only a question of official records; the cities wished to flatter Rome by using Latin. It is very evident that it was not used so soon in private life and every-day re-

* "Opera data est ut imperiosa civitas non solum jugum verum linguam suam domitis gentibus per pacem societatis imponeret."

lations. It takes centuries for one language completely to supplant another. When the ancient tongue has no longer a place in literary circles and reunions of good society, it survives in intimate conversation and among the lower classes. Nevertheless the new always wins, and, thanks to the instinct of vanity which makes one willingly look above oneself, and follow the example of those who occupy the foremost rank, it finally prevails. In the time of Apuleius good Latin could not have been spoken at Madaura, since it was necessary for him to learn it anew upon going to Rome. Two centuries later, St. Augustine, who was practically a native of the same country, tells us that everyone about him spoke Latin, and that a child needed only to listen in order to learn it.*

It is probable that the triumph of Christianity greatly aided in the propagation of Latin. The Church of Africa must at first have been wholly Greek; with time it became more and more allied with that of Rome. Therefore it used the Latin language almost wholly. It was in Latin that the Scriptures were read; it was in Latin that preaching was usually done, and this fact must have caused the knowledge of it to penetrate to depths hitherto unreached. In Africa, as elsewhere, and perhaps more than anywhere else, religion flourished among the lower classes. The natives furnished numerous victims to the persecutions, the memory of whom was piously preserved by the faithful.

* *Conf.*, I, 14, 23.

The Conquest of the Natives 317

When men of the world, confirmed pagans, accustomed to the elegant deities of Greece, heard of the honours rendered to Miggin, at Baric, and to the arch-martyr Namphamo, they ridiculed those barbarous names: *Diis hominibusque odiosa nomina!* But the Christians, especially those of the popular classes, were very proud of their native saints, and of their importance, and placed them without hesitation by the side of Peter and Paul.* These poor people, accustomed to speak the Libyan or Punic patois in their homes, strove in the churches, which they assiduously attended, to understand and to speak the language of the wealthy. Everything reminded them of it. If they looked about them, they saw engraved above the gates, along the walls, and around the mosaics, prayers or maxims, in Latin, intended to strengthen the faithful in the struggles of life: *Exaudi, Deus, orationem meam; Spes in Deo semper; Si Deus pro nobis, quis contra nos?* But what especially aroused their deep interest was the preaching of the bishop. Listening to Cyprian or Augustine expounding the truths of the faith or dealing with one of the questions of the day in which everyone was deeply interested, those even to whom Latin was not familiar succeeded by means of close attention in following and guessing at the meaning; this was the more possible, as those great speakers knew how to adapt their words to the comprehension of the most humble. St. Augustine, thorough scholar and experienced teacher

* St. Augustine, *Epist.*, 16, 17.

that he was, voluntarily committed grammatical errors and used incorrect words in order to be understood by everyone. "I would rather," said he, "have scholars angry at me, than that my listeners should not comprehend." Thus the Church was for very many of the poor people what the school was for the middle classes.

It was in the last centuries of the Empire, at the time when Christianity was beginning to triumph, that Latin must have become the dominating language of Africa. Not only was it spoken in the towns, but there is no doubt that it was used in the country also, as some of the twenty thousand inscriptions which compose our epigraphical collections come from there. It is the epitaphs which convey this idea; they show us that all classes, even the lowest, such as tailors, butchers, shoemakers, freedmen, and slaves wished to have some Latin words engraved on their tombs.

Naturally, the Latin of the common people is often very bad. It abounds in errors, but this is not at all surprising. Scholars have attempted to draw from it, however, very extraordinary conclusions; it has seemed a proof of barbarism, and it has been claimed that a people who spoke such poor Latin could not have been deeply affected by Roman civilisation. But it is precisely the contrary which is true. If the inscriptions were faultlessly correct, it might be supposed that they had been composed by professed scholars, and that the lower classes understood only the idioms of the country. The improprieties of language, the faults of grammar, the solecisms, and the barbarisms that are found in almost every line, show that we are dealing with ignorant people, that they spoke bad Latin—but that, at least, they spoke it. It was therefore not simply a pedantic and a formal language which a few scholars employed from vanity; it was a language that was in common use, and like all living languages, it adapted itself to the people who employed it, and underwent changes according to their degree of culture.

Although, as a rule, the epitaphs consisted of ready-made formulas that could be copied almost without being comprehended, there were some in Africa that escaped this banality, and in which, now and then, one unexpectedly comes upon a sincere and personal note. It must be believed, therefore, that the Africans succeeded in mastering a language which, at first, was foreign to them, since they used it to express their deepest sentiments. A native whose child had died wrote on the little tomb which he erected over it these touching words, into which he put his whole soul: *Birsil, anima dulcis!* * Sometimes it was difficult to find terms which expressed all that was felt. Epithets accumulated in the attempt to eulogise a deceased wife or mother (*piissima, pudica, laboriosa, frugi, vigilans, sollicita*, etc.), or, when it was the question of a young girl, Nature's most smiling images were borrowed (*ut dulcis flos, ut rosa, ut narcissus*), with-

* C. I. L., 16,582.

out giving complete satisfaction. Very often prose did not suffice for the disconsolate souls; they were inspired by grief to write verse:

"Hos pater inscripsi versus dictante dolore." *

Grief, it must be admitted, too often dictated wretched verses, but their very faults have the advantage of proving to us that Latin was spoken by every class of African society.

These faults, for that matter, are exactly like those that, at the same period, were committed elsewhere. This is what the publication of the *Corpus* of Latin inscriptions has helped to verify. It shows that there is very little in the solecisms and the barbarisms of the Africans, that belonged properly to Africa; as a rule they are similar throughout the Empire. We have previously seen that all those who spoke good Latin spoke it in almost the same manner; the inscriptions show that there were no different ways of speaking it poorly either. To refer here to the most frequent errors of the Africans, we see that they were confused over the grammar: they confounded the conjugations,† they were unable to distinguish the tenses of the verbs, they were ignorant of what cases the prepositions governed ‡; but if we open the epigraphical collections

* *C. I. L.*, 1359.
† St. Augustine tells us that in order to conform to popular custom he writes *floriet* instead of *florebit*.
‡ *Ob meritis—pro salutem—a fundamenta—apud lare suo—cum conjugem*, etc.

of other countries, we shall see by them that the people of Spain and of Gaul were neither better nor more careful grammarians. In Africa, as elsewhere, the genders were constantly being confounded; very little distinction was made between the masculine and the feminine, and the neuter was almost suppressed.* I do not lay stress on the African habit of taking no account of final consonants, which must have been sounded but very slightly, even when pronounced. This suppression was very convenient for those who desired to write verses, as, for instance, it allowed a bereaved husband to inscribe on the tomb of his wife,

"Et linquit dulces natos et conjuge dignu," †

for *conjugem dignum*, which cannot end a hexameter. But the old Latins wrote in no other way, and the Latinised provinces followed their example. ‡ As was natural, these changes became, in time, more serious. Latin, as it spread, became corrupted; it was spoken more and more incorrectly in proportion as it was used by the poorer and more ignorant

---

* On the tomb of a man whom his friends wished to congratulate on his talent and his cleverness, are found these words: *Cui artificius et ingenius exsuperavit* (C. I. L., 15,597). In order not to be too greatly scandalised, let us remember that the Italians whom Petronius brings before us readily say, *Bonus vinus*.

† C. I. L., 9117.

‡ In this way an inhabitant of Pompeii, wishing to commit to the anger of Venus the man who had effaced what he had traced in charcoal on the wall, wrote these words: *Abia (habeat) Venere Pompeiana iradam.* . . .

people. Toward the close of the Empire, in a little town of Byzacium, in order to say of a Christian that he had lived forty years, five months, and seven hours, the following expression was used: *Bixit anos qaragita, meses ceqe, ora setima.** This, apparently, was the height of barbarism, and a mode of expression which breathed of the Libyan and the Numidian; and yet there were, at the same time, in the very capital of the Empire, people who wrote no better. The catacombs are filled with equally barbarous inscriptions, and there is scarcely a word used by the Christians of Byzacium that cannot also be found in them. In like manner other errors noticeable among the common people of Africa were to be found almost everywhere else.

V

Latin, however, was not the only language spoken in Africa; there were others which disputed the territory with it, and which it did not wholly succeed in vanquishing. In the first place, Punic survived the destruction of Carthage; the habit of using it continued in the countries in which the Carthaginians had spread it by means of their commerce. We know that at Œa (Tripoli) and at Leptis it held its own for a long time with Greek and Latin, which had, however, one the prestige of age, the other that of conquest. The historian of Septimius Severus tells us that it was the language that this Prince used with the greatest ease: *punica eloquentia*

* C. I. L., 12,200.

promptior, quippe genitus apud Leptim.* As long as Carthage was dominant, the Punic was spoken in Northern Africa; it was the fashionable language even at the court of Masinissa, the great enemy of Carthage. Naturally, after the victory of the Romans, it fell back a step. Distinguished people ceased, little by little, to use it, and it constantly receded before the Latin; but it never completely disappeared. In the final centuries of the Empire, it still existed as a patois, used by the lower classes. St. Augustine, wishing to appoint a bishop to Fussala, a small town near Hippo, took care to choose a scholar who understood Punic.† At Hippo, also, there were people who spoke it, but they were few in number, ‡ and those who used it in their familiar relations must have understood Latin, as the preaching was always in that language. About the same time, the Circumcellians, a sort of rude peasantry, who were in the habit of roaming among the mountains, overthrowing churches, murdering priests, and demanding, as a favour, that they themselves be put to death, could communicate with the Donatist priests, that is to say, with the moderate members of their party, only by means of an interpreter, *per punicum interpretem.* And yet they had taken

---

* *Vita Sev.*, 15.
† St. Augustine, *Epist.*, 209, 3.
‡ St. Augustine in one of his sermons, quoting a Carthaginian proverb, translates it into Latin, and adds: "Latine vobis dicam, quia punice non omnes nostis." Latin was therefore the language that was best understood and most generally spoken.

for their watchword two Latin words, *Deo laudes*, to which the Catholics replied by, *Deo gratias*. It is not without emotion that, in the environs of Thamugade, where frequent conflicts took place, the traveller finds engraved on capitals or shafts of columns, these ancient formulas which, in the midst of the silence and the peace in which the places are wrapped to-day, seem suddenly to reawaken the din of the battles of former times.

There was another language * which must also have been wide-spread, but which seems to have been used quietly, and almost in secret; this was the Libyan, or, as we say to-day, the Berber. It is very strange that while the writers of the time very frequently refer to the Punic, none of them mentions the Libyan. St. Augustine is the only writer who says a passing word about it, and he speaks of it only as a jargon used by barbarous nations. There is no reference made to it by other writers, so that we should be ignorant of its existence were it not for some inscriptions which are beginning to be collected and deciphered.

It was, however, the ancient language of the country; but even the land in which it was spoken does not seem ever to have treated it with great respect. For instance, it was not deemed worthy of

* I set aside Greek, which was largely spoken among the educated classes of Carthage and in the neighbouring country as far as Mauretania, where, during the reign of Juba II., it held sway at Cæsarea. It is probable that from the second century it lost the ground that Latin was daily beginning to gain. From the time of St. Augustine even scholars rarely heard it.

being used to preserve the important memorials of national life; the history of the Berbers was written successively in Punic by King Hiempsal, in Greek by King Juba, and in Arabic by Ibn Khaldoun, but never in Berber. When Masinissa wished to civilise his people, he forsook the language of his forefathers, which probably did not seem to him susceptible of being perfected, for that of the Carthaginians. His subjects must have followed his example without much opposition, as there remain in Numidia many traces of the Punic. The new language, however, did not abolish the old, for most of the Libyan inscriptions have been found in the environs of Cirta, in the very heart of the kingdom of Masinissa. They are especially numerous a few leagues from Hippo, in a fertile and well watered valley, intersected by groves of wild olive and cork trees, which was called the Cheffia. Here, are tombs of natives; one of them is that of an old soldier, who had received military decorations, such as necklaces and bracelets, and who, having obtained his discharge, returned to his fatherland to die.* Almost all desired to have engraved beneath the Latin epitaph a Libyan inscription. It seems to me that it is easy to explain what took place at that time by similar results in our day. After the time of Masinissa many Numidians spoke both Libyan and Punic, as their descendants use Arabic and Berber; then Latin gained the ascendancy, as has the French to-day, and it took the place of the

* C. I. L., 5209.

other two languages, without causing them to be wholly forgotten.

But besides the natives who inhabited the subjugated and pacified countries, and who had assimillated with the Romans, there were others who were more independent, and who, without wholly escaping from the authority of Rome, continued to live their own life, and probably used only their ancient language. They were called nations (*gentes*)—tribes, as we say to-day. Some occupied the steppes and the plateaus, situated in the centre of the civilised country, but the greater number encamped beyond the frontiers, in the heart of the desert. We have only very vague accounts as to the way in which they governed themselves. The inscriptions mention a chief, called *princeps gentis*, who was aided by a council of the most important men of the tribe.* We do not know in what way the chief and his assistants were elected, but we may be sure that Rome was not without interest in a choice that might entail serious consequences. In any case, she reserved to herself the right of investiture of the chief. To-day we give to the sheik the red bornous, which is the mark of his authority; the Romans added to the white cloak buskins with gold ornaments, a silver sceptre, and fillets which formed a sort of crown for the head.† This was the costume of a

---

* This council appears to have been composed of eleven members (*undecim primi*). It probably consisted of the *princeps* and ten well known men.

† See Procopius, *De Bello Pers.*, i., 25; Ammien Marcellin, xxix., 5.

king; therefore the chiefs of the *gentes* were often called *reges* or *reguli*. The great thing then, as now, was to canton these restless tribes, ever ready to make raids upon the fields of others, especially if they were fertile and well tilled. We find, therefore, that the Romans were greatly occupied in assigning to them fixed limits (*fines assignati genti Numidarum*) and in keeping them therein. In order to prevent their crossing the boundary of this territory and to force them to live quietly within it, there was appointed over them a representative of Roman authority, called *præfectus*, or *procurator Augusti ad curam gentium*. These officers seem to have been chosen with great care; usually they came from the army, where they had been prefects of cohorts or military tribunes. Sometimes they belonged to the civil government. It is not known exactly what their duties were, but for a long time they have been compared to our chiefs of Arabian bureaus.

It is evident that these independent tribes, especially when separated by the sands or the shotts of the Roman territories, must have remained faithful to their national customs; and yet civilisation seems to have affected them more than might be supposed. We have seen that the influence of the Roman frontier cities, Theveste, Thamugade, Auzia, etc., spread very far, and that some of the barbarians who went thither out of curiosity or interest must have carried home with them the idea of, and the desire, for another mode of living. Moreover, many of them served in the auxiliary troops, and saw different countries while following the legions. The Moors of Lucius Quietus took part, under Trajan, in the campaigns of the Danube, and entered Babylon with him. When they returned to their homes, after roving about the world, they were no longer the same, and must have communicated to others the ideas and the knowledge that they had acquired from their travels. In order to appreciate the changes which time brought even to the savage tribes of the Aurès and the Hodna, we have only to compare the two men who, at the beginning and at the close of the Empire, led against Rome most formidable insurrections—Tacfarinas and Firmus. The former, who held the legions of Tiberius in check for seven years, was an incomparable leader, intelligent enough, no doubt, to comprehend and imitate Roman tactics, but, in short, a true Berber, who relied only on his fellow-countrymen, and who possessed all the characteristics of his race, especially that invincible obstinacy which was the strength of Masinissa and Jugurtha. Firmus, on the other hand, was half Roman. When he revolted against Valentinian I., he was aided by the auxiliary cohorts, and assumed the purple, like a Cæsar. We know that one of his brothers built a magnificent villa, in which he lived like a Roman; another, Gildo, who fought under Count Theodosius, was thought civilised enough to be chosen governor of Africa by the Emperor.

What seems very strange, is the fact that this

movement, which appeared to incline the barbarous tribes toward Rome, was not wholly stopped by the invasion of the Vandals and the fall of the Roman Empire. At the extremity of the province of Oran, a curious inscription of the year 508 has been found. It is a monument erected in honour of Masuna, King of the Moorish tribes and of the Romans, with reference to the construction of a strong citadel which had been built by Masgivin, prefect of Safar (*præfectus de Safar*),* and completed by Maximus, procurator of *Altava* (Lamoricière). Thus there was, near the borders of Mauretania Cæsariensis, under the last Vandal rulers, an independent kingdom, in which Romans and Moors lived together under the same authority. The King was, in fact, a native, but it is evident that he had been influenced by Roman civilisation. The inscription was written in Latin, and dated in the era of the ancient province (*anno provinciæ*). The formulas employed by the King were those used for the Cæsars (*pro salute et incolumitate*); he styled himself King of the Moors and of the Romans, and had around him representatives of both races; his prefect, Masgivin, was certainly a Moor, and the name of his procurator, Maximus, shows that he must have been of Roman origin.

*C. I. L., 9835. Note the expression, *præfectus de Safar*, and its resemblance to the French phrase, *préfet de Safar*. À *propos* of Apuleius we have seen how many words and phrases, in this elegant Latin, announced the approach of the Romance languages. There are naturally many more of them in the inscriptions, and many terms like *isposa* (épouse), *ceque* (Italian *cinque*, cinq), *depost* (depuis), etc.

We cannot read this inscription without thinking of what was taking place in Gaul at the same time. Masuna reminds us of the Merovingian kings who strove to speak Latin, who preserved the imperial traditions as much as possible, and who admitted among their followers, side by side with their Frankish generals, bishops, and such of the great Roman nobles as still survived in the country.

VI

CONCLUSION

From what we have just learned, therefore, it is evident that the Romans succeeded better than we in the conquest of the natives. It was an easier task then than it is now, but one which, nevertheless, presented great difficulties. We have seen that the Romans proceeded without haste or violence, leaving, so to speak, the assimilation of the various races to take place of itself. There can be no doubt that in time this was accomplished, at least for a part of Africa. The proconsular province and almost the whole of Numidia were counted among the most civilised countries of the world. Mauretania alone was more barbarous, especially in the regions near the ocean. The towns, which had become very numerous and flourishing, and of which there remain such beautiful ruins, contained, no doubt, many Romans, but a still greater number of native Africans. These two elements were combined and almost blended in them. We are less well informed about the outlying districts; but the large number of Latin inscriptions which have been found, and which originated from people of every class, seems to prove conclusively that Latin was spoken then to a great extent, and it is probable that those who, in their private relations, used another language, understood that of the conquerors, and employed it at times. Finally we believe that we have settled the fact that even the independent tribes of the interior and of the border were not wholly opposed to Roman civilisation, and that, to a certain extent, they submitted to its ascendancy.

These results, that history and, especially, epigraphy aid in proving, or at least in surmising, lead us to believe that the domination of the Romans must have produced the same results in Northern Africa as in the western countries of Europe, and that toward the close of the Empire, the conditions there must have been similar to those in Spain and Gaul. This seems to be proved by Salvian and contemporary writers, who make no distinction between these different countries, but place them all in the same rank. If this were so, it would be natural to suppose that the fate of each would be similar, and that what took place in Europe might have occurred also in Africa. May we not believe, for instance, that had it not been for unfavourable circumstances Africa might have developed a distinctive civilisation of her own, which, while preserving its individual character, would have borne the impress of Rome and its genius, as was the case with Western nations? I imagine that in going thither, our soldiers might have found a people, doubtless very different from us, but marked by the special characteristics usually left by Romans as a heritage to the countries they governed, and with a language bearing some affinity to our own instead of being wholly strange; a people, in short, ready to resume their part in the common work of the Latin races, and with whom we should have been in sympathy. This, alas! is not what happened.

While almost the whole of Western Europe, Gaul and Spain especially, were forming a language born of the Latin, and which preserves its characteristics, the Latin was disappearing wholly from Africa. Furthermore, it was not replaced by the Punic, which we know held its ground until the end, but by the ancient language of the natives, which, while it had disappeared elsewhere, seemed there to revive and triumph. Doubtless the chances of invasion count for much, but it is also very certain that since the Libyan, or, as we say to-day, the Berber, has been preserved there, it either must have had firmer root in the soil, or it must have been more favoured by circumstances than the Iberian or the Celtic.

How has this come about? How does it happen that this language of the people, which seemed thoroughly despised, and to which no writer refers, has held its own better than others?

The reason usually given is, that the conquest of Africa by the Romans was never completed, and that there remained in the interior and on the borders, territories almost wholly independent, where the Berbers continued to live their national life. This was a menace to Roman domination. Agricola, wishing to convince his son-in-law, Tacitus, that it would be necessary to follow up the conquest of Britain by that of Ireland, told him that a people are never wholly subdued while surrounded by nations not yet subjugated, and that in order to make subjection endurable, it is necessary to remove from before their eyes the sight of liberty.* This precaution was not taken in Africa, and it can readily be seen that the proximity of and the association with independent nations may have preserved some remnant of national character among those who were no longer free. Evidently the persistence of the ancient language in certain regions in which it freely dominated might easily have maintained it elsewhere.

But this reason does not explain all. If these people preserved their customs and their language better than others, it is not owing solely to exterior circumstances, but also to the fact that they were more disposed in this direction by their temperament and nature. In studying their history, strange contradictions have been noticed which are difficult to explain. They were assuredly brave, energetic, and tenacious, loving their independence; and yet, after having valiantly defended it, they seem to have adjusted themselves very easily to foreign rule.

* Tacitus, *Agric.*, 24.

Masinissa, the implacable enemy of Carthage, endeavoured to spread among the Numidians the civilisation of the Carthaginians, and succeeded in doing so. Juba made a Greek town of his capital, Cæsarea. While the Romans were masters, a large part of the country became wholly Roman. But what is most extraordinary is that, notwithstanding all these transformations, the national spirit was preserved. This race, apparently so changeable, so easily moved, so readily impressed with all forms of civilisation with which it came into contact, is one that has best preserved its primitive character and its individual nature. We find the inhabitants of Northern Africa to-day such as the ancient writers described them to us; they live almost as in the time of Jugurtha; and not only have they remained fundamentally unchanged by all the foreign influences which apparently absorbed them, but they have at length submerged and covered over the latter like a wreck. I have often said to myself when present at a gathering of natives, at some mart or fête, that I had before my eyes a remnant of all those who, from the most remote ages, peopled Northern Africa. Evidently the Carthaginians did not disappear in a body after the fall of Carthage. The tide of Romans which for seven centuries flowed unceasingly into African ports, did not ebb at the irruption of the Vandals. We hear nothing of the departure of the latter, who came with their wives and children, to establish themselves firmly in the country. The Byzantines also must have left more than one of their soldiers in the fortresses which were built by Solomon from the ruins of ancient monuments. Of all those races, the Berbers alone remain. They have absorbed the others. I do not know whether anthropologists, in studying the colour of their skin or the conformation of their body, will ever distinguish traces of the various nationalities which have disappeared; but in their ideas, their habits, their beliefs, as well as in their manner of thinking and of living, there is no longer anything of the Punic, the Roman, or the Vandal—the Berber alone has survived.

Thus there was in this race a blending of contradictory characteristics which no other race has combined in the same degree: it seemed to surrender itself, yet did not wholly give itself up; it adjusted itself to the manner of living of others, but at heart preserved its own; in a word, it was but little resistant, yet very persistent.

It belongs to those who see the natives from a nearer standpoint to judge whether they have retained or lost these characteristics. In either case, it is well to know that they once possessed them; it is information which I think we can turn to account. When, in our relations with them, we are tempted to be discouraged, let us remember that they have not always rebelled against the foreigner, that they did come into accord with their former enemies, that they did accept without repugnance their customs, their language, and their laws; but let us not forget either, in order to be on our guard, that in the end their nature conquered, that it freed itself from all these foreign acquisitions, and that it has remained permanent master of them. We have in this, both a cause for hope and a cause for fear; facilities of which we can make use, and an obstacle which we must strive to overcome.

This information has its value. In order to know what a people can become, it is first necessary to know what they have been. This is the service that history renders, and this will justify me, I hope, for having so long detained the reader in the study of Roman Africa.

TRANSLATOR'S NOTE TO CHAPTER VII

1. For interesting account of the sources and formation of the Latin, see essay in *History of Roman Literature*, edited by Rev. Henry Thompson, M.A.; *History of Roman Literature*, ch. i., by Charles T. Cruttwell; also *Encyclopædia Metropolitana*, and *History of Rome* by Mommsen.

INDEX

A

Abd-el-Kader, 24, 135
Ad Casas, 162
Ad Majores, 99
Ad Speculum, 99
Ad Turres, 99
Æmilii, 313
Æneas, 60, 61, 65, 69-72
Æneid, the, 59, 61, 68
Æschylus, 62
Æsculapius, temple of, 82, 126, 255
Africa, 1-5, 7, 8, 11, 13, 14, 20-24, 28, 34, 35, 40, 45, 46, 48, 52, 61, 64, 65, 73, 92, 93, 95-97, 100-106, 108, 109, 111-114, 116, 118, 119, 135, 136, 138, 139, 142, 143, 145, 147, 148, 151-153, 160, 162-167, 170, 171, 174, 175, 178-180, 185, 188, 192-194, 196, 197, 199, 208, 209, 214, 215, 220, 223-225, 228, 231, 233, 237, 242, 249, 251, 261, 263, 265, 266, 269, 271, 273, 276, 277, 279, 285-290, 295-297, 299, 301, 302, 304-311, 313, 314, 316, 318, 320-323, 328, 330-334, 336
African, 11, 21, 33, 51, 102, 114, 116, 138, 146, 150, 154, 156, 157, 160, 161, 164, 167, 188, 194, 206, 208, 213, 224, 238, 240, 243, 244, 246, 257, 261, 263, 264, 269-276, 285, 286, 299, 309, 311, 314, 319-321, 330, 334
Agricola, 333
Ahmed Bey, 19, 48
Ain-Drin, 126
Ain Tunga, 194
Alexandria, 35
Alexandrian, 62, 69
Algeria, 5, 6, 9, 28, 33, 95, 96, 101, 109, 136, 142, 160, 220, 291, 296
Algiers, 32, 33, 95, 104
Altava, 329
Amphitruo, the, 225
Ampsaga, 14, 104
Annona Sancta, 165, 296
Antioch, 35
Apollinaris, Sulpicius, 243
Apollo, Promontory of, 49
Apollonius Rhodius, 62, 63
Appian, 73, 76, 81, 94
Apuleius, 223, 224, 244-247, 249-264, 266, 268-270, 316
Arab, 1, 5, 9, 15, 31, 53, 55, 111, 112, 116, 145, 147, 153, 156, 168, 227
Arabia, 28
Arabic, 6, 325, 327
Argonautica, the, 62, 63
Ariadne compared with Dido, 66
Aristophanes, 62
Armenian, 3, 44
Arnobius, 224, 269
Aryan, 7, 8

Assyria, 42
Athens, 49, 241, 246–248, 250
Atlas mountains, 34
Audus, 7
Augustine, St., 238, 249, 255, 269, 271, 274, 300, 315–317, 323, 324
Augustus, Emperor, 35, 116–118, 132, 161, 163, 300, 306
Aumale, 138, 231
Aurelius, Marcus, 119, 243
Aurès, 7, 14, 99, 100, 118, 195, 196, 198, 230, 235, 328
Aurosius, 7
Auzia, 138, 231, 327
Avitta, 315
Avitus, St., 281

B

Baal-Hammon, 57, 304
Babor, 137
Bacax, 303
Bagradas, 50, 151, 180
Balbus, Cornelius, 97
Balearic, 11
Baric, 317
Batna, 196, 229
Baths, Roman, 168
Begua, 162
Beja, 22
Beled-al-Jerid, 7
Benzerta, 144
Berber, 9, 10, 12–16, 19, 20, 27, 34, 40, 147, 148, 154, 245, 302, 306, 313, 324, 325, 328, 332, 333, 335
Beulé, description by, 49, 51
Biskra, 99
Bithecusæ, 92
Bizerta, 144
Blidah, 96
Bougie, 138
Britain, 333
Bugeaud, General, 96, 135
Bûjaya, 138
Burgi, 110
Byrsa, the, 48, 49, 51, 55, 56, 59, 60, 81, 82, 255

Byzacium, 142, 148, 158, 212, 263, 272, 311, 322
Byzantine, 112, 195, 226, 227, 237
Byzantines, 334

C

Cæsarea, 30, 31, 33, 34, 104, 138, 334
Calama, 22, 152, 213, 232, 239, 244, 315
Calceus Herculis, 110
Caligula, 35, 97
Calypso compared with Dido, 70
Capsa, 26, 142
Carmen de Deo, 280
Carpis, 305
Cartagena, Cape, 51
Carthage, 3, 11, 12, 16, 18, 19, 46, 48–55, 57–61, 72, 73, 75, 77–83, 92, 94–96, 100, 103, 108, 112, 118, 137, 154, 180, 182, 187, 193, 228, 238, 239, 243, 246, 247, 249, 253, 255, 273, 275–277, 297, 302, 303, 305, 307, 313, 322, 323, 334
Carthaginian, 1, 8, 11, 12, 17, 18, 46, 47, 50, 55, 57, 60, 72, 79, 80, 82, 92, 94, 101, 156, 208, 244, 255, 309, 310, 322, 325, 334
Castella, 110
Cato, 67
Catullus, 63
Celtic, 300, 332
Celts, 299
Chaouia, 7
Chateaubriand describes the Byrsa, 49
Cheffia, 325
Chélia, 227
Chemtou, 138
Chiniava, 144
Christians, Tomb of the, 31
Cicero, 67, 295
Cidamus, 97

Index

Circe compared with Dido, 70
Circumcellions, 323
Cirta, 8, 11, 14, 16, 18, 30, 159, 202, 243, 244, 274, 295, 314, 325
City of God, the, 271
Claudii, 313
Cleopatra Selene, 29-31
Commagenian, 119
Confessions, the, 271
Constantine, 8, 14-16, 19, 25, 96, 167, 220, 232, 314
Cornelii, 68, 313
Cupid and Psyche, 256
Curulis, 315
Cyprian, St., 137, 185, 186, 227, 228, 269, 270, 317
Cyrenaica, 9, 113
Cyrene, 101

D

Dacian, 115
Delattre, Father, 54, 55
Dido, 61, 64-71
Diocletian, 118, 119
Donatist, 323
Dracontius, 277-282
Dugga, 194

E

Egypt, 7, 9, 30, 31, 42, 163, 164
Egyptian, 30, 33
El Afroun, 31
El Begar, 162
El Jemm, 143-192
El Kantara, 109
El Kram, 76, 79
El Mersa, 51
Epithalamium Thetidis, 63
Euripides, 62
Europe, 33, 331, 332
European, 294, 296

F

Fazzen, 97
Felicianus, 277
Ferikia, 19

Festus, Postumius, 244
Fezzan, 97
Firmus, 328
Florida, the, 251
Florus, Annæus, 244
Fondouks, 111
France, 96, 153
Fronto, Cornelius, 243, 244
Fussala, 323

G

Gabes, 142
Gades, 7
Gætuli, 2, 3, 97, 118, 147, 244
Gafsa, 26, 99, 142, 149
Gallic, 300
Garamantes, 97, 118
Garas, Mt., 98
Gargilius, 278
Gaul, 11, 45, 51, 136, 240, 242, 252, 271, 276, 295, 299-301, 321, 330-332
Gauls, 300
Gela, 11, 12
Gellius, Aulus, 243
Germania, 130
Geta, Hosidius, 98
Ghadames, 97
Ghamart, 51
— Cape, 51
Gibraltar, Straits of, 7
Gildo, 328
Giufi, 305
Golden Ass, the, 256
Goums, the, 116
Greece, 31, 33, 34, 45, 56, 58, 261, 263, 304, 317
Greek, 4, 19, 28, 29, 33, 41, 43, 51, 56, 62, 127, 193, 237, 239-241, 255-258, 261, 263, 264, 266, 269, 303, 315, 316, 322-334
Guelma, 22, 152, 213, 232
Gurza, 310, 315

H

Hadrian, 119, 151, 172, 181, 184, 186

Hadrumetum, 75
Haïdra, 158
Hannibal, 11, 51, 59, 94
Hanno, 57
Harbours of Carthage, 75
Hasdrubal, 12, 16, 57, 82, 83
Hebrew, 40
Henchir-Tina, 92
Hephæstus, 43
Heraclidæ, 4
Hercules, 3, 4, 110
— Straits of, 47
Hexameron, the, 281
Hiempsal II., 2-4, 6, 9, 325
Hippo, 244, 323, 325
— Zarytus, 144
Hodna, 99, 155, 328
Homer, 63, 70, 71
Homeric, 63, 69
Husch-el-Cheme, 26

I

Iberian, 299, 332
Icosium, 32
Ieru, 303
Ilerda, 272
Iol, 30
Italicus, Silius, 151
Italy, 45, 51, 95, 105, 163, 164, 188, 230, 252, 285, 294, 297, 308

J

Jason, 63
Jebel Armour, 60
Jebel Bou-Kurneïn, 304, 306
Juba I., 26
— II., 27-31, 33-35, 104, 325, 334
Jugurtha, 9, 20, 22, 24, 26, 27, 135, 242, 295, 328, 334
Julii, 313
Juno, 57
— Hill of, 56, 59
Jupiter, Fields of, 159
Jurjura, 7, 137, 154
Juvenal, 134, 165, 242, 308

K

Kabyle, 3, 5, 6, 9, 10, 147, 157, 235, 262
Kabylia, 6, 16, 137
Kafsa, 26
Kairwan, 142
Kanga, 100
Kasrun, 143
Kêf, 22, 306
Khaldoun, Ibn, 325
Khamisa, 245
Krenchela, 99, 131

L

Lactantius, 269
Lamartine describes Dido, 61
Lamasba, 155
Lambæsis, 99
Lambèse, 99, 108, 116, 118, 121, 125, 127-132, 134, 155, 167, 198, 199, 205, 213, 214
Lamoricière, 329
Lamta, 243
Latin, 49, 95, 240, 241, 248, 255, 257, 260, 261, 263-267, 269, 274, 275, 277, 285, 293, 309, 310, 313-325, 329-332
Latium, 60
Latro, Porcius, 242
Leptis, 243, 315, 322
Libya, 28, 41, 50
Libyan, 2, 3, 8, 161, 263, 265, 309, 317, 322, 324, 325, 332
Liternum, 170
Louis, St., 48, 54, 55
— — Chapel of, 82
Lyons, 118, 300

M

Mactaris, 158
Madaura, 238, 244, 246, 255, 257, 263, 316
Magalia, the, 51
Mahadda, 27
Malagbal, 110

Index

Malga, 187
Mapalia, 156
Mascula, 99, 131, 167, 198
Masculula, 306
Masinissa, 4, 8, 12, 13, 16-18, 26, 27, 35, 92, 96, 148, 299, 323, 325, 328, 334
Masuna, 329, 330
Matero, 144
Mateur, 144, 145
Matron of Ephesus, the, 262
Mauretania, 28-36, 104, 105, 108, 114-116, 138, 330
— Cæsariensis, 104, 329
— Tingitana, 104, 105
Maxula, 305
Mazippa, 135
Medea compared with Dido, 63, 64, 66
Medeah, 96
Medes, 3
Medinet Kadina, 143
Mediterranean, 49, 50, 303
Megara, the, 51, 74
Mejerda, 50, 194
Melcart, 4
Metamorphoses, the, 248, 249, 253, 258, 268
Metellus, 25
Micipsa, 19, 20
Milesian, 258, 262
Milève, 167
Misua, 305
Mokrani, 227
Moorish, 30, 53, 175, 303, 329
Moors, 3, 9, 98, 115, 328, 329
Morocco, 7, 9, 28, 98, 101, 109, 296
Motman, 303
Mussulman, 13, 56, 147, 162

N

Nævius, 72
Negrin, 99
Nepos, Cornelius, 166
Niger, 7
Nomad, 3, 9, 14, 96, 113

Numidia, 2, 3, 11, 12, 14, 18, 20, 26, 27, 35, 96, 101-105, 108, 114, 116, 117, 120, 137, 162, 167, 186, 196, 216, 245, 325, 330
Numidian, 3, 4, 8, 9, 16, 17, 19, 24, 25, 112, 135, 147, 148, 159, 170, 186, 242, 244, 245, 262, 263, 295, 306, 307, 309, 312, 322, 325

O

Octavia, 29
Œa, 250, 322
Oran, 96, 104, 329
Ostia, 297
Oued-Atmenia, 167
Oued-Djedi, 99
Oued-Ghir, 98
Oued-Kebir, 14, 104

P

Palmyra, 110
Parthians, 205
Paulinus, Suetonius, 98
Paulus, Æmilius, 68
Pergamus, 34
Petreius, 27
Petronius, 258-262
Phædras, 62
Phazania, 97
Philippeville, 164
Philosophical Dialogues, the, 271
Phœnician, 4, 8, 30, 40, 42, 43, 46, 47, 49, 55, 56, 58, 154, 303
Phrygia, 65
Phrygian, 60
Piscina, 99
Plato, 246, 252
Platonist, 246, 259
Plautus, 225
Pliny, 161, 172
— the Elder, 166, 193
Plutarch, 28
Polybius, 49-51, 73, 81, 148
Pompeian, 27
Porto-Farina, 14
Procopius, 155

Index

Proculus, Eutyches, 244
Propertius, 68
Punic, 2, 9, 11, 52, 54, 57, 58, 72, 94, 263, 265, 266, 302, 305, 313, 315, 317, 322–325, 332, 335
Puteoli, 164
Puzzuoli, 164, 166, 297

Q

Quietus, Lucius, 115, 328
Quintilian, 278

R

Roman, 1, 9, 12, 16–18, 20, 25, 28, 35, 52, 72, 74, 75, 79–81, 92, 93, 96–100, 102, 103, 105–110, 112–118, 120–123, 125, 128, 130, 135–137, 139, 142, 144, 145, 148–152, 154–156, 161–163, 165, 166, 169, 171, 173, 174, 182, 184, 188, 189, 192–194, 196–199, 202, 208, 209, 215, 218, 220, 223, 225, 228–230, 234–237, 240–242, 245, 246, 250, 252, 258, 261, 267, 269, 275, 276–279, 286, 290–303, 306–312, 314, 315, 318, 323, 326–336
Rome, 2, 11, 12, 17–19, 22, 26, 27, 29, 35, 49, 56, 58, 72, 73, 92, 95, 101, 103, 107, 113, 115, 128, 134, 135, 138, 145, 160, 163–165, 167, 168, 171, 172, 178, 188, 197, 208, 214, 216, 217, 220, 223, 224, 238, 240–246, 248, 249, 259, 261, 267, 272, 277, 279, 293, 298–305, 309, 310, 313, 315, 316, 326–329, 331
Rummel, 14–16
Rusicade, 164

S

Safar, 329
Sahara, Great, 7, 9, 96, 110, 113, 118, 146, 198, 206, 290
Sahel, 31
Saldæ, 138
Sallust, 2–4, 6, 14, 19–21, 24, 26, 94, 149, 156, 157, 235, 295
Saltus Buguensis, 162
Saltus Burunitanus, 180
Salvian, 331
Sardinia, 45, 47, 163
Sbîtla, 143
Schemtou, 186
Scillium, 143, 158, 272, 311
Scipio, 12–14, 17, 54, 58, 73, 74, 79–82, 92, 101, 120, 295
— the Elder, 170, 295
Selimonte, 221
Semites, 304
Semitic, 40, 58, 264, 315
Seneca, 35, 170, 225, 242, 278
Senegal, 7
Septiminiana Via, 125
Setif, 167, 236
Severus, Septimius, 107, 121, 124, 243, 257, 322
Shelliff, 137
Shershell, 30–34, 152
Sicca, 244
— Veneria, 22
Sicheus, 66, 67
Sicilian, 51
Sicily, 45, 47, 60, 95, 163, 164
Sidi Bu Said, 51, 78
Sidi Okbah, 99, 156
Sidonian, 43
Sigus, 186
Silanus, Servilius, 244
Simittu, 138, 186
Sitifis, 167
Sittii, 314
Slippers of Philetærus, the, 262
Soliloquies, the, 271
Sophonisba, 12, 16, 17
Soudan, 5, 7
Soukara, 245
— Lake of, 48
Souk-Arrhas, 5
Sousse, 310
Spain, 3, 11, 12, 45, 47, 51, 113, 242, 272, 276, 299, 321, 331, 332
Spaniard, 296

Statius, 243
Subeitla, 143
Sud-Oranais, 156
Sufetula, 143
Suffetes, 57
Susa, 75
Suthul, 22, 25
Syphax, 11-14, 16, 17, 96
Syria, 110, 112, 113
Syrian, 44
Syrtes, 243
Syrus, Publius, 225

T

Tabarca, 92
Tabraca, 92
Tacfarinas, 135, 328
Tacitus, 115, 128, 130, 163, 214, 240, 333
Tadert, 99
Tagaste, 5
Tagilt, 5
Taine, 92
Takape, 142
Tangiers, 104
Tanit, 55, 57, 58, 303, 304
Tanja, 104
Tarâbulus, 250
Tebessa, 99, 118, 142, 162, 196, 203, 213, 227, 245
Teburba, 305
Tebursuk, 194
Tell, 19, 146
Tertullian, 270, 304
Tezzût, 99
Thabudei, 99
Thagaste, 238, 309
Thala, 26
Thamugade, 99, 131, 196, 198, 200, 204, 205, 217, 234, 324, 327
Thapsus, 27, 75, 101, 313
Thelepte, 26, 143
Themistius, 115
Thenæ, 92
Theveste, 99, 118, 142, 199, 213, 327
Thibica, 315

Thibursicum Bure, 194
Thignica, 194
Thuburbum minus, 305
Thubursicum Numidarum, 245, 308
Thugga, 144, 194
Thule, 242
Thysdrus, 143, 153, 192, 295
Tiberius, 128, 135, 328
Tibur, 172, 186
Tidsis, 167
Timegad, 99, 194-198, 200-202, 205, 206, 209, 211, 213, 216-224, 226, 227, 229-231, 237
Tingis, 104
Tipasa, 152
Tipech, 152
Tivoli, 172
Trajan, 115, 198, 199, 203, 205, 215, 328
Trimalchio, 260
Tripoli, 250, 322
Tripolis, 243
Tripolitana Provincia, 101, 109, 296
Trojan, 60, 66
Troy, 65
Tuarick, 3, 7-10, 147
Tub, the, 262
Tuliusii, 96
Tunis, 9, 44, 48, 99, 101, 109, 124, 142-144, 160, 162, 219, 245, 292, 296, 304, 305
— Lake of, 48, 51, 78
Tupusuctu, 154
Tyre, 44, 46
Tyrian, 44

U

Udena, 305
Ulysses compared with Æneas, 70, 71
Uthina, 305
Utica, 14, 19, 46, 75, 272, 305
— Gulf of, 50

V

Vacca, 22
Vaga, 22, 295

Valentinian I., 328
Vandal, 155, 226, 275, 277–279, 329, 334, 335
Vegetius, 111, 132
Velisci, 96
Verecunda, 131
Vespasian, 107, 108
Victorinus, Marius, 281
Vicus Augusti, 142

Virgil, 57, 59–72
Vitruvius, 201

W

Wadi el Kantara, 109

Z

Zaghouan, 159

POPULAR ARCHÆOLOGY.

By GASTON BOISSIER.

Rome and Pompeii.—Archæological Rambles. Translated by D. Havelock Fisher. With maps. 8° $2.50

"Gaston Boisser is a refreshing writer with whom to travel. . . . He gives us ideas and improves our knowledge, while improving his own, and adds to the treasures of his memory what can be gained by direct contact with events and even with ruins ; . . . particularly interesting and valuable are the notes to be found in his archæological rambles."—*Paris Correspondent of N. Y. Evening Post.*

Cicero and His Friends.—A Study of Roman Society in the Time of Cæsar. Translated, with an Index and Table of Contents, by Adnah David Jones. 12° $1.75

"M. Boissier's brilliant work is as excellent as it is a delightful introduction to the politics of the period in which Cicero and Cæsar were, each in his own way, so great."—*London Saturday Review.*

The Country of Horace and Virgil.—Translated by D. Havelock Fisher. With maps and plans. 8° $2.00

"American lovers of two of the most popular and enjoyable Latin poets will find delight in the translation of 'The Country of Horace and Virgil.' The writer, who has evidently a most affectionate intimacy with both his authors, has very skillfully set them in the volume against the background of the places in which or about which they wrote."—*The Outlook.*

Roman Africa.—Archæological Walks in Algiers and Tunis. Translated by Arabella Ward. With maps. 8°.

G. P. PUTNAM'S SONS, NEW YORK AND LONDON.

POPULAR ARCHÆOLOGY.

Rome of To=day and Yesterday.—The Pagan City. By John Dennie. With 58 Illustrations and 5 Maps and Plans. Tourist's edition (the fourth), full flexible morocco, with round corners, $4.50.

"Rarely is so much excellent and instructive archæological matter presented in a style so lucid and so instructive."—*American Magazine of History.*

"We are not surprised that a third edition of Mr. John Dennie's readable and scholarly 'Rome of To-day and Yesterday' has been called for in three years. Seldom does one meet with more animated description in a field where it is difficult to escape being as dry as a guide-book. . . . The fifty-eight illustrations from photographs are unhackneyed in a quite unusual proportion, with fresh points of view even for familiar objects. No better popular introduction to Roman Antiquities could be named."—*The Nation.*

"Rome's eleven pagan centuries have never been more thoroughly and attractively treated than in John Dennie's 'Rome of To-day and Yesterday.' The book was first published three years ago, and its merits have now won for it a superb third edition, illustrated with five maps and fifty-eight full-page reproductions of Roman photographs bearing upon the early life and architecture of the Eternal City. Buckram binding, deckle-edged paper, and faultless typography add all that could be desired in externals.—*Chicago Tribune.*

"Since reading this book we have been full of regret that we did not have it in hand when in Rome. It would have reduced to historic sequence and order that which is now a jumble of magnificent suggestions and half-located impressions. . . . It is not too much to say that to the student at all interested in that strong conqueror of time—Architecture, this handsome volume will throw a new light on the most marvellous history recorded among men, while to the reader contemplating a visit to Rome, it will prepare the way for an intelligent and delightful view of that city."—*The Outlook.*

Egyptian Book of the Dead.—The most ancient and most important of the extant religious texts of ancient Egypt. Edited, with introduction and a complete translation, by Charles H. S. Davis, M.D., Ph.D. With 99 full-page Illustrations from the Turin and the Louvre Papyri, and 25 Designs representing the Egyptian Gods. Large quarto, *net*, $6.00.

"Dr. Davis's work has made it easy for the general reader to learn what has hitherto been confined to the innermost circle of Egyptologists. He has performed his task well and faithfully, and deserves the gratitude of all scholars and students."—*The Churchman.*

G. P. PUTNAM'S SONS, New York and London.

POPULAR ARCHÆOLOGY.

The Riviera, Ancient and Modern.—By CHARLES LENTHÉRIC, Chief of the French Government Department of Civil Engineering. Translated by C. West, M.D., F.R.C.S.L., Foreign Associate of the National Academy of Medicine of Paris. Large crown 8vo, with maps and illustrations . $2.00

"This is certainly, besides being a very readable book, the first systematic account of the Riviera which has taken into consideration both the needs of the historian, the archæologist, and the traveller."

A Manual of Archæology.—Containing an Introduction to Egyptian, Oriental, Greek, Etruscan, and and Roman Art. By TALFOURD ELY, Author of "Olympus: Tales of the Gods of Greece and Rome." With 114 illustrations, 8vo . . . $2.00

"For a brief yet comprehensive account of the earliest art, we know of nothing better. . . . After a careful examination, we say that Mr. Ely's statements are scholarly and trustworthy."—*Christian Union.*

Egyptian Archæology. By G. MASPERO. Translated from the French by AMELIA B. EDWARDS. With 229 illustrations. 8vo, gilt top . $2.25

"A rich and enjoyable book in every way satisfactory and fascinating. It is delightful to find frankness, accuracy, and scholarship united in the production of this work, which makes the humanity of vanished Egypt live again."—*The Critic.*

Nippur; Or Explorations and Adventures on the Euphrates. The Narrative of the University of Pennsylvania Expedition to Babylonia, in the years 1888–1890. By JOHN PUNNETT PETERS, D.D., Director of the Expedition. With over 100 illustrations and maps. Two volumes, 8vo, each $2.50.

"A splendid work, which is to be classed among the most remarkable of modern archæological researches."—*New York Times.*

G. P. PUTNAM'S SONS, NEW YORK AND LONDON.

POPULAR ARCHÆOLOGY.

Primitive Man in Ohio.—By Warren K. Moorehead, Fellow of the American Association for the Advancement of Science, author of "Fort Ancient, the Great Prehistoric Earthwork of Warren County, Ohio." 8vo. Fully illustrated . . $3.00

This book which is a companion work to Nadaillac's "Prehistoric America," is the result of the observations of the author and his collaborators in Ohio during a number of years; their deductions are made from the testimony of the burial-places, village sites, and fortifications marking various epochs in primeval man's existence. It is a comprehensive statement of their discoveries related without ornamentation.

Prehistoric America. By the Marquis de Nadaillac. Translated by Nancy Bell (N. D'Anvers), author of "History of Art." Edited, with Notes, by W. H. Dall. Large octavo, with 219 illustrations. Popular edition $3.00

"The best book on this subject that has yet been published, . . . for the reason that, as a record of facts, it is unusually full, and because it is the first comprehensive work in which, discarding all the old and worn-out nostrums about the existence on this continent of an extinct civilization, we are brought face to face with conclusions that are based upon a careful comparison of architectural and other prehistoric remains with the arts and industries, the manners and customs of 'the only people, except the whites, who, so far as we know, have ever held the regions in which these remains are found.'"—*Nation.*

"His book is one which no anthropologist should be without. It gathers into one critical and incredulous volume all that is most solid, sure, and trustworthy in the whole realm of American archæology."—*Pall Mall Gazette.*

The Customs and Monuments of Prehistoric Peoples. By the Marquis de Nadaillac. Translated with the permission of the author, by Nancy Bell (N. D'Anvers). Large octavo. Fully illustrated $3.00

"To the student of archæology and anthropology this book is invaluable, to the class interested in the knowledge and speculation concerning the primeval races it will be a rare book for the library, for the world at large it will be a contribution to scientific literature not to be forgotten."—*Columbus Despatch.*

G. P. PUTNAM'S SONS, New York and London.

www.ingramcontent.com/pod-product-compliance
Lightning Source LLC
Chambersburg PA
CBHW032043220426
43664CB00008B/837